"Reading *Escape from Texas* was like listening to a story someone had written about my life. My childhood was very similar to that of don Jesus, and prior to finding his work I never believed it possible to find true happiness. He accurately articulated so many of the emotions and opinions I had locked up inside, but didn't know how to express, even to myself. Although I physically left home so long ago, I am just beginning my spiritual escape from Louisiana. As don Jesus says, 'We all start where we are.' Thank you, don Jesus."

-Virginia Holloway, Retired Nurse, Cleveland, Ohio

Book Reviews

Excerpts from letters sent by readers from all over the world

"My experiences with workshops held by self-named masters of the Toltec discipline were comical and entirely useless. I am grateful beyond words that amongst these frauds a true practitioner of the Warrior's discipline remains. Although he refuses to be known as anything other than a Warrior, I will say that I have found a teacher in don Jesus."

-Kevin Wilkinson, Civil Engineer, Vancouver, Canada

"Shockingly awakening! *Escape from Texas* provides Seekers with a roadmap to follow. Don Jesus guides and encourages us to find our own path to freedom by taking action. A Warrior's knowledge and true liberation from a hurtful past cannot be inherited or shared with anyone. We must earn freedom ourselves, and we must do it alone. Thanks to don Jesus, we now know what to do, we just have to do it!"

-Elizabeth Stafford, M.D., Palo Alto, California

"Don Jesus does it again! In this heroic autobiographical tale he demonstrates a true mastery of storytelling, while illuminating the path towards knowledge. Ancient Toltec wisdom has never before been translated in such an accurate and practical manner. Seekers need only follow his example to find the spiritual freedom he speaks of."

-Desmond Archer, Author, San Francisco, California

"As a Native Tejano whose ancestors fought alongside Davy Crockett and Jim Bowie within the walls of the Alamo, I have longed for a genuine Warrior to appear. Without apology or reservation, don Jesus strips away the shallow veneer of so-called 'race relations' in America, particularly in Texas. As a retired teacher and perpetual student of history, I have been sickened and dismayed at the blatant omissions of Tejano accomplishments to Tejas history. Thanks to don Jesus, thousands of bigots will be turning over in their graves, as a new generation learns what it means to be Tejano, while simultaneously learning how to be a Warrior."

—Gabriel Esperanza, Retired Teacher, San Antonio, Texas

"I spent eight years in prison as a member of a major white supremacist gang. For safety reasons I've chosen to not share its name. Although it's been years since I learned I was lied to and brainwashed about the myth of white supremacy, *Escape from Texas* reopened my eyes and gave me a deeper understanding. I saw the true impact this cycle of hate has on the culprit and the victim. In realizing the harm I helped perpetuate upon my fellowman, I was consumed with regret and self-loathing. If don Jesus were an average man he would have left me with my pain, but instead showed me how to live like a Warrior. Thanks to him, I too can escape from Texas, and my painful past. I may be the only Anglo person who refuses to be called White, and just wants to be known as a human being."

—Scott Freeman, Electrician, Dallas, Texas

"*Escape from Texas* demonstrates why lies repeated over generations become accepted as 'truth.' The veil of self-deceit has been removed, exposing the cost of government approved racism. Native Tejanos have found a genuine hero in don Jesus."

—Richard A. Steinberg, Ph.D., Durham, North Carolina

Escape from Texas
Born into Darkness

Also by don Jesus M. Ramirez

Sorcerer's Secrets, Book 1
Translated Secrets of Carlos Castaneda

Sorcerer's Secrets, Book 2
A Modern Guide to Ancient Toltec Wisdom

Escape from Texas, Book 2
Journey out of the Abyss

Sorcerer's Disagreements, Book 1
Searching for Nirvana

Sorcerer's Disagreements, Book 2
Tearing the Thin Veneer

Sorcerer's Disagreements, Book 3
A Facade of Freedom

Sorcerer's Disagreements, Book 4
A Warrior's Greatest Challenge

Escape from Texas
Born into Darkness

Book 1

Don Jesus M. Ramirez

Edited by Christopher Kiyosaki
Cover designed by Angel Valadez

Copyright © 2013
All rights reserved

In accordance with the U.S. Copyright Act of 1976, no part of this publication may be reproduced or stored in a retrieval system, or transmitted in any form or by any means, electronic, mechanical, photocopying, recording, or otherwise, without the prior written consent of the author. For information regarding permissions, contact Toltec Institute.

Toltec Institute
PO Box 6552
San Jose, CA 95150
www.toltecinstitute.com
info@toltecinstitute.com

The author is not responsible for websites (or their content) that are not owned by the author.

ISBN 978-1-939163-08-0

Disclaimer

This work addresses highly controversial subject matter. The majority of the names, places, dates, and identifying characteristics have been changed to protect the innocent and not antagonize the guilty. In addition, many of the illustrations, examples, and events described within this work have either been altered or are fictitious. Any similarity to real persons, living or dead, is coincidental and not intended by the author. The content found within this work is the sole expression and opinion of the author, created with the intention of providing information. No warranties or guarantees are expressed or implied, and no part of this work is intended as a substitute for the medical or psychological advice of physicians. Neither the publisher nor the author offer any type of psychological, legal, or any other such professional advice, nor shall they be liable for physical, psychological, emotional, financial, or commercial damages, including, but not limited to, special, incidental, or consequential damages. This work is distributed with the understanding that the publisher and author suggest extreme caution. You are responsible for your own choices, actions, and results.

Cover Artwork
Designed by: Angel Valadez

During the crusades thousands of knights traveled to the Holy Land seeking their fortune, and a few their salvation. The few who sought a cleansing of their souls did so earnestly, swearing celibacy and devotion to Christianity. Having sworn fidelity, they contemplated upon the skulls of dead saints and religious relics, considering themselves already dead. These warrior monks swore to be fearless before their enemies, honest and upright. They spoke only truth, protected their king, and swore to safeguard the helpless, even if it meant their death. The image of the hooded monk skull symbolizes a Warrior's awareness of his death. Death then becomes his greatest motivator, ally, and adviser. The cover artwork was selected and designed to convey our awareness and sense of urgency.

Dedication

For my grandfather, Jesus M. Ramirez
A hero of the Mexican Revolution

An unforeseeable series of events led to my grandfather becoming an unwilling participant of the Mexican Revolution. While traveling to México City, the train on which he was a passenger was attacked and captured by Pancho Villa's forces. When soldiers confiscated the horses he was transporting, he protested against the injustice. His actions were interpreted as bravery, and as such he was offered the opportunity to join the famous División del Norte, or face a firing squad. With no alternative he reluctantly joined the rebellion. As a man of action, he accepted his fate, acknowledging there was no turning back. He earnestly played out his role and via his deeds advanced to the rank of officer, becoming a recognized and trusted companion of the General.

Contents

	A Warrior's Aloneness	I
Prologue	History Will Always Repeat Itself	1
Chapter One	Looking Back	25
Chapter Two	The Instinct of Survival	40
Chapter Three	The Boy Who Loved Norma Jean Slaughter	84
Chapter Four	To All the Girls I've Known	99
Chapter Five	Close to Hell and Far from God	117
Chapter Six	Bandits, Drunks, and Fools	146
Chapter Seven	Christmas Ghost	152
Chapter Eight	Visit from an Exorcised Ghost	200
Chapter Nine	The White Pony	208
Chapter Ten	The Moon Watcher	223
Chapter Eleven	A Tejano Greek Tragedy	227
Intermission	Standing at the Edge of the Precipice	254
	Essential Concepts and Vocabulary	A1

A Warrior's Aloneness

"Fighting loneliness with writing is like fighting fire with prayers. It seems just as powerful, but in the end, words are just words and not what you need."

-don Jesus M. Ramirez

Many years of solitude created a distant personality within me which I once found troubling. I have spent much time alone and have developed strategies to manage loneliness. Today I am no longer lonely, and have learned that loneliness and aloneness are not one and the same. However, it has taken years for me to arrive at this point. I now prefer to be alone, but only because average people are so toxic. I've not met anyone from Epitaph, the town in which I currently reside, whose company I enjoy. I've come to prefer my own company to the best average person I've ever known. I have several students, who aside from the few who are more advanced, I only care to tolerate intermittently. Burdened by their averageness, after several hours their energy becomes too taxing, heavy, and unpleasant. In search of a defensive weapon to combat loneliness I sought to become a writer, and have worked endlessly to develop my skills. I often found myself surrounded by crowds, yet always feeling alone. One of these times was in a college cafeteria, which was flooded with students making enough noise to wake the dead. In the midst of this madness I began to write.

The first time I heard voices as a child I knew I would not be an ordinary man. I was only nine-years-old or so and thought I was dreaming, but then the voice told me to look outside and listen to the birds. I did. The trees in our front yard were filled with sparrows singing their happy songs. I assumed the voice was God's, and it never occurred to me that it might have only been my imagination. Perhaps the brainwashing I received by the obsessive sisters of the Church was responsible. Whatever the explanation, I felt special and happily behaved as if I had a secret, which I did. However, this inner happiness was not met with curiosity by my teachers at school, but seen as a sign of concern. They assumed I was disturbed, which by today's standards I would have been. I had no idea that I was in the company of muses, madmen, and prophets, as poor Native Tejano children in Texas were not supposed to feel happy or special. The experiences of hearing voices impacted my life tremendously, but as a child I never knew how the knowledge of these occurrences would have been received by others. I never knew that some would have preferred I be burned at the stake like Joan of Arc, or be ordered to commit suicide like Socrates. Today, after all these years I've accepted that the voice I heard belonged to power. It is then no wonder I never fit in. I would not have fit in even amongst others who did not fit in. I was never a rebel seeking to burn down society or free political prisoners, but I am in a constant state of revolution. I am more of an extremist than the enraptured religious zealots who attack their enemies with bombs strapped to their chests. I find there is an ocean of distance between myself and the average man. The ability to *see* has haunted me throughout my life. As ordinary people chat around me, I've learned to carry a book to read or a notepad to write in. I used to envy their commonality and simple, uncomplicated lives. I don't have a best friend, nor do I belong to a group. Not for the lack of wanting, but because I know none worthy of receiving or capable of giving true friendship. My oldest and most trustworthy companions have always been words, and even they only serve to distract me. In the past I admired men whose words appeared to hold truth — those who allegedly loved their principles and raged valiantly against evil. Now, after so many years on the Warrior's path, the words that matter most, those that move and stir my blood, are my own. I am by definition an author, philosopher, thinker, and a loner. This is no passing fancy, but an extreme affliction, an illness of the heart that is incurable by modern standards. There is no ancient ritual or alchemy which can remove the memory of the voice that spoke to me as a child. I suffer from a self-imposed punishment, driven by a hunger for understanding. Whether by habit or affliction, I write when I am happy and while I am sad. Mostly, I write to keep myself company. Like many other writers, I am surrounded by a self-made fortress of solitude which no one can penetrate. My words imprison and protect me, while at the same time confuse and liberate me. In those rare and precious moments when I am able to put together a poignant phrase, words also free me beyond the bonds that restrain average men. It is in these instances that time stops, and if only for one moment, I catch a glimpse and can almost grasp understanding of the power that can only be called God. I find myself soaring, lifted by the beauty and mastery of words, while at other times I think myself an egotistical fool.

    I have been alone many years and have grown accustomed to my isolation, as I feel a part of something bigger than myself. I belong to the millions of unknown and unheralded fellowship of Seekers, who sought understanding via the power of words. I belong to a fellowship that has no membership, no roll, and does not exist. I've found efforts to belong to my fellowman below standard and unworthy of association. These men and women cannot be the best mankind can produce. Instead of friends to offer advice, or a comforting touch, these average people seek to soil my spirit and contaminate me with their greed and vanity. These are not friends to share secrets with, so I share mine with my journal, and even then, only in code, in the event unwanted eyes should uncover my secrets. Untrusting of casual friendships, I hide myself from the unworthy and claim no peers. Daring to say so, yet truth, I am no stranger to myself. It is impossible to discover who we are unless we are alone, as growth can only be measured in solitude. Seekers of the past offer solace, but only superficially. As I roam the halls of academia I find only confused children wearing adult masks. I have to believe this must be a joke, as this just cannot be. Can these really be the best professors and allegedly learned professionals society has to offer? There must be more. Somewhere out there amongst the millions of supposedly educated people, there must be a group which holds themselves to a higher standard. These cannot be the people who I was brainwashed to believe could guide me. It is devastating to discover they cannot teach what they've never learned, no more than the ghosts of the dead.

    I've learned that the ramblings of professors seeking tenure could not guide or assist me. Instead of a Warrior's dedication to a challenge, they exchanged their quest for money and prestige. They are mere self-serving hypocrites calling themselves teachers, and their arrogance smells like dung. Their presence is repulsive and their pomposity ridiculous. In all their years of living they have yet to discover that time is fleeting, and as their faces will wrinkle, so death will expect them. These fools believe they are important and immortal, not recognizing that their place would be filled in an instant. In their hunger for accolades they forget that we will all die alone. These self-deceiving frauds fail to inspire and betray the trust bestowed upon them by knowledge hungry students. I once moved like a phantom on the periphery of these academic hallways, seeking passage through the barriers blocking my entry. I struggled to fit in and unravel the mystery, like a modern-day Doctor Frankenstein. I often felt exiled into purgatory, where I could not hear, feel, or be touched.

Throughout the years of searching I found not only my own failings and self-indulgence, but those of whom I came to for answers. I discovered that these learned individuals had not obtained knowledge. Instead they had gathered information which had been passed down from others like themselves, seeking a position of respect in false society, made up of lies and liars. These men are frauds, liars, and thieves, and are not worthy of respect or dedication. My discovery was revolting, and yet social obligations forced me to continue on my quest for an academic degree. A Warrior's quest is a learned habit of solitude. It is not a self-imposed sentence, but a journey for freedom. I willingly adopt it and once more sit in a crowded room, surrounded by people, yet still alone, but not lonely. There are other silent Seekers who long to feel a part of the Universe, yet like myself are unable to bridge the gap. The riddle of how much to surrender to the average man's world in exchange for membership is not worth entertaining. Like broken tree limbs lying upon the ground, I have been beguiled with compromises and hypocrisy. My memories of broken promises have faded. All that remains is the bitterness of betrayal and isolation, as well as the knowledge that the magical passage which will release me from myself is... silence. It is the same silence in which I first heard the voice that spoke to me as a child, telling me of birds singing in the trees outside my window.

I've asked myself a hundred times where I learned this and who or what terrible event caused it. For many years I lived as a stranger to myself, surrounded by the sounds of the living, while moving like a spirit through the crowd. Like one of the souls of the charging Light Brigade I was just following orders, never replying or reasoning why, riding into the Valley of Death. I longed for a band of brothers to shed blood with me, and I found a battle worthy of sacrifice; my quest for freedom. Something no fool dressed in academic robes or religious ceremonial gowns can provide.

I am unwilling to surrender my independence for membership in cliques, gangs, clubs, frats, or groups of any kind. I no longer seek to believe or belong. I suffer the common affliction amongst modern-day Seekers and live like a Rōnin Samurai without a master, teacher, or Shogun lord. A faithful apostle without a savior, I struggle beneath the cross of this knowledge and journey through the Valley of Death. Like an ancient knight lost among his obligations while still trying to solve the riddle of life. I no longer seek a quest worthy of my mettle, and accept that outside of myself there are no causes worth fighting for. Although I sharpen my sword daily, read and write unceasingly, I acknowledge that life amongst average men is folly.

Texas escapee,
don Jesus M. Ramirez

PROLOGUE
History Will Always Repeat Itself

"Born into a hostile environment one becomes a wolf or a lamb. You either become the hunter or the hunted, but everyone suffers."

-don Jesus M. Ramirez

Motivated by greed and the desire to acquire land, the first Anglo immigrants of Texas swore an oath which they never intended to keep. Of their own free will they agreed to prerequisites established by the Mexican Government for admittance to their country. Among these were the promises to forgo slavery, behave as proper citizens, adopt Spanish as the official language, and Catholicism as the religion. Upon voiding their agreements soon after obtaining what they desired, these immigrants contributed to the tainted history of American treaties. They gathered together, and in October of 1835 launched the Texas Revolution. In a legal effort to maintain and protect its borders, the Mexican Government sent an army led by General Antonio López de Santa Anna to squash the rebellion. The Battle of the Alamo soon followed. This legendary massacre and pivotal point in Texas history has been recounted countless times by Anglo historians. Thanks to their contributions we know of alleged heroes Colonel James Bowie, Lieutenant Colonel William Barret Travis, and Davy Crockett. We also know that Santa Anna's defeat and capture at the Battle of San Jacinto led to the signing of the Treaties of Velasco, which both recognized Texas' independence and guaranteed his life. The Anglicized version of this history has become standard

1

curriculum in the Texas educational system. Yet it was only through my independent research that I learned there were Native Tejanos in the Alamo who helped fight against Santa Anna's attack. Although these men fought and died alongside supposedly legendary heroes, most people are unaware they even existed. Anglo historians and teachers maliciously and deliberately kept this fact hidden from Native Tejanos like myself. Had this truth been made known, millions might have been spared a life as a second class citizen, years of racist hatred, discrimination, and an oppressive hostile environment. Fortunately future generations can benefit from the work of historians like Professor Jesús F. de la Teja of Texas State University, who enlightens thousands via teaching the history of the Texas Revolution from a Tejano perspective.

On February 24, 1836, William Barret Travis, Lieutenant Colonel Commander at the Alamo wrote a letter addressed "To the People of Texas and All Americans in the World." His request for assistance was denied. At the tender age of sixteen, while a student at "Andrew Jackson High School" in Corpus Christi, I wrote a similar letter. Addressed to the Texas legislature in Austin and the office of President Lyndon B. Johnson, much like Lieutenant Colonel Travis, my request for assistance was ignored.

> To the people of the United States, and freedom loving individuals around the world,
>
> I am surrounded by millions of bigoted and intolerant citizens, led by racists disguised as conservatives. They are the self-proclaimed "real Americans," who hide behind the flags of religion and patriotism. I have sustained a continual bom-

bardment of hate crimes, violence, government legislated racist laws, and physical attacks. I have been denied equal rights and protection under the law, and my people have endured generations of oppression. They have demanded our complete surrender and submission so the entire population can continue to be subjected, harassed, illegally arrested, convicted, and imprisoned, or possibly killed by law enforcement officers. I have refused to surrender my cultural heritage and ethic ties to my people. I stand beside the American flag, along with millions of other Americans who refuse to submit to tyranny, racial discrimination via political oppression, or overt violence. I shall never surrender or retreat. I come to you in the name of liberty, of patriotism, and everything dear to the American character, asking that you come to our immediate aid. Our oppressors have endless resources, and due to a complete use of government troops, are armed and determined to end our struggle. If our request for assistance is neglected, I am determined to sustain myself as long as possible, and die as a "free American" who was due, but denied equal representation under our laws. I will never forget what is due to my honor and that of my country.

We pray the Lord is on our side, but it appears God favors the wealthy and powerful,

Jesus M. Ramirez
Andrew Jackson High School student, 1967
Corpus Christi, Texas

An escape from your past without a solid spiritual discipline and merciless self-examination is impossible. Millions of self-indulging average people attempt to disconnect themselves from their painful past via traditional therapy without success. Traditional counseling methods are not designed for spiritual freedom, life, or self-actualization, and as a result these efforts are doomed to fail. Eventually these wayward and lost individuals surrender to the wisdom of the Toltec discipline, accepting that there is no "why," nor a satisfactory explanation for their suffering. Regretfully, most of these average people will abandon their desire for freedom, thereby accepting a sentence to misery and a mediocre existence. Attacked and bombarded with never-ending insane logic, conclusions, and behaviors, the pressure to conform and surrender is more than they can resist. They will emulate behaviors learned from their parents, who learned from their parents, who never recognized that the world is what it is because they contribute to the insanity. This is how senseless logic and ridiculous self-defeating behaviors become accepted standard practice. Tragically, thousands of therapists unashamedly work towards keeping their patients sick and dependent on therapy. They claim the solution to filling voids of the soul lie in discovering why something happened. Realizing that it does not matter why something happened is the first of many lessons upon the Warriors path. It is time to stop indulging. Having suffered the same disillusionment, I offer my heartfelt condolences to anyone who stubbornly denies reality and refuses to stop asking why. Unbeknownst and unexplained in counseling circles, they are in fact being squashed by self-importance, and being defeated by the multi-headed monster that it is. The actual chances of an average counselor leading another average person to freedom are zero. Regretfully, they will only succeed in reopening old wounds and releasing the horrific memories of those experiences. This is common and very dangerous, and usually results in a relapse, madness, and acts of revenge or suicide. I speak from the wisdom of experience after having relived all the pain I was trying to escape. I discovered that without the spiritual rebirth found within this discipline I would have never survived long enough to write my tale. The story of my escape from Texas has been broken into two parts: *Escape from Texas, Book 1: Born into Darkness*, and *Escape from Texas, Book 2: Journey out of the Abyss*. The second installment of this work is a direct continuation of the first. As such, characters, themes, and experiences relating to the storyline will not be reintroduced, but rather continue in a fluid manner. Those wishing to obtain the most from their reading experience in terms of storyline and entertainment value are recommended to read this series in sequence. However, Seekers and Warriors should note that this recommendation only pertains to the storyline. Beneficial information concerning the Toltec discipline is present and accessible throughout both works, regardless of the order in which they are studied. As a deliberate act of war made by a Warrior in the course of his development, this series has been written and examined from a *detached* perspective. Great effort has been made to describe experiences precisely as they occurred, without exaggeration or indulgence. To accurately portray the environment, characters, and mood, as well as convey the desired message, the occasional use of vocabulary which may be deemed inappropriate or vulgar is essential. Readers who have not read my book, *Sorcerer's Secrets, Book 1: Translated Secrets of Carlos Castaneda* are directed to *Essential Concepts and Vocabulary*, located at the back of this book. This section will provide the essential introduction for concepts, themes, and vocabulary used throughout this work.

My painful spiritual rebirth cleansed me of unresolved childhood issues. While doing so it also shattered any remaining innocence, leaving my soul open and unprotected. My screams for justice and desire for vengeance caused me to suffer tremendously. As I wallowed in self-pity and hate, I came to understand how destructive these emotions are. I struggled to adopt a Warrior's discipline and shed the clouded mind of an average man. I began to apply the discipline of impeccability, using energy only upon matters that advanced my position. As I did, I felt my spirit begin to soar. After many years of merciless self-examination, I arrived at the eye-opening conclusion that the most impactful influence upon my life was not my brutal childhood experiences, nor was it my paranormal awareness, ethnicity, education, poverty, social status, religion, culture, or even my being one of twelve children. Although all were significant, the most powerful influence upon my life was the racist and hostile environment into which I was born. This cannot be overstated, and must be studied carefully by readers as a warning that their environment may be equally as toxic. Like millions of other Native Tejanos and various peoples of color, I lived under the yoke of racist oppression and endured the indifference of the "good" descendant of European immigrant (DOEI) people of Texas. As such I was sentenced to an inferior role in a racial hierarchy, established for the sole perpetuation of the dominant race. Readers should note that I generalize this group of people with the word "DOEI," yet acknowledge that not all descendants of European immigrants are ignorant individuals who believe ridiculous distortions of racial superiority. My oppressors however, were, and these are the individuals I am referring to when I use the word "DOEI," as well as to those who share their beliefs and ideologies. I have stated many times before, 96ers, as well as Four Percentors, come in all shapes and sizes. Race, ethnicity, education, occupation, status, money, gender, age, and etc., does not matter. Behavior is all that matters. Warriors *see* everyone in terms of energy, and know that death makes all things equal. This makes the idea of any person believing their race grants them a level of superiority completely ridiculous. How can one biological creature be superior to another, if they are both going to die? I ask readers to keep this in mind, as the experiences described throughout this book are told accurately, and often not in a politically correct manner. The corrupt system in which I was raised included politically dangerous circumstances which existed as ordinary occurrence. Readers should be aware that the criminal justice system of Texas deliberately subjugated people of color. These were very troubled times, filled with death, imprisonment, or worse lingering around every corner.

Born a Native Tejano in a state with strict racial codes and popular discrimination, I was punished by an accident of birth. Common sense, which is not common, would easily demonstrate that no one would deliberately choose to be born into a socially inferior position. Yet, those born into a superior position behaved and believed that their accident of birth granted them divine privileges. This accident of birth is an impossible variable to defeat — one which Tejanos have been fighting against since DOEIs first invaded Tejas. These self-proclaimed people of God made it their life's goal to oppress and subjugate all Tejanos. This is true the world over, but my story pertains to South Texas and Corpus Christi in particular.

As a Native Tejano in occupied Tejas, I was legally marginalized and politically ostracized from society, which included participating in ordinary high school activities. Native Tejanos attending Andrew Jackson High School (AJHS) in Corpus Christi during the Sixties and Seventies were forced into a racial hierarchy, which had been in place since the Declaration of Independence. As yet still unrecognized by the DOEI elite who write the history books, it began the moment our Founding Fathers denied freedom to African slaves who fought alongside them during the American Revolution. In doing so, these men created the American institution of slavery, which has not officially been assigned to their actions. This unprestigious title has been well documented by African American historians, but ignored by popular media. The men known as heroes of the American Revolution created this American system of racism with the same stroke of the pen that declared them free from the British Empire. The Declaration of Independence, which stated all men were equal, endowed with certain inalienable rights, excluded Black people, and as a consequence, all persons of color. This deliberate omission has impacted millions of people over the course of many generations. It was founded upon the same greed which demanded our Founding Fathers fill their pockets off the sweat and toil of slaves. Their actions declared that their creed was greed, and profit is always before people, justice, kindness, or common sense. The descendants of these men became rich as a result of their inhumanity, which was bequeathed via religion, culture, and government decree. All these men and their descendants created America's cast system based upon the concept that their ethnicity made them superior. The Civil War, which followed 85 years later, nurtured the seeds of hatred already engendered throughout the South. Though started by wealthy landowners, the war was fought predominantly by DOEI sharecropping farmers who never owned slaves or claimed the privileges of American royalty. These overly romanticized country gentlemen and Southern belles, who were "gone with the wind," were invented by Hollywood and endorsed by DOEI culture. In reality, the ignorant and poor DOEI people of the South transformed racism into a malignant disease which continues to infect the United States. These deliberate criminal distortions in history that brought on the Civil War were used by Southern state governments as justification for an undeclared war; discrimination based upon racism. This tribalization of cultures, grouped by income, region, religion, and ethnicity continued. By the 1960s racial divisions were blatantly hostile. DOEI hypocrisy and indifference towards racist treatment of Americans turned injury to insult, while Black, Hispanic, and Asian Americans returned from various wars wounded or in coffins. The Cold War, regional racist practices, and blatant political injustices turned American streets into battlegrounds for equality.

As a child born into an inferior social status due to my accident of birth, my cries for justice in light of blatant discrimination in Corpus Christi, and at Andrew Jackson High School, would have been suicide. Racial tension had been building for years, but I stood alone against the passive nature of fellow Tejanos, and the entire DOEI student/staff population. History once again repeated itself as people of color were blamed for everything from the bad economy to droughts and teen pregnancies. The United States-Mexican border of Arizona, California, New México, and Texas continues to be a point of conflict. Anti-Mexican sediments expressed via conservatives screaming for balanced budgets, along with the Tea Party movement, are once again urging deportations. The same as those which took place in 1933, when the government legally deported over 16,000 supposedly illegal Mexican aliens, who were blamed for competing with Americans for jobs, as is occurring in Southern states today. The unspoken but very clear message is that anyone not of European ancestry is inferior and a criminal suspect. These screams for balanced budgets are code for bigots, and reinforce the racial caste system, which translates into hate crimes that are seldom punished or acknowledged. The return of hate groups and popular white fraternal organizations has quadrupled in recent years. Newly arrived immigrants and practicing Muslims have been attacked, beaten, and murdered by children of these conservatives. They have proven that the only person more heartless than a "good American Christian" is a Nazi. Religion has too often been connected with horrible examples of behavior, long since and before the Crusades. As when our government refused entry to the *MS St. Louis* in 1939, filled with 937 Jewish refugees who were fleeing Nazi Germany. After being denied access into the United States, Canada, and Cuba, they were forced to return to Europe and face the threat of concentration camps, ovens, and eugenics experiments. Historians estimate that after their return, approximately a quarter of the ships population died in concentration camps.

Political oppression via state mandated ordinances and codes were implemented to prevent poor people of color from voting, as was the case when Jim Crow laws prohibited Southern Blacks from voting in 1941. Today, racism disguised as conservatism runs rampant, and may include placing Pakistanis, Arabs, or Mexicans into concentrations camps. As FDR did in 1942 when he imprisoned 110,000 Japanese Americans living on the West Coast into concentration camps in Arkansas, Arizona, California, Colorado, Utah, Idaho, and Wyoming. Today there is an increase in murders of Black, Hispanic, and Asian citizens, but there has never been an official record made of hate crimes, as in the case of Emmett Till. In 1955 14-year-old Emmett Till of Chicago was visiting relatives in Money, Mississippi. According to historian, David Halberstam, Till was kidnapped, beaten, and murdered by Roy Bryant and J. W. Milam for whistling at a white woman, (Roy's wife) Carolyn Bryant. Both men were found not guilty by an all-white jury. Soon thereafter Rosa Parks made world history by refusing to give up her bus seat to a DOEI. She was arrested and jailed. Martin Luther King Jr. organized a bus boycott the same year which lasted 385 days. The following year, on May 17, 1957 he spoke at the nonviolent demonstration "Prayer Pilgrimage for Freedom" in Washington, D.C., in front of the Lincoln Memorial, drawing a crowd of 25,000. After a career of civil rights work, being awarded the Nobel Peace Prize in 1964, and giving his infamous "I Have a Dream" speech to over 200,000 people in Washington, D.C., he was assassinated, allegedly by James Earl Ray while standing on the balcony of a Memphis hotel on April 4, 1968.

Several years earlier in 1958, President Dwight Eisenhower dispatched federal troops to Little Rock, Arkansas, to protect nine Black students from mobs of angry DOEIs. That same year the National Association for the Advancement of Colored People (NAACP) staged counter protests to support desegregation in Oklahoma City, Oklahoma. In 1960, African American college students staged sit-ins at the Woolworth in Greensboro, North Carolina. Within a year there were over a hundred sit-in protests across the South and Border States. The Civil Rights Act was passed in 1964. Freedom Riders traveled through the South to test compliance with federal laws, integrating bus stations, and were attacked by angry DOEIs. Civil order was restored only after Attorney General Robert Kennedy sent in federal marshals, who made arrests and cracked some heads. In protest of continued exploitation of farm workers, César Chávez organized the National Farm Workers Association in California in 1962, which merged with an AFL-CIO affiliate and formed the United Farm Workers of America (UFWA). The South continued to burn, as the Ole Miss Riot of 1962 broke out between Southern segregationist civilians and federal and state forces at the University of Mississippi, after the forced enrollment of Black student, James H. Meredith.

On November 20, 1962, President John F. Kennedy ordered a ban on racial discrimination in federal housing, but these laws were never enforced in Corpus Christi. Tensions continued to worsen in South Texas and across the country in 1963. All hell broke loose in Birmingham, Alabama, when police used water hoses and attack dogs on peaceful demonstrators led by Martin Luther King Jr. In response to overt racial oppression, race riots broke out across town where a significant population of Black Americans lived in Corpus Christi. Local news of the event was not published in order to keep from stirring up angry reactions from Blacks in Houston and Dallas. The DOEI teaching staff at Andrew Jackson reacted to the news and tightened the screws on Black and Native Tejano students, while civil rights leader, Medgar Evers, was murdered in Mississippi in 1963. Southern DOEI determination to maintain the status quo was made clear. It was at this time I was told point blank to tone down my attitude by a DOEI administrator.

Fear and violence was no match for peaceful demonstrations, and public opinion slowly began to turn upon race haters. Much to the chagrin of the DOEI power structure across the country, race riots erupted in Chicago and New York City, causing race to become a major theme in music and film, along with the number one cause of interracial conflict in Corpus Christi. In response local police were given riot gear and training, as National Guard troops were ordered to prepare in the case of riots in Black neighborhoods. Unbeknownst to state officials, a large number of National Guardsmen were Hispanic, Black, or Asian, and were reluctant to attack protesters. The ongoing racial tensions grew, and open conflict irrupted within National Guard units. The Governor threatened action against the troops and tensions continued to rise. Angry Native Tejanos and DOEIs waged open warfare at drive-ins, shopping areas, and popular locations throughout town. The assassination of Martin Luther King Jr. in 1968 added fuel to the fire, and race riots continued to erupt across the United States, including Corpus Christi. Once again, news of these riots had been squashed by the only newspaper in town, which refused to print the story in order to avoid more rioting. The city council and mayor agreed that the tourist industry would suffer if the truth had been made known. Local community organizers and church leaders were quietly rounded up and dealt with outside of media attention, while the status quo was upheld and protected.

In Corpus Christi DOEIs refused to bend with the winds of change, and local political officials openly defied civil rights legislation. Farm workers, of which I was one, were routinely exploited and paid one dollar for every one hundred pounds of cotton picked by hand. Local traditional racial hierarchy determined where I belonged and which job I would be assigned. DOEIs were traditionally in charge and given less physically demanding work, while Native Tejanos and Blacks were predominately used as manual labor. Racism ran rampant in Corpus Christi and was popularly supported by the mayor and chief of police. This was the social and political climate which existed while I went through adolescence. I was surrounded by angry racists screaming against the demands for equal freedom by millions of Americans. It is not necessary to be a psychologist to agree that a child's school experience is one of the most powerful influences upon their life. The meaningful events which mark school experiences will either bind or give youth wings. The opportunity to grow and spread their wings was stolen from millions of people of color, and thousands more were marginalized via racial bigotry throughout American history. The best way to describe what occurred in Corpus Christi, and the Andrew Jackson School District in the Sixties and Seventies is "Texas apartheid."

All escapes from tyranny must start with the idea of freedom and the willingness to risk the consequences. As a result, few will endeavor to achieve it. My story of escape offers examples of how the state of Texas, led by a DOEI population during the Sixties and Seventies, deliberately denied Tejano heritage and instilled a sense of inferiority into the minds of helpless children. This systemically imposed inferiority was conveyed via a corrupted educational system that perpetuated lies, of which there are many. One such example is the case of Thomas Jefferson and the slave woman, Sally Hemings. Annette Gordon-Reed's book, *Thomas Jefferson and Sally Hemings: An American Controversy* exposed America's hypocrisy and confirmed what all African Americans have always known; our Founding Fathers were rapists, fornicators, and slave masters. They were not great men who sought freedom and fought to gain it. They were self-serving, greedy average men who denied freedom to others, while claiming it for themselves. Countless American historians have deliberately ignored the damage and distortion they caused. This can only be called what it is; self-perpetuating blatant lies. It proves once again that perspective, and those in power to enforce their will, can and do perpetuate the fantasies told in American history books. Imagine if you can, the sense of betrayal I experienced upon discovering there were many Native Tejanos who played a vital role in Texas Independence, as well as in American wars over hundreds of years. I began researching history, and after doing so never looked at another teacher with respect, nor trusted anything history books said. I learned that amongst others, Benjamin Franklin was a member of the "Hellfire Club," which held orgies attended by many powerful members of British Parliament. Some have accused him of being a Satan worshiper and allege the remains of ten human bodies (four adults and six children) were discovered hidden beneath his former home in London. These allegations were immediately rebutted by the Sons and Daughters of the American Revolution, who would not tolerate challenges to their assumed pedigree. These important details were kept hidden from generations of students via the same educational system which enforced a sense of inferiority upon others. I can only compare my sense of betrayal to that felt by Jewish Americans after learning about Auschwitz in 1945, or Japanese Americans who were incarcerated during World War II. There are millions of Native Tejanos who have surrendered spiritually and died long before their bodies expired, never having known their history and the role their ancestors played in it. Unlike Auschwitz, there are no death chambers in Texas, which makes identifying the guilty much more difficult. There are no grave markers or memorials for the millions of Native Tejanos who were stomped on by the merciless, racist caste system imbedded in the hearts and minds of their oppressors.

  I was twelve-years-old when I began dreaming of escaping Texas, and of California, where people were said to be less violent and more accepting of racial differences. My struggle to survive and eventually escape from Texas took place over many years. The majority of the names, places, dates, and identifying characteristics in this work have been changed to protect the innocent and not antagonize the guilty. I realize that pointing a finger at racial injustice perpetuated by an entire society is as useless as begging God for justice. I do so nonetheless. Not because it will do any good, but because popular racism has not faded. Sharing the story of my escape has helped me offload emotional baggage collected over many years. This is an essential requirement for a Seeker, who must be free of emotional burdens in order to have complete use of their energy. The disciplined use of personal energy via deliberate action also demonstrates the differences between the behavior of a Warrior and an average person. Self-indulgent 96ers carry their emotional baggage with them throughout their lives, which causes a distortion of their spirits. They increasingly grow irrational, indulging in self-serving and destructive behavior that eventually destroys them. Reactions to crimes perpetuated by the DOEI population have many social consequences. Amongst them is the loss of credibility. From a political standpoint it makes everyone distrust politicians in general. On a personal level, the average person will react with avarice, greed, gluttony, jealousy, vanity, anger, envy, lust, and pride, all of which lead to tremendous conflicts. Tragically, these behaviors are popular and feed into the never-ending cycle of violence and hatred so common in today's society. My escape from Texas required I battle these monsters, which demanded I learn an attitude of no self-pity. My eventual freedom from such behaviors came at a high cost, and I paid continuously as I slowly developed.

 My journey upon the Warrior's path required I conduct a merciless, in-depth evaluation into myself. I recognized that what DOEIs believe in matters of race is deeply stained by ideologies born over hundreds of years of self-disillusion, and based upon an invented racial hierarchy. The choice to either endorse and perpetuate, or reject and acknowledge this propaganda as being what it is, is what separates the group of people I am describing from those who simply happen to be of European ancestry. This distinction is extremely significant, and also a part of what separates 96ers from Four Percentors. As I mentioned before, not all descendants of European immigrants are ignorant individuals who believe ridiculous distortions of racial superiority. It is paramount to acknowledge that those who believe in the concepts of racial supremacy have been nurtured and advanced via legal mandates, and repeatedly validated by government endorsement. There are many examples of racist legislation made into law by men who swore to protect freedom. Beginning with our Founding Fathers and continuing down through the generations, all DOEIs who either endorsed or stood idly by while benefiting from this racial caste system, deserve the responsibility for today's "racist America." Of the thousands of so-called professors who assume the roles of leadership, none have explained this twisted condition. None have ever presented this phenomenon as a mental illness, dysfunction, or distortion of reality. Academia has failed to challenge to the status quo and launch independent studies and investigations. Independent thinkers should not expect change to occur naturally, as such growth is painful and accompanied by tremendous upheaval. As stated before, you'll observe that many of my positions are not politically correct. I have no interest in supporting or endorsing such belief patterns, stereotypes, or accepted norms. I am not exaggerating or falsifying information, but simply relating it via my experiences. Those who find offense in my statements are forewarned against proceeding through this work. Although finding offense in statements which challenge your reality is average, those who do are not ready to approach the topic of sorcery. For many, this book will serve merely as fuel to feed the fires of hatred. For others, perhaps at best an entertaining read. However, only a genuine Seeker with steadfast discipline will be able to set aside their self-importance, challenge what they know, and truly examine the content impartially.

I understand that one cannot point their finger at a city, state, or country and say, "You are to blame." I can however give names of places where this history occurred, in hopes of bringing attention to the problem. I doubt those responsible will consider themselves guilty or see themselves as monsters. The relatives of the students I attended high school with may still live in Corpus Christi, and may wish to know who their parents, grandparents, uncles, aunts, and etc., are. Some of these people may wonder how their behavior affected their fellow classmates. Although, I doubt many have given it much thought. My DOEI classmates perpetuated Texas apartheid, and are responsible for the hate, racism, and ignorance alive today in Corpus Christi.

I am not by formal training a cultural anthropologist or sociologist. I am however an educated, well-traveled, multilingual student of history and cultures. I am a proficient historian, and reject the concept that Tejanos were ever a conquered people. Native Tejanos living in Tejas during the DOEI invasion were farmers, not soldiers. They were passive, hard-working people who battled the elements and Native American tribes who raided along the border. Tejanos never surrendered and are amongst the most resilient, creative, determined, tough, and brave people in the country. This work is specifically about my own personal misadventures and survival, and though not focused on Texas history, some must be included. Comparisons between cultures and ethnicities are inadequate and superficial, but can serve as examples.

For instance, I will draw from the case of Hispanic gang members in Los Angeles, who consider themselves brave and deeply connected to their ethnic roots. These ignorant unfortunates have little connection to their culture, and have completely surrendered their identity to popular trends. What they consider to be the Mexican culture is a mixture of hip hop, alcohol and drug use, vulgarities, violence, self-absorbance, and dishonesty. None of which has any redeeming quality in any culture. What they present as bravado is in fact an absence of humanity, and confirms that they have been brutalized via their environment and peers. From a political perspective this also exemplifies how generations of people have disconnected from a political and educational system that has ignored, abused, and abandoned them. As every disenfranchised and politically oppressed people (Irish, Scottish, Italians, Native Americans, Blacks, Jews, Poles, and etc.) have done throughout history when faced with consistent legal inequality, they formed gangs for defense and survival. These same tactics were used by the so-called Fathers of our country. However, American historians have called them revolutionaries, not criminals. The trait of self-preservation has been accepted wholeheartedly when it supports the myth of American independence, but never in cases of minority populations demanding justice. Our Founding Fathers formed a popular front and declared themselves independent, outside of the laws of the British Empire. These men sought and formed a political system that recognized their legal claims, and were supported via taxes which led to open warfare. In here lies the difference between criminals and revolutionaries, (those that formed gangs in Los Angeles). Although there were thousands lacking political representation, financial backing, weapons, and man power, this difference reduced them to the category of criminals, resulting in their being hunted down, imprisoned, or killed on the streets by police. Constant infighting, such as in the case of Native American tribes who warred against each other, made identifying and defeating them much easier. The gangs failed to unite, and instead warred amongst themselves in a counterproductive manner, which led them towards self-destruction. Los Angeles gang history is filled with tragic endings, murders, and blatant brutality usually only witnessed in civil wars. I teach my students to avoid all gang members. I have never believed gang behavior to be worthy of my participation, and have always considered such individuals to be bullies and cowards. However, I recognize that many of those living in overcrowded and crime ridden neighborhoods have joined gangs as a method of survival. I offer my regrets to these people, who might have been so much more.

Popular authors have stated that we are a reflection of those who surround us. If this is so then I can only conclude that I, along with hundreds of other Tejanos, was invisible at Andrew Jackson High School. None of the DOEI students or teachers ever saw us as real people. To them we were simply "Mexicans." The culture of Corpus Christi ignored and pushed us aside, never considering us of value. It's no wonder Native Tejanos were randomly murdered and imprisoned unjustly throughout Texas history. Readers who consider my statements farfetched are reminded of the genocide of ethnic minorities in Rwanda in 1994, which should serve as proof that ethnic cleansing can occur anywhere.

The story of my escape from Texas is much more than simple relocation, change of attitude, and spiritual rebirth. It is a worldwide search for identity and validation of the Warrior's discipline. It is a story of how personal power, *focus*, dedication, and adherence to the Toltec teachings overcame impossible obstacles. More importantly, it is an instruction manual and blueprint for Seekers hoping to find freedom from their past. Much to my own chagrin let me add that due to the continuous brainwashing by DOEI society, I was once one of the millions of Native Tejanos who simultaneously hated my oppressors, yet sought their recognition. This generated tremendous conflict and caused my awakening to falter. Under the direction of the racist Texas educational system, which denied participation of Tejanos in its history, I was systematically programed to feel inferior. Tejano teenagers were seen as predisposed towards crime and violence. No one questioned whether we had a reason to be angry or why we fought against oppression. Readers should note that had we been DOEIs behaving in the same manner for the same reasons, America would have rallied to our support. I was told repeatedly via Texas history that we, as the descendants of Mexican ancestors, had been defeated and conquered by the DOEI Texans. As such, we were expected to behave in a subservient manner. This delusional self-report tells how Texas fought for independence against an evil Mexican Government, under leadership of the tyrant General, Santa Anna. I was categorized as inferior because of my Mexican roots, and therefore associated to Santa Anna, who massacred the heroes at the Alamo. Simultaneously I was also never informed that there were Native Tejanos inside the Alamo, who fought and died alongside DOEIs. I am still at a loss for words at how so many people who unashamedly assumed to title of "teacher," allowed this discrimination to continue. These so-called educators never corrected ignorant statements and misinformation. They never taught us about Colonel Juan Nepomuceno Seguín, a real Tejano hero of the Texas Revolution. He eventually became a Texas Senator, and later the mayor of San Antonio, but was eventually run out of town by racist, land hungry, recently arrived Northerners. Unfamiliar with Native Tejano history, they challenged his loyalty to Texas, claiming that because of his ethnicity his allegiance lied with México. Despite this consistent overt discrimination, I sought and struggled to receive acceptance and recognition from my oppressors. I hated, and yet wanted to be acknowledged by the same people who treated me as an inferior. Imagine, if you can, my self-loathing and disillusionment when I discovered that their sense of superiority would never permit them to see me as an equal.

This all too common distorted sense of superiority has been created and reinforced via government mandates throughout American history and across the world. Although these self-promoting lies have been rebuffed and rebutted hundreds of times, the myth of DOEI supremacy continues. This delusional sense of ethnic privilege is so deeply ingrained it has become common ignorance, and there is no known cure for self-imposed blindness. It was only via the Toltec discipline that I was able to gain *detachment* and perspective on how such individuals view people of color. Over forty years of research has gone into writing and documenting this book. It will without a doubt be rejected, misinterpreted, misquoted, and maligned. Regardless, thanks to this discipline, I am no longer concerned with validation, acceptance, or public recognition, especially by those who oppressed me as a child. Those upon this path who remain *focused* will eventually transition out of the mad race of the average man, and no longer consider anyone superior or inferior, including themselves. Warriors *see* people in terms of energy, and know that behavior is all that matters. Race is nothing more than a powerful social idea which has developed over time, creating a hierarchy based upon physical characteristics. A Warrior acknowledges how he is identified and categorized by the average man, yet knows that he is not bound by his classification or prejudices. As such, a Warrior does not belong to any race, nor does he identify with any group of average people. Reaching this point will not be easy and requires tremendous effort and discipline, which will only be accomplished via a Warrior's *intent*. This concept is essential to this work. As I have mentioned before, the most powerful influence upon my life was the racist and hostile environment into which I was born. As such, it molded who I became. I spent a great deal of my life feeling connected to my ethnic roots and my people. However, as a Warrior, this is no longer so. This is a point of great consequence, as the average reader will undoubtedly interpret this work as being ethnically biased. Language is incapable of accurately describing the concept of a Warrior's *detachment*, and without said understanding, the context in which this work is written will be misinterpreted. Once again, I am not exaggerating or falsifying information, but simply relating it via my experiences.

Any genuine spiritual path would include an absence of ethnocentricity or religious superiority, and yet this is not the case with the average person. A focus on ethnocentricity makes a person ill-qualified to be honest or demonstrate integrity and humanity. This is something that has troubled me throughout my life, and after many years of contemplation I've accepted it. I've never believed myself to be superior to anyone, yet at the same time I've never considered myself inferior. I've never felt less worthy than someone who had more wealth than I, and never felt more worthy than someone who had less. I am not less than anyone, nor am I more, and neither are you. This is a revelation that only comes with *seeing*, as Warriors know death will eventually make everyone equally meaningless.

These matters are relevant to the study of the Toltec discipline, although every so-called spiritual teacher thus far has failed to address social injustice in their teachings. This was not accidentally omitted, but a sign of their reluctance to confront the cost and ugliness of American racism. Take notice that whether you agree or not makes no difference, as long as you act upon your beliefs. As you read, remember that while you may have a position, it is imperative to never become that position. Toltec Warriors were able to survive because they moved unseen throughout their lives, with clear objectives, forethought, planning, and steadfast discipline. To move about in a blatantly reactionary manner is to invite destruction. Having a position means you can change it if new information demands it, while becoming your position means you must defend it. Anyone who refuses to change despite new information is not utilizing all their alternatives, nor living the disciplined life of a Warrior. Reality is a harsh teacher, and an ever-present reminder of the contrast between the way things should be and the way things are.

Texas escapee,

-don Jesus M. Ramirez

Chapter One
Looking Back

"A Warrior's history differs from that of an average man. He does not wear it like a badge of honor or shame, but simply recognizes it as the person he used to be."

                                                                    -don Jesus M. Ramirez

Turning points in history can occur at any corner. In the words of Edward H. Carr, "Nothing in history is inevitable except in the formal sense that, for it to have happened otherwise, the antecedent causes would have had to be different." I wonder who I might have become if I had not been subjected to a systemically imposed inferiority. I am awed by how much work, discipline, and determination it has taken to defeat the years of systemic brainwashing. It is equally impressive how much injustice, discrimination, and poverty has played a role in my development. These hardships were the keys to my freedom. I have discovered that even those who live a disciplined life may have many questions. Anyone who has ever made hard choices wonders what might have happened if they'd acted according to how they felt, rather than to what they believed was right. It's not true that time heals all wounds. Time won't heal anything. Memories don't fade away, and they don't watch the clock. They'll go on living until you disconnect from them. This requires constant vigilance and steadfast determination. It demands merciless self-analysis and proper self-talk. Painful memories will consume you until you eject them from your life via discipline. In the end, both the strong and the weak are equal, but a Warrior makes seeking *detachment* a goal and a strategy. A Warrior struggles equally as hard with life as an average man, but suffers much less. These struggles take place while surrounded by 96ers, who he lives amongst, but never as one. It is a worthy struggle, but not one without sacrifice. It can only be obtained by implementing discipline, which can only be compared with going to war. Each Seeker must decide to commit fully while acknowledging the odds of winning are minimal.

I began writing my Warrior's inventory as a strategy when I decided to stop indulging in my past. At the time I had been following the Warrior's path for nearly thirty years, during which I had fanatically studied the work of Carlos Castaneda. Much to my disappointment, after years of dedicated examination and implementation, I discovered Carlos had deliberately misled readers. He intentionally misrepresented extremely significant aspects of this discipline, while making others inaccessible via casting a fog of confusion around them. As I conducted my Warrior's inventory, I soon recognized that this concept was another area where Carlos omitted momentous information. For instance, I discovered via application that conducting a Warrior's inventory is a lifelong process, not be a one-time event. Genuine Seekers and advanced Warriors will agree that self-awareness is as painful and difficult as any challenge. Every aspect of conducting an in-depth self-analysis is comparable to entering alien territory, yet essential for anyone seeking spiritual freedom, emotional healing, and through it, personal power. The idea of writing out my Warrior's inventory came from an editor of the *Calallen Herald*, a newspaper for the Corpus Christi suburb; Calallen, archrival in football of AJHS. The editor was asking former AJHS students to write an essay describing what it was like being a student there. I saw it as an opportunity to begin another phase of my development, and it was without a doubt the most difficult challenge I have undertaken. I experienced a hurricane of troubling and conflicting emotions, along with tearful and heartfelt recollections of painful experiences. I was caught in a torrid of anger, sadness, joy, rage, and despair. Oceans of painful memories engulfed me with remembrances of my years at Andrew Jackson High School, and living in Corpus Christi.

Imagine being asked to describe your feelings about the people who oppressed and humiliated you throughout your childhood and adolescence. Imagine what you might say about the people who stood idly by as you were beaten and subjugated. I struggled to find the best manner in which to describe my experiences, and when given the restrictions of the Calallen Herald's publication, I found it impossible to do so adequately. The best I could have done was use the limited space to describe and convey a tiny percentage of what it was like to be a Native Tejano in the racist culture of South Texas during the Sixties and Seventies. The problem was that it was also true throughout the entire state of Tejas. This was an impossible challenge. There was no way in which to convey what it was like to have your childhood stolen, and your dignity stripped from you so completely as to make you question your self-worth. I still believe it is impossible to convey. Although this document cannot adequately communicate what I had to endure, it will give readers an insight into the life of one Native Tejano who escaped Texas. In order to do so, I've decided to share some of my memoirs of AJHS and Corpus Christi, Texas. I know that I will be misquoted, criticized, and maligned. I am aware my philosophies, statements, and suggestions will create anger in those who seek to maintain the status quo. Nevertheless, I continue without apology. Even at its best, my endeavor will only serve as a symbolic gesture and meaningless stone thrown against a racist educational system that perpetuated DOEI superiority in this so-called "land of the free."

I was not surprised to learn former President George W. Bush's grandfather, Prescott Bush, was a supporter of Nazi Germany ideologies. As much as I've tried to understand, I have no explanation for how such individuals justified their cruelty and violence towards innocent children. Hurting a child of any culture, under any circumstances, has always been forbidden throughout the world. Much like how the film *The Birth of a Nation* was used by the Ku Klux Klan (KKK) to justify murdering Black Americans, the Alamo has been the cause of an endless number of hate crimes against Native Tejanos throughout Texas history. You should bear in mind that although this is my personal story, it's also true of most Native Tejanos. There are millions of Texas escapees with similar experiences, and although most remain silent, no one ever forgets their high school experiences.

I was one of hundreds living on Main Drive, a once upon a time migrant camp which transformed itself into a community. Main Drive, or Hudson Acres as it's called, was not located within the city limits, and built upon a former oil field. The DOEI landowners saw nothing wrong with selling migrant farm workers polluted land they couldn't do anything else with. I was one of the thousands of unwanted children born to women who were not permitted to use birth control by the Catholic Church. I am the grandchild of revolutionaries that fought in the Mexican Revolution, born of blood spilled so America could grow richer. Like millions of other Hispanics, I am the great grandson of Pancho Villa's dreams, who became American when México relinquished territorial claims in the Treaty of Guadalupe Hidalgo. We are American as a result of manifest destiny. President James K. Polk's desire and greed to expand the country's borders bestowed the gift we were told was a dream. Yet, after experiencing racist double standards and broken promises, my American dream has become a nightmare. I've learned via many harsh lessons that although my accident of birth was not of my choosing, I must bear the consequences. Although I am promised equal justice and opportunity, I am denied, discriminated against, and excluded from partaking of the cornucopia. I have yet to find the land of opportunity which I was told existed, where hard working people can prosper. Like millions of others, I have found that the best opportunities are reserved for those whose parents and relatives own banks and run civic and private organizations, which offer loans and bestow recognition. I've learned that the system is firm against the average citizen, yet inviting towards the preselected children of the rich. This brand of inferiority is not regional, nor a passing notion of ignorance, but a permanent fixture. Until I found the Toltec discipline I feared my only salvation was to become that which I loathe. Without this discipline I would have been lost, doomed to never find freedom.

My mother, now deceased, instilled within me a pride of culture and heritage. She tried to teach me how to be a man. This seems absurd given that my father, also now deceased, drank and chased women, and instilled distorted values, inferiority, and fear via physical abuse. Much to my chagrin, adopting his behavior multiplied my problems and added to my humiliation and suffering. He was the most influential person in my life, as was my older brother whom I refer to as "Beelzebub" throughout this endeavor. These individuals taught me who not to be.

Many of my most powerful lessons were learned while attending Andrew Jackson Elementary and Junior High School, where I was subjected to racial discrimination by bullies and DOEIs. This included society, which fed into the indifference and distorted sense of superiority demonstrated by the DOEI population. Even though I now understand DOEI delusions are a result of hundreds of years of self-deception and government mandates, it did not make the racism easier to tolerate. I look back and feel fortunate to have survived Andrew Jackson and escaped Texas. I feel like a refugee from a war-torn country, homeless and forcibly deposed from his own land. To remain would have required I surrender to the ignorance and hatred that has broken the spirits of thousands who attended AJHS and lived in Corpus Christi, Texas. Unfortunately, return trips have confirmed my worst fears, as little has changed. Tejanos are still viewed as an inferior population, and not as Americans, but as "Mexicans." Our ancestors were living in Tejas long before European land thieves arrived, but it is pointless to continue to explain why we are not Mexicans. Their refusal to accept recorded history validates and explains why racism continues to be America's ugliest secret.

My survival at Andrew Jackson required I deliberately subordinate my feelings and bite my tongue, something which has taken years to learn. To openly rebel against injustice would have resulted in beatings, death, or imprisonment. Like slaves did in the South, most Tejanos learned to keep silent. As a result of being shunned, openly hated Tejanos moved through Andrew Jackson like ghosts. Most crept around as if we had done something wrong, and used silence as a protective shield. We were called Mexicans and had no voice, representation, or defenders. Similar to Jewish people in Nazi Germany, we were hated for something we had not chosen to be a part of; our ethnicity, culture, and language. As it was with the Holocaust, the passive acceptance of the "good people" cosigned our demise. Under the disguise of "boy will be boys," it was "normal" for groups of DOEI thugs to pummel, humiliate, and drive Tejano students out of school. All this was done with the passive indifference of DOEI administrators. It was also normal for administrators to knowingly permit after school beatings, and "it's not our problem" was their attitude, leaving us at the mercy of hooligans of all ethnicities. Most Tejanos surrendered, but the few who fought back were beaten and branded as "trouble makers." We lived under a constant threat of violence, and hopelessness and despair filled our souls. The police were instruments of terror, used by the DOEI power structure to enforce illegal practices and punish any who protested. Many police officers were blatant racists who used their authority to maintain the status quo. To demand justice would have been to willingly place ourselves on the bullseye and become the target of DOEI scorn, possibly resulting in death. Edmund Burke's words were once paraphrased in reference to Nazi arrests of Jews in prewar Europe, "The only thing necessary for the triumph of evil is for good men to do nothing." I experienced the same indifference by fellow students that "good Germans" demonstrated towards Jews during the Holocaust. These shocking and eye-opening events are pivotal, and so devastating that survivors never fully recover. Tejanos of that period have much in common with Holocaust survivors. I have presented these experiences to many Jewish people, but none have agreed. Amazingly, those whom I've met lacked compassion and empathy, which resembles the same indifference they have complained about throughout their history. It is a regrettable condition of man that our personal experiences must outweigh everyone else's, and explains why things never change. I have also spoken of these experiences to Japanese, Chinese, Black, and every other ethnicity I've come into contact with. None have demonstrated an understanding of what I spoke of. None agreed that our suffering was comparable to theirs. I have no answer to this riddle. It is a reality which has caused me many sleepless nights.

My very first day of school will live in my memory forever. My total unpreparedness compounded by not knowing the language, or even where I was supposed to go, caused me to wander into the high school gym. I came across a group of high school DOEI basketball players who accused me of trying to steal something, and no more needed to be said. They beat me, and then dragged me into the shower room, where after closing the door, formed a circle and urinated on me while laughing. I emerged soaking wet with urine, shocked, terrified, and in tears. The DOEI teachers ignored me and I simply walked off campus and continued three miles home. The incident was swallowed up into a dark hole of racial injustice as if it had never happened. It became one of many shameful secrets which I never spoke of to anyone.

This experience set the tone for my years at Andrew Jackson Elementary School, which were a series of beatings and humiliations. Gangs of DOEI and Tejano thugs picked on me for stuttering and being small. They would steal my lunch and torment me without repose. I grew to hate them and fought back as best as a child could against a gang of thugs. I took countless beatings, but stubbornly refused to be cowed. I complained to my teachers and begged them to intervene, but they weren't interested in protecting a "Mexican" kid. Besides, my oppressors weren't stupid, and never attacked me in front of them. I quickly learned to always stay within sight of a teacher, or not go out to the playground at all. Everywhere I went I moved in silence, always alert for an attack. Amazingly, not going to the playground was also the reason why I grew to love reading. I stayed in the classroom reading the books off the shelves, developing a love for books that continues today. Elementary school was a memorable time of sad experiences and hard lessons, interrupted by random acts of violence which materialized out of nowhere. As a result I developed primal instincts; *reading* the setting and never depending on adults to protect me. I learned to always have an avenue of escape, carry a weapon, and be ready to fight for my life. Although I had many brothers, I endured all this alone because my father never taught us to watch out for each other. We were all alone, together.

I carried these secret painful memories until the demands of taking my Warriors inventory caused me to realize that I had also been sensing my mother's sadness and despair. I discovered I have always sensed what was going on around me. The ability to perceive what others cannot has been both a curse and a blessing. It gave me an understanding far beyond my years and ability to articulate. It left me stunned and silent, as you can imagine what such knowledge might do to a child. Far and beyond anything else, watching my father beat my mother caused me to withdraw into an imaginary world. It is impossible to convey how much my life was affected by watching him beat her and my siblings. It is even more difficult to express how understanding my mother's pain made her behavior towards me even more heartbreaking. Lost in indulgence and ignorance, she never realized I could sense the depth of her suffering. It was also at this time that I came to sense the ominous dark inorganic entities surrounding the region. The land between the Nueces River and the Rio Grande is soaked with the blood of massacred Native Americans, murdered Mexican farmers, and unlucky Tejanos. The entire area has witnessed years of violence, injustice, and sadness. The bones of thousands are scattered across the land. My childhood is filled with memories of perceiving the presence of wandering spirits. Additionally, my father's abusive behavior left horrible impressions. As a result, my siblings withdrew into protective shells to survive. It essentially became every man for himself. To my regret, this pattern of behavior continues, and on top of stealing our childhoods, my father also stole our relationships with each other. He role modeled behavior which Beelzebub adopted and excelled in. It was his approval and indulgence that planted the seeds of criminal conduct into Beelzebub's mind, giving him the corrupted idea of what it meant to be a man. It didn't take long to learn that my chances for survival were few at best. I was literally surrounded by individuals who saw themselves as superior, endowed with the right to torment me at their whim.

The DOEIs forced us to feel inferior and changed the rules to benefit themselves. When challenged, they used all their power to maintain the status quo. They also used the legal system to incarcerate, lynch, murder, and make suspects disappear. It was a shameful time in Texas history, and as a result much of what I learned about DOEIs was negative and destructive. It has taken years to develop the necessary *detachment* and ability to *see*, in order for these experiences to not negatively impact new interactions with people who so happen to be DOEIs. Even after years of world travel and education I cannot understand or comprehend such senseless evil. To this very day I am still unable to fathom how anyone honestly believes their ethnicity makes them superior. According to Noel Montgomery Elliot's book, *Finding Anyone, Anywhere, Anywhen*, many scientists now estimate that everyone on Earth is no further apart from each other than a 50th cousin. While others believe we are no further apart than a 32nd cousin.

All the incidents which I describe took place at Andrew Jackson, occurred within sight of countless DOEI students, who never took a stance against injustice. Keep in mind, we all attended the same elementary, junior high, and high school together. We all read the same books and heard the same history lectures about America, the land of the free and home of the brave. We saluted the same flag and said the same Pledge of Allegiance every morning before class. Yet, none of them saw any discrepancy with what they said and how things actually were. As for myself, I'd been so brainwashed, I used to actually feel chills when I looked up at the flag and heard "The Star-Spangled Banner" before the Friday night football games. I am stunned at the power that constant brainwashing and misinformation has upon a young person. To this day, their lack of a moral barometer has no comparison, but demonstrated that what is considered normal is not always right. It also explains how and why genocide can happen anywhere. Even as we pledged an oath to a flag representing freedom and justice, we, the Native Tejano children, were routinely denied it. I am still revolted by the blatant hypocrisy, and realize there was nothing I could have done to protect myself from the bigotry that existed. I used to believe that only in Texas could such a system have been tolerated, endured, and publicly funded. It wasn't until years later, after much travel that I discovered my experiences were not unique to Texas, and that Texas was simply a microcosm of our entire country and its racist epidemic. It was only one extension of the hatred that has lingered since the Civil War. It would be impossible for the teachers to justify themselves. It would also be equally impossible for the principals to explain how this was the appropriate conduct. Unfortunately, Texas was and continues to be a moral vacuum, where DOEIs believe it is their divine right to subjugate all people of color. In their racist minds we were Mexicans, a "conquered people," and therefore subject to their whims. To point out such delusion and hypocrisy is as meaningless today as it was then, as my complaints fall upon deaf ears. Not because they are unjust, but because 96ers reading this material have been desensitized by the brutality of their life experiences. I've learned it's impossible to instill a moral barometer or a conscience into a 96er, especially a DOEI 96er when it comes to matters of race. I cannot conceive any possibility of DOEI 96ers acknowledging they are not superior to people of color. I don't believe they are capable of admitting what science has consistently proven. Texas was founded on the principles of a racial hierarchy, which has not changed. At its core, Texas continues to believe in the institution of slavery and white supremacy. I am still unable to fathom the degree of depravity that was considered normal amongst the DOEI population. Keep in mind that Corpus Christi is a port city, a Mecca of tourism, and was the home of Farrah Fawcett, Selena, Freddy Fender, Eva Longoria, and other celebrities. I am lucky to have survived Andrew Jackson and escaped from Texas. I was systematically and brutally stripped of my innocence, subjected to cruelty and indifference, and forced to move from childhood to adulthood. I was stunned and left unable to understand. After years of torment, preferring death to living life as a lesser human being, I volunteered to fight in Vietnam. I left Texas and Andrew Jackson in the manner spoken of in the Bible. I wiped the dust from my feet, walked away, and never looked back. I am still surprised the entire population was not destroyed by a rain of fire and brimstone, as in the destruction of Sodom and Gomorrah.

While working on the first draft of this book I awaited the release of the 2004 film *The Alamo*. I had hoped this remake would do what its predecessors failed to do, and use actual historical facts to tell the truth about what really happened at the Battle of the Alamo. I had hoped it would include the names of Tejanos who fought alongside DOEIs, against Santa Anna's invading army. Unfortunately, once again such details were deliberately omitted, denying Native Tejanos knowledge of their place in history. It was only after researching Texas history myself that I discovered the first Vice President of Texas was Lorenzo de Zavala, who also signed the Texas Declaration of Independence. I'll bet you a penny to your dollar that George W. Bush never knew that. My only satisfaction came from discovering the film did horribly. It was immortalized as being the official second biggest box office bomb in cinema history. As a child I was attacked and subjected to racial hate crimes by DOEIs who wanted to avenge the Battle of the Alamo. If left unchecked, another generation of Tejano Americans will suffer due to the same ignorance. Those in power will never publicly admit they deliberately subjugated Tejanos via keeping the DOEI population ignorant. Unless history is truthfully taught in schools, racism based upon ignorance will continue to thrive.

The desire to write my experiences has provoked several return trips to Corpus Christi. I have placed several advertisements in the local newspapers and have combed libraries for information. I visited my old stomping grounds, including Andrew Jackson High School, and found that nothing has changed. The unconscious brainwashing of Native Tejanos continues, and is demonstrated via their incessant need to seek approval, recognition, and acceptance by their oppressors. Although Native Tejanos are now employed in the Andrew Jackson School District, and are members of the board, DOEIs continue to view them as criminal suspects, not as professional colleagues worthy of respect. Tejano Americans have fought a continuous uphill battle, and have much to be proud of with regards to the advances students, teachers, and administrators have made. This is merely scratching the surface, and the battle for justice and equality continues. As an example, the DOEI clerks in the administrative office at AJHS treated me with amusement, reluctantly loaning me the old year books, all the while watching me with suspicion and scorn. I was not surprised, as this is considered "normal" in Texas, especially in Corpus Christi, and particularly at AJHS, where students and staff have inherited intergenerational racist attitudes. The manner in which they treated me was inherited from their parents, and bequeathed to their children in an endless cycle of hatred. Not surprisingly, you'll never hear or read about inherited intergenerational racist attitudes concerning DOEIs in Texas. Who amongst the millions of DOEIs would have the courage to admit such a thing exists? By the same token you'll never hear of mass deportations of German, Irish, Scottish, English, or any other such people. You'll never hear of these people being placed into concentration camps and having their property confiscated and sold at auction. You may have heard of the racial cleansing of one group of European population upon another, but this only occurs during civil wars, when old scores are settled. As I said, no one forgets nothing. I make no apology for my statements, nor do I seek endorsement or support. These are my observations and I assume full responsibility for expressing them. I will not be surprised to learn my books have been burned in protest. Should I find this book has been banned in Texas, I would feel complimented, considering it a red badge of courage. Such anger and rejection is nothing more than disguised cowardice and ignorance. However, the events I describe are real, and expressed from the perspective of a Warrior who *sees*.

I have asked several former classmates to contribute to this work, but none chose to participate. Among these people are my younger sister and her husband, a former football teammate. Another was a woman named Samantha Rojas who was living in Houston at the time, and also did not wish to contribute. I also contacted Bill Chancy, another former football teammate, via email. He never responded. I requested assistance from the library and was allowed to make copies. I was also asked to pay for the copies, which I gladly did. I have no ill will towards those ignorant wretches who are only acting out as they were taught by their racist ancestors. The problem is that understanding someone is emotionally disturbed, and even understanding why they are, does not help make them easier to deal with. This is the catch-22 of a Warrior who *sees*, while having to survive in an ocean of disgusting behavior, yet is unable to change anything. In the end, we are who we are, and that's why we find ourselves where we are. If I had been treated as a welcomed guest and valued alumnus, I might have had less to say. As it is, their behavior only served to validate my experiences.

Texas escapee,

don Jesus M. Ramirez

Chapter Two
The Instinct of Survival

"It is not true that there is always a light behind every cloud. Sometimes there are monsters. There have been millions of helpless souls who died waiting to be saved by the good people of America; civil rights marchers, Jews in concentration camps, and countless others. How many opportunities did former President George W. Bush have to demonstrate clemency, yet instead chose to earn another conservative vote?"

-don Jesus M. Ramirez

During the darkest storms we sometimes see a glimmer of light that gives us hope. To this day I cannot explain how I happened upon this optimism. Although I stuttered and had freckles, and my ears stuck out like lampshades, I believed love would win. Perhaps I watched too many late night movies, or maybe I stared towards heaven too often. No matter, one morning after a restless night, I awoke to a singing bird who taught me the secret of happiness. During that magical moment, what I then believed to be the voice of God spoke to me. It said the singing bird sings because he lives, and he lives because he sings. A Native American shaman told me birds bring the spirits of loved ones to say hello via a happy song. This may be fairytale nonsense, but I have loved birds ever since. My mother used to whistle as she hung the wash on the clotheslines and cleaned the house. After all these years I continue to love birds and smile whenever they're near.

As a child I was intuitive and insightful with an endless curiosity, which urged me to seek adventure and take chances. I slowly learned not to attract attention and move about like a shadow without a sound. When I silenced my *internal dialogue*, surprisingly it attracted attention like a beating drum, until I learned to quiet my spirit. This was how I discovered the spiritual connection that links us all, making us aware of one another. We sense other people's energy the way we sense heat, wind, or a coming storm. Average people can be sensed at great distances, especially when involved in emotional turmoil, but everyone can be sensed. I have sensed the presence of bodies, which baffles and scares most people, but only because they failed to observe I was sensing the dead person's spirit. I have always been able to sense the presence of animals as well. This made my childhood journeys into the woods especially interesting. I had not yet discovered the reason for my being able to do so was in part because I stuttered so badly. I rarely spoke, which resulted in the silencing of my *internal dialogue*. After my discovery of the Toltec discipline, I learned this ability is nearly impossible to acquire, and is as rare as finding a cave. I no longer doubt my intuition or ability to sense and perceive what others ignore or simply are not aware of. This ability has nurtured me throughout my life. It has kept me energized even while facing seemingly insurmountable obstacles.

    Speaking of which, I discovered an unknown cave while hiking as a child. I was making my way across an open pasture which had a large canal running through it. The canal had been enlarged via rains that eroded the cliffs. I was leaning over the bank, gazing into the creek, when I sensed a breeze. It was as if someone was blowing wind through a tube towards me. I looked up and saw a giant hornet's nest. Behind it was a hole in the wall of a large cliff, with an opening approximately four-and-a-half feet wide. The breeze I felt seemed to be coming through it. Guided by my curiosity, I crossed the canal, and climbed up and around the entrance to find another opening in the ground. The rain had eroded a hole through the wall of the cliff, all the way down towards the creek, creating a thirty foot long cave, approximately five feet tall. I was happier than I'd ever been in my whole life, and even more so when I discovered I could stand up inside. I kept the secret of the cave for years, and periodically returned to spend time there alone. I sometimes brought along hotdogs, mustard, ketchup, slices of Wonder Bread, and had a weenie roast. They were the best hotdogs I ever ate. Discovering the cave was as close to magic as I could find, and made me into a believer of improbable possibilities. Perhaps this experience is the reason why I have always been able to believe in things that cannot be seen, explained, or conform to scientific requirements.

The more time I spent alone in the woods, the quicker I learned to be my own best friend. I discovered something few have ever learned; my relationship with myself was more important than any other. The beginning of my awakening came in finding this open yet hidden secret which few ever see. It is this simple self-interest that shapes us, determining whether we become sheep or independent individuals with our own thoughts and ideas. Few 96ers ever come to know themselves, which explains their chronic disassociation. They spend their lives seeking gurus and spiritual leaders to give them an identity and direction. Most never accept that we are alone, no matter how many people surround us. My ability to perceive feelings and thoughts also taught me that although we are physically alone, we are never alone spiritually, as we are all connected to one another and the Universe. After being confronted with this truth many alleged spiritual leaders claim it to be commonsense, yet Warriors know this is not so. If it were commonsense, then these supposed masters who claim to impart wisdom and guidance would have addressed the topic sooner. Regardless, accepting this truth as reality is shattering to most. Learning not to be afraid of being alone is a skill which few 96ers will ever know. Unlike most, I actually preferred being alone. It was while alone that I practiced speaking out loud, rehearsing what to say and how to say it. I imagined myself speaking to a group, which helped me overcome stuttering. At the time I did not recognize this as cognitive therapy. I didn't realize that it was self-actualization and positive imaging. I also never knew it was a Warrior's strategy. Seekers should note that strategy is implemented during a crisis, when a Warrior utilizes perfect *timing* via discipline. Hard work on my own, *focus*, and dedication became the manner in which I defeated my obstacles. I eventually recognized that the only way to conquer stuttering and my fear of public speaking was through action. Abstract ideas and theory must always give way to action. Without it, theorizing and philosophizing is useless. I therefore began constructing a Warrior's challenge, which requires abandon and control, the paradox of a Warrior's strategy. My deliberate act of war against my weakness took the form of performing stand-up comedy. Over the course of several years I worked various comedy clubs and bars in San Francisco, Sacramento, Fresno, and around the entire Bay Area. Although at this point in my development I no longer stuttered, I could not claim complete victory while my fear of public speaking lingered. As I acquired experience and learned the subtle secrets of performing, this weakness slowly began to fade away. It was a very difficult process, during which I discovered that there is nothing easy about trying to make people laugh. Average people are as critical of others as they are of themselves. Twisted and envious of everyone, including performers, they ignorantly believe they could do better. When the self-importance of a 96er is engaged it reveals their true nature. Haven't you ever wondered why there are so many hecklers in comedy clubs? Were we as a society not calloused to this concept it would appear as absurd as it actually is. Think about it. Of their own free will hecklers chose to attend a show, under the premise of allegedly seeking entertainment, yet decide to attempt to ruin that show via creating a disturbance. Only in the mind of an average person could this make sense. Beginning comedians discover many subtleties and accept many disappointments. This is all a part of learning, as wisdom cannot be obtained via observation. As expected, I hit the same wall all Warriors crash into when interacting with 96ers. This stage of my development was very challenging, frightening, and fun all at the same time. I met dozens of comedians, including Lewis Black, who along with Bill Maher were my comedy heroes. I've always admired their ability to challenge our way of thinking and help us look at situations differently. My last show was at the Improv in San Jose, California. If I had the time which this art form demands its practitioners dedicate, I would still be performing now. As I have said before, my only regret is that there will never be enough time to do all the things I've wanted to do, and my time on this great earth will be altogether too short.

    I spent countless hours alone in the woods without a single thought, word, or picture in my head. I found peace in my aloneness, as it was the only time I did not have to worry about the unpredictable and dangerous nature of average people. These experiences heightened my awareness and made me even more sensitive to people's energy. Being so perceptive as a child left me confused, and it took years to learn how to differentiate the energy, thoughts, and emotions of others from my own. Aside from thoughts and bodily functions, there are not many things a ten-year-old child can control. I discovered that simply not attracting the attention of undesirables was not enough. I spent months trying to unravel this mystery, and finally settled upon a strategy to not get caught up in someone else's drama by accident. This required constant self-monitoring, vigilance, and discipline, of which I had very little at the time. Plus, there were so many distractions in my barrio, which was a combat zone. I felt like I'd been drafted into a war I didn't want to fight. So I ran, dodging bullets from one foxhole to another. I learned to dodge and weave in and out like a hummingbird, moving like a desert roadrunner, silently and quickly. I moved in the shadows, making the least amount of noise as possible, always expecting trouble. Things never got easier, and in place of one tyrant there was always another.

    I was able to disappear from time to time, as I didn't look like much. I was skinny as a toothpick, and quiet as a mouse. I hardly spoke due to my stuttering, and didn't have much to say when I did. What would a ten-year-old boy who'd been raised to be seen and not heard have to say? When I did have something to say, I had to get it out quickly, which was precisely why I stuttered. In my rush to speak, my tongue twisted into a knot. Everyone laughed, and I lived in constant fear of humiliation. Even my parents never missed an opportunity to laugh, which resulted with my being ridiculed by my older brother, Beelzebub. I now understand my stuttering was the result of having witnessed countless acts of violence, and enduring them in silence. My parents never spoke to me unless I was forced to explain why I'd done something wrong. I still find this puzzling, as I have no idea how my parents expected me to know how to speak or behave. They acted like crazy, angry children, rather than adults. I never understood how they demanded I do what they said, while behaving as they did. They never spoke to me or took the time to explain anything, and I literally mean nothing, which still seems absurd. It is a miracle I survived.

Things at school were a little better, but not much. There was always a fight on the way to school or coming back. Kids from Main Drive were driven in on huge yellow/orange school buses, which seated between sixty and eighty kids. No one spoke, and there was always an element of danger in the air. The older junior high and high school kids were always fighting about something. I tried not to get caught up in anyone else's trouble, but it got harder as I got older. All the fighting going on at home sharpened my instincts and enabled me to perceive violent explosions before they occurred. I usually did pretty well. However, I wasn't always right. When I was wrong and something happened, I risked getting smashed by the combatants. I also had to keep an eye out for bullies who picked on anyone they wished. Life as a kid on Main Drive was scary and dangerous. I wasn't the only kid getting hammered on the school bus, and everyone lived under constant danger. One minute everything would be peaceful, and then suddenly fists would fly. Sometimes knives flashed as rivals clashed over whatever they were fighting about that day. The fights were usually over an insult or a girl. Personally, I never saw any girls on Main Drive who were worth the trouble. I've never understood fighting over women. For that matter, I never understood jealousy. No one had anything worth stealing, and everyone was equally as poor. Nevertheless, it seemed like there was always a fight about to happen, just ending, or expected in the near future. Years later I realized brutality runs downhill, just like shit. Those who are brutalized inflict the same punishments which they endured upon others, and the endless cycle of violence continues.

Most of the kids in elementary school were in awe of the older guys who fought all the time. I never cared who they were or what they were fighting about. I was always trying to predict conflicts so I could avoid them. Most of them were bullies, and I hated bullies. Many of the older migrant kids wore their hair like Elvis Presley, long on the sides and in the back, with lots of hair cream. It made their hair greasy, which is why DOEIs called them greasers. This got real confusing, as there were also groups of DOEIs who worked on cars or rode motorcycles, and they were also called greasers. Everyone wore a different uniform which designated where you lived, what kind of work you did, and which group you belonged to. I identified with the California teenagers I saw dancing on *American Bandstand*. I figured being called a greaser always meant trouble, because of the manner in which it was said. The word was used as an insult, and usually followed by a larger and older DOEI making aggressive gestures towards you. I learned that in these situations it was always best to run away. It was even better to keep an eye out for these individuals, and just not be there at all. The bigger, older DOEIs were often football players, and were just as cruel as the thugs. Everyone was subject to being harassed, beaten, or sexually molested by these bastards. I never had protection and was always afraid of getting cornered in the bathroom or boy's locker room. It wasn't any safer around Tejano thugs either.

During the Sixties and Seventies it was guaranteed you were going to get picked on at school. The best you could do was to not get caught in the wrong place at the wrong time. For instance, you didn't want to be in the bathroom or parking lot during class. Things could get real ugly if there were no teachers around to intervene. The only thing that helped was having an older brother. Unfortunately, my older brother, Beelzebub, was a coward. My oldest brother, who I refer to as "Bumper" throughout this endeavor, was a legend amongst street fighters, known for his fast hands, great kicks, and courage. He had married his high school girlfriend, who I'll refer to as "Lilith," and dropped out of sight. Lilith, as you might know, was the name of Adam's first wife, who refused to be subordinate to him, and was cast out of the Garden of Eden for disobedience. She became the queen of energy sucking demons who preyed upon men, literally sucking the life out of them via sexual conquest. I don't think Bumper loved Lilith. She was just the prettiest Tejano chick in school, so he had to have her. The story, which has become family legend, and may not be true, is that they stayed out too late one night and her father refused to let her back inside the house. Today, it would be a joke, but back then it was serious business. They spent the night at our house, which was tiny and already filled with too many people. She slept on the sofa in the living room, while he slept in the double bed we shared in the back of the house. We lived out in the middle of nowhere, long before enforced building codes, so when my father decided to add another room to our house, he just built one. My father was a jack of all trades, or at least he thought so. He could construct a frame, lay cement, and do electricity without consulting anyone or getting permission. He used us as workhorses, particularly during labor intensive projects, like roofing. One of the many problems which accompanied our lack of experience, considering we were just children, was that we made a lot of mistakes. My father resolved this with beatings. Another issue was that he didn't want to spend money for building materials. He was a master scavenger and we were part of his crew. Before beginning a project he gathered discarded materials from old buildings that were about to be torn down. Whether he had permission to remove scrap materials or stole them is still a mystery to me. I recall gathering two-by-fours, discarded nails, old windows, and sheets of aluminum from construction sites and trash heaps. When I was eight-years-old he had me sit in front of several five-gallon buckets filled with bent, twisted nails, which I had to spend hours straightening with a hammer. No one gave a damn about what went on out there, as long as we paid our taxes and never killed anyone. Our house was built like a train, in a long line with one room attached to the other. There was no indoor bathroom and no privacy.

The morning after Bumper's girlfriend had stayed the night, my father should have taken her back home and just dropped her off. Instead, he drove them to get married. This is typical of average people with horrible judgment, inherited stupidity, and dysfunctional logic. Seekers need always remember that all average people are great at making bad choices, and then making them worse by involving other people and the law. The newly married couple then moved in the house across the street from ours, and fought like cats and dogs. Ten years later Lilith pointed a .22 cal rifle at Bumper and pulled the trigger. Luckily it wasn't loaded, but she didn't know that. They divorced, but continued hating each other, and it looks like they'll die before ending their feud. Sorry, if you're waiting for a happy ending, you're reading the wrong book. The best I can do is present the truth in a comical manner, because it's the only way to manage stupidity. The guy was my hero, and he turned out to be a loser. The fool thought sex was love, and the only way to find happiness. Like all average people he continues to do the same things while expecting different results. After five divorces he still has not discovered that sex and happiness are distinct. Women learn this very early in life, which is why most don't consider sex to be an essential part of love. Most prefer money, endless attention, diva status, celebrity, power, and lots of men kissing their ass. I wish I could say Bumper learned his lesson and is finally happy, but average people don't change, they just get older. The truth is he's just an older version of the same fool he's always been.

My brother Beelzebub has always been, and continues to be a coward. Supposedly he now has a lot of money, but has never been generous. The wealth of others has never interested me, and I've never met anyone with money whom I enjoyed. I like doing things, not having things. Beelzebub was the source of my jokes at the Improv Comedy Club in San Jose, California. As an adult he changed his last name and married a blonde-haired, blue-eyed DOEI woman, and engendered two unwanted children. I have not spoken to him in years and have never met his children, nor do I wish to. While I have spent years working on the Warrior's path developing my spirituality, he seems to be destroying his. He now wears blue contact lenses, pretends he is a DOEI, and even made up a fake family tree leading him back to England. Why, you might ask? I don't know. I cannot understand it either, but I do find him very amusing. I get a great laugh at how he demeans himself. I am not surprised he is so self-loathing. Even as a child he wanted blue eyes. He's traded his identity and roots in exchange for a position amongst a group of people who rejected him. True to form, his greatest love is money. Not what it buys, but the power it conveys. He became an insurance salesman. Let me simply say that he lacks character and has gotten worse with age. Character is something you either have or you don't. As a kid he wanted to be the center of attention, a typical Leo who always wanted to be in charge. He went out for football once, but quit because he wasn't any good. He wanted to shine, but wasn't willing to put in the work. Like so many guys who cannot cut it, he stopped trying and never played sports again.

Birds of a feather flock together, and so do skunks. Beelzebub used to hang out with a guy named Joe Hernandez, who everyone called "Little Joe" because he was so tiny. He was Bumper's brother-in-law, and he was a trash talking loser. He was just another victim of too much television, and was without a clue. Little Joe was randomly cruel, intermittently sadistic, and subject to manic mood swings. Like millions of other teenagers he was obsessed with fame. On top of all this, he had that strange mixture of behavior which occurs in short, good looking poor males. He was a mixture of grandiose ego, self-loathing, anger, and inferiority complexes. I've generally discovered these individuals have a grandiose obsessive defiance syndrome, and are hell bent on self-destruction. Little Joe became my rival over a girl named Toni, who was the only girl I knew at Andrew Jackson High School willing to have sex before marriage. Although, unbeknownst to me at the time, there must have been a whole lot of screwing going on, as girls kept getting knocked up. Keep in mind that this was before birth control pills, when finding a girl who'd give it up was like finding gold. This may be hard to understand today, as finding sex now is less trouble than fishing, and requires a lot less skill. I don't remember why I was willing to fight over Toni. She was ugly and no fun to be with other than for sex. This may sound mindless today, but back then it made perfect sense. In typical average person fashion, it got settled when she dropped both of us for Ruben Luna, the biggest guy on the football team. She found the biggest, most popular guy, and declared herself in love. They even ended up getting married. Lucky guy, right?

The only time I ever saw Beelzebub get into a fight was

against Little Joe. Like I said, Beelzebub was a coward, and wouldn't fight anyone outside of our house. His one and only fight was with a trash talking runt. It wasn't even a real fight, as Little Joe was a pipsqueak with a big mouth, who suffered the same delusion as Beelzebub. I don't know what they were fighting about and never gave a damn. The short story is Beelzebub beat up a kid who was a foot shorter and forty pounds lighter. Beelzebub sort of pushed him around a little, and the twerp ran home crying. In typical deluded fashion, the runt later joined the Marine Corps in a ridiculous stereotypical effort to prove his mettle. He served in Vietnam for eighteen months as a tanker, and then like all losers, returned to Main Drive. Only he was more screwed up than he was before leaving, as he was using drugs and acting rebellious. In truth, he never had a chance, as he'd never learned discipline. His father was even worse. Little Joe, the self-centered, full of shit, mean little bastard who survived Vietnam, later died of a heart attack. God works in mysterious ways. Little Joe joined the ranks of losers and dropped dead. It's only too bad that before doing so he married Beelzebub's ex-girlfriend's sister, knocked her up, left her, and spent his remaining years in and out of jail. Today, Little Joe's memory is proof that death does not ennoble a man. He was a loser throughout his entire life, and then he died, and is now buried somewhere, costing money which could be better spent on anything else.

    About the same time Beelzebub had his one and only fight, I'd had ten fights with just one kid. His name was Frankie Abundez, and the entire ordeal was ridiculous. We should have been best friends, but ended up trying to kill each other. We were neighbors and had grown up together. I have no idea what we were fighting about. The experience I got from fighting Beelzebub, who tormented me relentlessly as a child, helped a lot. I beat the hell out of Frankie so many times I got swollen knuckles from pounding him. I do not claim to have been the "good guy," nor am I apologizing. I did what I did, for whatever reason I had at the time. I was as much a victim of Main Drive psychology as everyone else. In truth, I was half-nuts from the brutality. Once while fighting on church property I sprayed Frankie in the face with green spray paint. Lucky I didn't blind the poor guy. I felt bad about myself and vowed never to inflict such punishment on someone in a fight, a promise I never kept. Years later, during the time I did my first Warrior's inventory, Frankie still lived in the same house where he grew up, next door to the Vallejo's, who purchased our old house. Now, many years later, I've learned he died. His mother Lily, who became a "party girl" on Main Drive, died earlier from some kind of illness. Allegedly, as per rumors, she'd been banging my father.

  At one point during the storm we moved from 1015½ Main Drive, across the street to 1515 Main Drive, which we called the "Big House." Unbeknownst to anyone, my father had purchased a lot and hired a contractor to build the new house. The contractor was a DOEI man who worked alone. He built the entire four bedroom house by himself. I was very young, but recognized that this guy was one hell of a worker. He worked like a dog under the hot Texas sun, which is nothing to laugh at, especially during the summer. The trouble was my father hired me out to him, without consulting me. I'd come home from school and have to go help out by bringing him lumber or whatever he asked for. I never stayed long, as I was still young. He needed real help, not some skinny little kid. At the time I had no idea what the neighbors thought or said about the house. To be honest, it never crossed my mind. I later learned that many of them hated us, because according to them, we thought we were high and mighty. This came as a shock to me. I had no idea they gave us any thought at all. I never gave much importance to what anyone else did, so long as it didn't impose upon me. I quickly learned that this way of thinking is not normal. I discovered that 96ers will hate you for no reason at all. I've yet to understand the driving force behind this delusional sense of superiority. More importantly, I've never understood why anyone would care what another person thinks or says. Associating with 96ers is a necessity due to their sheer numbers, but none of them are worth a damn. Very little of what comes out of their mouths is worth listening to. Average people love to hate and spend all their time comparing themselves to others, which leads to jealously, conflict, death, or imprisonment. My being independent had many positive side effects, yet just as many drawbacks. At this point in my life I had not acquired the discipline of a Warrior. I had no idea that 96ers were judging and hating me without ever having spoken to me. I didn't know that they received their information from gossip and skewed views, and used it to fuel their hate and ignorance. I never cared what any of my so-called peers thought until they attempted to impose themselves upon me. I've always found the notion of being concerned about someone's idea of me to be ridiculous. As I grew older my sole objective was to graduate and get the hell out of Texas. Even then I knew I was not going to live in the South. To this very day I still dislike the South, with its backward thinking, racism, injustice, and ignorance. The notion that any group of people would believe themselves better than others is ludicrous. Distorting scripture, science, and etc. in order to justify inhumanity is the heart and soul of a 96er. Even more distressing is the fact that this manner of thinking is the core of the nation. Additionally, I wanted to escape poverty and horrible weather. Any story of Texas has to include the weather. It was oppressive and added to the misery all Tejanos suffered. It also gave the DOEIs something more to use as a comparison. For instance, one time Norma Jean, a little girl who I loved, asked me if we lived in a brick home or one made of wood. She also asked me if we had air conditioning. To be honest, I assumed everyone lived the same. I had much to learn about economic differences and racism.

The fighting at home never ended. It just came and went in waves. Years later as an adult, during the Persian Gulf War, while living under the threat of rocket attacks, I was reminded of my life at home. One never knew when an attack might take place, and one was never truly prepared. One moment you could be sitting quietly enjoying a cup of coffee, and the next you'd be terrified, running for your life towards shelter. Only as a child there was no shelter, no place to hide, and no one to go to for help. Hopelessness and despair were as real as the darkness that surrounded us. I have no idea how many times I asked God to let me die. I would have preferred to be attacked by rockets, as we at least had an early warning device. During the Persian Gulf War we received a warning several minutes before the rocket struck, blowing the hell out of whatever it hit. I'd have given anything to have had a warning device before a wave of violence struck our home. Sadly, there was none. I'd have given anything for an M-16. It would have made dealing with a tyrant like my father a whole lot easier. Like Saddam Hussein, he only picked on weaker people.

After moving to the Big House the pace of action picked up. We moved across the street from an extended Mexican family named "Flores," and another called "de León." These families were notorious for killing people and having done time in prison. The kids were nuts, the men were pissed off, and the women wore too much makeup and tightfitting clothes. In Epitaph, where I currently reside, they'd fit right in and look average by today's standards, but back then it was outrageous. Everyone called them whores behind their backs, but no one dared say it to their faces. These women were said to carry razorblades in their hair, which they wouldn't hesitate to use. They were vulgar, nasty, hot, and oozed sexuality and danger. As a kid their primal sexual allure excited me, while their brazen harshness and violence frightened me. I didn't know whether I should try to be nice to them or run away. It was one of the many paradoxes of my childhood. At the time their coquettish, seemingly carefree nature seemed both wonderful and scary. Today, I recognize they were simply ignorant and abused women who were angry and beaten up. Their self-destructiveness had eaten away at their souls and tormented their lives. I learned to dislike such women, as I *saw* they did not possess any endearing qualities. Once again, I learned that this was another area where I differ from the average man. Many men are attracted to women who ooze sexuality. Perhaps this is why women who dress suggestively are so popular. Throughout my travels, I've never found a woman who oozed sexuality to actually possess it. Those who do are emotionally disturbed and troubled. These wild families had been raised as migrants, moving across the country from one camp to another — a Tejano version of European Gypsies. Who knows how many bodies they'd left buried along the way. All of them were tough, dope smoking, hard-drinking, half-crazy, evil individuals, who lived in a separate reality. Perception of reality depends on an individual's personal power. This subculture of people were known as pachucos. Today, in California they would be called cholos. I've always called them idiots. These punks took pride in their rebellious manner of dressing, talking, and daredevilish behavior. All of them lived by a street code that demanded they fight anyone who insulted them, and take revenge to the extreme. Beating, stabbing, and even killing someone was perfectly acceptable within their Code of Conduct. The word "pachuco" was a sort of style or club amongst the poorest of the Mexican migrant families. It was just another method of survival wherein extended families gathered under their flag name and fought to survive. Their manner of dress was a uniform and the most important aspect, which included starched khaki pants, tangerine shoes with no heels, and triple or quadruple soles. They also wore a white t-shirt worn under a heavily starched short sleeve shirt, with a single pocket over the heart for cigarettes. You'd usually find them smoking a pack of Camels or Winston Cigarettes. Their hairstyle was also very important. It was the Elvis Presley look with a duck tail, usually long and always greasy. In addition to the manner of dress, the person usually carried a knife or some kind of weapon. These guys were the reason why I later began carrying a battery cable inside my pants, down alongside my leg. Some were said to carry guns. I saw many of all calibers, styles, and models. Knives were very important, because as I said earlier, it was dangerous and everyone was armed. Another significant detail was that everyone knew how to fight, and would for any real or perceived insult. They might pick a fight with you because they didn't like the way you looked, talked, walked, or just because. They had their own language, culture, rituals, and code of honor. None of them saw themselves as bad people, only as part of a tribe. They were half-mad homicidal maniacs, and they were the people I grew up with. It was scary as hell. You either became a wolf or a lamb. You became the hunted or the hunter, and unless you had money and could leave, there was very little middle ground. It would have been a great place to raise future terrorists or suicide bombers. They were nuts and all of them believed in the kind of law that demanded loyalty to family first, no matter what. They all had balls, and once in the mix they were as deadly as any of today's Taliban or Jihadist.

The Flores family lived next door to the de León family, and there was always something going on. Someone was always fighting, getting out of jail, or just about to go in. The cops were always in front of their homes. There was never a dull moment or end to the anticipation. Naturally, my mother forbade us from associating with them, especially the women, who were supposed to be wild and sexy seducers. Following these commands was easy for me because in truth, I was afraid of them. There really was no need for the warning, as the few times I had anything to do with any of them were always unpleasant. They were part of 96 percent of the population that infects the world, who enjoy watching others suffer, and will steal from anyone when given an opportunity. Just like today, a 96er's idea of being good has more to do with getting caught than with respecting other people or their property. They lived on the border of society, like many families do presently in Epitaph. It was primitive, tribal, and very dangerous, just like it is in the Valley of Tears. I find it comical that I ended up amongst the same kind of people I find the least appealing. My research into regional customs and characteristics exposed several areas of dysfunctional conduct. The regional hatred amongst races is a phenomenon which has not yet been studied or explained. As it stands, there is no known cure for racial bias. The willingness to inflict lethal harm upon another human being is a reflection of brutalization handed down via generations. The number of people within our society who have had one or both parents in prison is staggering. The disparities between the rich and poor continue, as does how people harm each other. The indifference demonstrated by the average person is alarming. Innocent people remain in jail and children are allowed to suffer in emergency rooms.

An extended Tejan migrant family might have up to twenty or thirty people living and moving about together. They'd move around the country following the migrant labor trail, like tribes of dangerous nomadic invaders. The more sons they had, the larger their family got, as each of them married and brought along a woman. They would have children like it was a contest, and the kids grew up just as wild and violent. It was tribal. I don't recall ever speaking with any of those people in a friendly manner, although I did have to fight several of them years later. The badass, Joe Flores, was shot and killed after a dispute over a dog. Like I said, it was crazy. If gossip is true, which it probably isn't, it seems badass Joe Flores got into an argument over his dog, who attacked a neighbor's dog who was feeding in his own yard. Joe never spent money fixing his fence and the dog came and went as it pleased. He threatened to shoot his next-door neighbor's dog and actually fired at it with a gun. The neighbor, who was equally as stupid and from the same background, fired several shots into Joe's house, and one of the bullets hit Joe, killing him dead on the spot. Joe died not forty feet from where I lived. The neighbor claimed he fired in self-defense because Joe had shot at him. He got away with it too, as it was considered to be so, at least by Texas standards. He and his family disappeared because the Flores Clan was gathering, along with several drug dealing Mexican biker clubs with whom Joe was friendly. As I said, some of these battles go on for years, and there are usually several bodies that are never found. Keep in mind, these people lived next door. This was my barrio.

The gangs of Main Drive, like all gangs, were comprised of mostly cowards and losers. Average people like Curly Perez, Joe Salas, Joe Flores, Roberto Trejo, Alejandro Garcia, Joel Cantu, Ernesto and Nacho Chapa, and half a dozen others. They were like a horrible pestilence, but nonetheless a force to be reckoned with. None of them were worth the trouble it would take to kill them, but the thought never left my mind. This gang of losers made life on Main Drive similar to living in a Western movie, only the blood, bullets, knives, and dead bodies were real. Aside from a select few, alone, they were as dangerous as dog dung on the sidewalk. So like dogs, they always attacked in packs. I learned the tactics of Sun Tzu's *The Art of War* before I ever heard his name or read about Miyamoto Musashi. These bastards forced me to learn about guerrilla warfare tactics, ambushes, dirty fighting, hate, and vendettas. If I'd had a little help, things would have been very different.

The worst bully of all, only rivaled by my father and the Devil himself, was my older brother Beelzebub. Like all bullies, outside of a safe environment he was coward. He hid behind his size, which is how I learned it's not the man's size that's important, but his willingness to get into the mix that makes him dangerous. A smaller determined man armed with a blade can take down a much larger man with a few quick slices and stabs. There will be lots of blood, consequences, and he'll be hunted forever, but it sure beats the alternatives. Throughout the years I've had to face dozens of taller men in battle, and discovered that taller men are rarely truly tested. They're size has cushioned them from life's indignities and insults, while men of smaller stature get tested every day. They must either be willing to fight, take a beating and endure, or surrender to being insulted by every asshole who decides to pick on them. Let me add, a beating is a lot easier to get over than being humiliated in public. Bullies know this and make it a part of their torture. It's better to do real harm in the least time possible and be ready to face the consequences. The end result is that it's the tested man with actual combat experience, willing to fight, who wins. Sun Tzu would agree that this has nothing to do with righteousness or justice. Tactics are just as important in a street fight, but sometimes it's simple mad dog fury that gives you the edge. Losing a fight isn't as bad as it sounds, especially if you're able to get in a few good shots. Remember, once someone attacks you, it's not over until they're dead. This should be kept in mind before engaging in street battles. Once you give yourself over to revenge, vendettas become a lot more than the theme of a great movie. Everyone knew about vendettas long before Mario Puzo's book *The Godfather* was released. Michael Corleone seemed cool in the books/movies, but it's a lot less romantic when people are actually hunting you. Being hunted changes you in ways which those without the experience cannot imagine. Hate became an obsession which swallowed my whole life and stole my innocence. Looking back, I don't know how I managed to stay alive and escape. It didn't matter whether I was wrong or right. All I knew was I had to get those bastards, and stay alive long enough to get the hell out of Texas. I fought almost every day, almost anywhere, and at any time.

At home Beelzebub picked on me mercilessly, and I fought him a thousand times over everything imaginable. My father solved these ongoing conflicts by beating both of us. He used extension cords, rubber hoses, broom handles, or whatever else he could find. My father looked like Genghis Khan, the warlord, except The Great Khan earned respect via his bravery, leadership, and fighting skills.

The only people my father fought were his wife and children, and just like Beelzebub, his cruelty was real. He never demonstrated an ounce of remorse for the terrible beatings or humiliation he inflicted. He beat all of us at the slightest provocation, including my mother. Unfortunately, she was just as stubborn and often as cruel. Looking back upon these experiences I realize why it took so many years and countless attempts to stop hating my father. I have learned via experience that hating anyone is a terrible waste of precious energy. I cannot overstate this, as it is a major stumbling block for many who seek freedom.

In addition to adverse conditions within our family, Texas as I mentioned has terrible weather. The heat along the Gulf of México is so humid it sucks the life out of you. Thank goodness it's also very windy. The skies are deep blue with great big beautiful clouds that float across it, providing temporary shade from the sun. It was amidst these magnificent details I was made aware of how inconsequential I was. I was the fifth child in a family of twelve, and third in line for hand-me-downs. I was skinny, sad, and got pushed around and ignored. I bought my first pair of new pants when I starting picking cotton in the cotton fields surrounding Corpus Christi. The only thing significant about me was how insignificant I was. In a world where the squeaky wheel gets the oil, I was afraid of being the target of negative attention. Nearly everyone on Main Drive picked cotton during the summer to buy clothes for the next school year. It was a harsh existence. If you've ever wondered how hard African slaves worked, take an opportunity to do a little cotton picking along the Gulf Coast in Texas. You'll discover a new appreciation for the term "manual labor." You'll also discover why being poor in Texas was equivalent to slavery, and why DOEIs looked down on Tejanos. The large multimillion dollar agribusiness demanded cheap labor, and the lack of industry, job training, and discrimination guaranteed it. It was also the only kind of work available to ex-felons and thugs. The rest of us just got caught up in the horrible mix of events. Yet, not even the hot sun or brutal weather conditions affected how these brutes saw the world or treated each other. The constant battling for alpha dog status scared the hell out of everyone, and set the standard for what tough was on Main Drive. At the age of ten I saw the Garcia brothers beat each other bloody, as the older used a dirt clod to crack the skull of the younger. He beat his brother like an animal, without an ounce of concern for the consequences. It's no wonder all of them ended up dead or in prison. The surrounding conditions were only a little less dangerous than the people. Every year people were bitten by rattlesnakes, but there were hundreds of other ways to get hurt in that environment. You could stop a bullet, be gored and killed by an escaping bull, run over by a drunk driver, or simply die of heat exhaustion and malnutrition. You could get run over by a tractor or truck, or be stabbed and beaten to death by thugs. Amazingly, very few people went mad or died from a broken heart or chronic disillusionment. We lived simply because we didn't die, which proves biology always wins.

Even with eleven brothers and sisters I grew up alone. I have no idea what my brothers were doing while I was fighting off thugs on the streets, but the brutalization at home left me unable to relate to other people. One of the reasons I never had any friends was because my parents would not let us associate with other kids, so I never learned how to make or have friends. I now realize that the kids on Main Drive were emulating the alpha dog bickering of the older teenagers, and it never would have worked. I was not going to put up with someone else trying to squash me at school, the way Beelzebub tried to do at home. I would have preferred to die fighting than submit to more torment. My mother often said all the kids on Main Drive were lazy good-for-nothings, and that they were dirty ignorant people with head lice and other diseases. My father, who did not want any of us talking about him, further separated us from the rest of the community by building a five foot fence around our home, then adding two feet of barbed wire on top of it. I spent my childhood behind those walls, lonely and scared. To add salt to an open wound, my parents never instilled a sense of family, but rather pitted us against one another like fighting dogs in a pit. We had to compete for approval and attention from my father, who lacked an ability to nurture and never demonstrated any affection. My mother was not nurturing either, and the fact that I had been born sickly made me an unwanted burden. True to his form of brutal indifference my father reacted with disdain. I often wondered if I might not have been someone else's son and was there only by accident. I entertained the notion of being the son of an alien space traveler who impregnated my mother and then returned home. My ability to sustain myself via fantasies proved invaluable and literally saved my life. Too bad there was no extraterrestrial to take me home or beam me up. It's amazing what a kid will do to explain why his father hates him and his mother shuns him. My father's example of parenting convinced me not to have children, as I feared I might harm them as seriously as he harmed me. I also realized I was not prepared for the demands of helping someone else learn how to be a human being, especially since I'd never seen an example of it myself. I have never regretted not becoming a parent. I was fortunate my mother passed me along to my oldest sister to have her raise me. As proof of their ignorance and my father's delusional concept of manliness, my mother got pregnant again. My younger brother, who I'll refer to as "Punk" throughout this endeavor, is only nine months younger than me. My eldest sister, who out of respect for her privacy I will refer to as "Precious," became my surrogate mother. I love her beyond words.

Picture the environment I've described. The violence, racism, poverty, weather, and the terrible child abuse which I endured. Now, add a slice of happiness. Not a big slice, but just enough to give me hope. For some unexplained reason, I loved going to school. I loved learning. I loved listening to the stories my teacher read to the class after lunch. She'd have us put our heads on our desks and would read to us the adventures of *Johnny Texas* by Carol Hoff. I now know these stories were just a lot of lies, about how DOEIs are better than anyone else, but at the time, I thought he was great. I wanted to be just like him. I loved listening to her read. I could imagine every detail she described. When the book had a drawing she'd ask us to look up, and she'd let the class examine it. It was one of the few happy moments of my childhood. As a result, I loved school. I tried very hard to please my teachers. Yearning for their attention, I did everything I could to be a good student. I'd ask questions. I'd try to sit up close to the front, and worked hard on my lessons. I am sorry to admit, I was not very good at schoolwork, even with all my extra efforts. In my defense, I had no help whatsoever at home. Everyone was left to fend for themselves. It was swim or sink. Those who got good grades never received any appreciation, as we were expected to graduate and get out of the house soon thereafter. My father made it perfectly clear he didn't want us around after we completed high school. He didn't care where we went, just so long as we got out of his house. Everyone was just trying to survive. Harsh environments tend to brutalize people, and my parents were not interested in helping me study or offering an encouraging word. I was given constant reminders that as soon as I finished school I had to get out of the house. I guess my father didn't like having to compete with so many angry males who would eventually become a threat to him. I don't know what they told my poor sisters, but I certainly got the message. It never occurred to me that this was abnormal, as it was such a constant theme while growing up. However, I never understood how we were supposed to survive, as none of us had any training, schooling, or anywhere to go. What in the hell were we supposed to do. At the time the only option open to poor Tejanos without an education was to join the Army, go to Vietnam, and hopefully survive. Trouble was, you could get killed, seriously hurt, or permanently damaged. No one gave a damn about patriotism, democracy, freedom, free speech, voting, or being represented, as it never made a difference to us. No one treated Tejanos like Americans. We were hated and treated as aliens. Hundreds of guys from Corpus Christi joined the military after graduation, some eventually returning with a burr haircut and a uniform. Most were sent to Vietnam, and many never came home. Those who returned arrived with new attitudes about their place in society. They refused to be pushed around and squashed, which created problems that upset the racial hierarchy. Strangely enough, political leaders failed to realize that those who go to war and learn to kill will not easily submit to injustice. The racist Texas legal system responded with more laws, harsher punishments, and even shootings. Those who witnessed it hated the cops, but recognized that war against them was suicide.

    My mother grew up hating DOEIs, or "gringos" as they were called for their many offenses, and she conveyed this to us. She hated them for the invasion of Columbus, New México, during which they hunted down Pancho Villa. Her relatives were killed in New México during the Mexican Expedition, while Pancho Villa tried to find the DOEI gunrunners who'd cheated him. He was attempting to recover his money or get the guns he'd purchased from them. It should be noted that no charges of gunrunning were ever filed against these alleged criminals who sparked an international incident. My mother had grown up listening to stories about drunken, angry American soldiers murdering innocent people who lived along Pancho Villa's escape route back into México. Interestingly, the American Government never conducted an investigation as to how many "alleged banditos" were killed trying to escape, and how many of the dead New Mexicans were just murdered as revenge. It's just another one of the thousands of unanswered questions in America's racist history. As an act of defiance my mother refused to learn to speak English, which was fine with my father, as he didn't want her to learn anyway. He liked her being totally dependent on him, which must have been horrible for a person like my mother. Surviving without English may sound impossible to some, but thousands of newly arrived immigrants do so today. My mother also never drove, and only late in life learned how to use a telephone. I never understood how my father could think of himself as such a big man when he couldn't speak English well enough to help his children study, or take a position against injustice. I never knew him to do anything for anyone other than himself. He was nevertheless my greatest teacher. The most impactful lesson he taught me was that the opposite of love is not hate, but indifference. It makes sense in primitive cultures and tribes that the chief would not want his most ardent opponent to surpass him in anything, but this man was allegedly my biological father. Neither of my parents studied beyond elementary school, but the real tragedy is that they had no idea how to solve a problem, resolve an argument, compromise, or even speak proper Spanish. As a result, I never learned proper Spanish, and grew up speaking the same vulgar Tex-Mex Spanish used amongst the poorest and most ignorant migrants. It was another dark shadow which loomed overhead, branding me like a sign saying "LOSER" around my neck. I overcame this obstacle many years later, which was accomplished via dogged determination.

We were under constant pressure to assimilate into the mainstream of things, but from what I'd witnessed, doing so wouldn't have made any difference. DOEIs didn't want Tejanos hanging around them. No matter what you did or said, you were still not one of them. Yet, the pressure to fit into the mold created by the Texas educational system was relentless. Every sign of independence was squashed, so as to humiliate you into obedience. When it came to homework, it was understood that you were on your own. If you didn't comprehend it, too bad, you failed, and then your failure was made public by the teachers. You were then categorized, placed in a group and forgotten. No further testing or assistance was given to those who didn't make the grade. You were told it wasn't your fault, and that you were simply defective and not as bright as the other students. No one ever challenged the idea that it was a racist system that demanded everyone be the same and have the same manner of learning. You were publicly embarrassed and cast aside as defective, inferior, and forgotten. I seemed to have been playing in the wrong game and holding all the wrong cards. I was shy, quiet, and scared, which they interpreted as a lack of determination and an absence of personal qualities. I seemed to be the only one who saw we were being ignored and neglected, which made me angry. I hated being treated as a dummy without having been given a chance to learn. I remember once being handed a test and staring at it as tears ran down my face. I cried until the teacher, who never took an interest in helping me, came and took it away. She then wrote a big zero in red ink on it before walking off. I don't remember her offering to help me, explaining the material, or asking if I understood it before she gave us the exam. Somehow, and much to my amazement, which was beyond my ability to understand, I *saw* that the DOEI teachers did not expect me to stay in school and graduate. Similar to how today's Central Valley Native Californians of Mexican ancestry (NCOMAs), are expected to dropout and join the unskilled labor force, without which the Valley would die. It was the same in Corpus Christi. Without a constant influx of cheap manual labor it could not survive. These so-called "teachers" and self-proclaimed educators were descendants and relatives of the rich cotton and cattle ranchers, who exploited Native Tejanos and needed an endless supply of cheap labor. I never saw or heard a DOEI teacher help a Native Tejano student. Added to the racist stereotype casting, the fact that my parents did not speak English guaranteed a disaster. I was doomed to fail and literally behind the eight ball. A monkey surrounded by wolves would have had a better chance. It is proof of my ability to *see*, that I knew I had to escape Texas. It's also proof of how I used anger to motivate me to excel, which is a Warrior's strategy; using his weaknesses as strengths. The problem was that I wasn't aware of my shortcomings. I simply indulged, as I'd learned by example and behaved like everyone else. I didn't know how to learn, think, or solve a problem. Young guys like myself were expected to become adults via a magical formula which no one knew or understood. We were supposed to manage our emotions, sexuality, peer pressure, and somehow make good decisions without ever having seen an example.

Everyone was under tremendous pressure by society, parents,

school, and DOEIs to fit in, and do so gracefully. I was expected to learn about life, work, craftsmanship, reading, math, history, and everything else without any assistance or explanation. I have no idea how my parents or teachers could have honestly demanded I simply absorb this information without some explanation. My inability to fit in, in addition to the absence of actual teaching resulted in my failing the first grade. I had to repeat the year, and because there were no special classes for Tejano kids who could not speak English, I was placed in a class with the mentally handicapped children, who were referred to as being "retarded." Please keep in mind that this was the term used in the days before political correctness, and the educational system administrators never thought it insulting. This was common at the time, as Tejano children were shunned and shoved aside, doomed to fail. I might not have known how to speak English, but that did not make me "retarded." I might have been emotionally withdrawn and shy, but that's a hundred miles away from being mentally handicapped. The problem was the racist teachers and Texas educational system didn't care. They wanted you to fit in nicely, behave, never say a word, and move on out of sight. If you deviated one percentage from the norm or were a little different, you were singled out and identified as a failure. I can only imagine how much damage they did to thousands of Native Tejano children of Mexican ancestry. The Texas educational system was set up to produce functioning robots to enter the workforce, with enough education to do the job, but not enough to challenge the system. Colleges taught teachers that our alleged inferiority was inherent and could not be changed. As a result, Tejanos were discouraged from attending college, and expected to join the unskilled and semiskilled labor force.

    Getting stuck in a classroom filled with mentally handicapped children was very interesting. It taught me not to judge, and that the first sign of character is kindness. Being with the mentally handicapped kids was an eye-opening experience. I remember a girl named Sally Rogers. She must have been older, because she had bosoms. She would have probably been considered a bombshell by today's standards, with her blonde hair, blue eyes, huge pink lips, and big butt. She had a few problems however. One of which was that she picked her nose all the time and wet her pants daily. When she soiled her drawers the teacher would ask us to go outside while she cleaned up the mess and called her parents. All the mentally handicapped students were DOEIs. I was the only Tejano kid. I have no idea what poor Tejano families did with their mentally handicapped children back then, as things were awful. I wouldn't be surprised to learn that they put their own children to death. You got to remember, Texas was still in the dark ages when it came to managing mental illness. The people calling themselves conservatives, or "real Americans," ensured there was no system for helping anyone who could not afford it. Their concept of Christian values stopped as soon as it cost them money. If you were poor and had special needs of any kind, you were on your own. In South Texas mentally handicapped people were oftentimes hidden away in basements like some dirty secret. Some were killed and buried in a cow pasture, and then the families would simply move away. It was crazy, and I mean that literally. Not speaking English was apparently considered a mental defect, and as such I was kept in a class with the so-called "retards" until they transferred me into a regular classroom, with the supposedly "normal" students. In this case normal just meant average, yet none of them seemed normal to me. At least the mentally handicapped kids were friendly.

After six months of being around nothing but mentally handicapped children who threw up, pissed and shit all over themselves while I simply didn't speak the language, what can be considered normal? I was already very intuitive. I perceived and understood much more than I could explain. When I suddenly found myself around "normal" kids, which translated into self-centered, spoiled, temperamental, compulsive, and trained to fit in, I was more alone than ever. It never occurred to them that I was one of millions of children who'd been abused, neglected, and beaten at home. I needed kindness, acceptance, affection, and a little help learning the language. You won't be surprised to learn that during the Sixties and Seventies, despite thousands of Tejano kids in the Tejas school system, there were no bilingual teachers. The teachers were never taught to appreciate differences in culture and language, even though America is called the "Melting Pot," a supposed mixture of cultures. Amazingly, at one point in Tejas history there were so many German immigrants that they printed state legislative news in German. In typical average person fashion, they wanted understanding, acceptance, and accommodations, but were unwilling to give any. The teachers had been brainwashed to believe, as have all DOEIs, that they are the acme of humanity. DOEI Four Percentors are those who have acknowledged this brainwashing to be exactly what it is; pure fantasy and delusion. Teachers at Andrew Jackson believed Charles Darwin was describing them when he spoke of the "fittest." Looking back, it's difficult to believe that those self-absorbed, mean-spirited people saw themselves as having been created in the image of God. This delusional ideal has been backed by racist pseudoscientists since before the English began to invade and enslave other countries. Teachers were supposed to be educated and enlightened individuals, who loved children. The ugly truth, and a slur upon all teachers, is that very few people go into teaching as their first choice, or because of a love for children. Teaching is perceived as an easy job by those who have not taught, which is why so many delusional individuals flock to it. They soon discover it is a tough, low paying, thankless occupation. In Tejas teachers only liked you if you looked like them and spoke English.

Another interesting detail about school was how stupid the teachers were. I don't mean mentally handicapped, but socially stupid. Try to imagine a teacher today not knowing how to pronounce Spanish names or having no understanding of other cultures. The idiots calling themselves teachers at the time thought you could translate any name or word literally. As an example of how little they understood the people they'd grown up around all their lives is this illustration. There was a kid named Domingo Nieves. The two words are translated as, Domingo, or "Sunday," and Nieves, meaning "snow." The idiot teacher decided the poor kid's name was "Ice Cream Sunday." You can imagine how funny all the DOEI kids thought this was. It amazed me that the teacher was actually trying to entertain them. Another kid was named Maria Luce Dominguez. The same teacher called her "Mary Light Bulb Sunday," and the poor girl was called "Light Bulb" for the rest of the year. My name, Jesus, which in Spanish is pronounced (heh-soos), was automatically changed to the English pronunciation of Jesus (jee-zuhs). It's simply amazing that these people were considered to be educators. Keep in mind, this is the same educational system that produced such world-renowned characters as George W. Bush, whose granddaddy, Prescott Bush, attempted to assassinate President Franklin D. Roosevelt and overthrow the American Government. As Well as American grown terrorist, Charles Whitman, who murdered people from the Tower at University of Texas at Austin, and Lee Harvey Oswald who shot

President John F. Kennedy. It also produced the most murderous state in America, with more executions than any other state in history. Texan DOEIs have behaved so inhumanly towards Native Tejanos they've become legend even amongst other DOEIs who find their behavior unacceptable. In the book, *The Rope, The Chair, and the Needle: Capital Punishment in Texas, 1923-1990*, Authors James W. Marquart, Sheldon Ekland-Olson, and Jonathan R. Sorensen suggest the practice of executing prisoners reflects pre-Civil War, Southern cultural traditions of the concept that non-white populations are less human, don't adhere to their idea of normal, social, and legal standards, and are easier to detach from. This translates into legal lynching, which serves to reaffirm the concept of "them and us" to Southern society. Unsolved murders of Tejano and former slaves caused overt rebellion which has led to more violence and legal executions. These state sanctioned executions reflect Southern resentment of post-Civil War federal intervention and insecurity towards Blacks. Today, the pro DOEI educational and legal system continues to reflect the racist exclusive mindset of South Texas DOEIs, and is in conflict with overwhelming evidence of intergrading cultures.

At the time my child's innocence protected me from the horrible truth that teachers saw me as a burden. Unaware of their hated, for my own part I loved school. I loved some of the teachers, how they looked, smelled, dressed, acted, and pretended to care. Due to the fact that I'd been sexualized via listening to my parents having sex at home, I saw them as women, not as forbidden or unobtainable. Of course this was absurd, but in my imagination I was fornicating with all of them. In my mind it wasn't dirty, nasty, or illegal. It was just a great fantasy, which I enjoyed. As a result I wanted to please them and gain their approval, so I struggled to improve and learn, and did my homework. I loved being able to raise my hand and answer the teachers questions, especially when I got it right. I really didn't mind being wrong, I just wanted to get into the mix. Plus, it helped me with my stuttering. Things started to get dicey in the third grade. My little brother Punk was now in the same grade because I'd had to repeat a year. I have no idea why I felt I had to protect him, as I was skinny as a pencil and hardly ever spoke. Yet, I always watched out for him. One day I saw a big Tejano girl, who must have weighed two hundred pounds, push Punk off the merry-go-round. He hit the ground like a sack of cement, rolled over, and then got up crying. I rushed over and dusted him off, and then followed her as she made her way towards the big slide. She was a large, dark-skinned, ugly monster, whom I'd never seen before. She was running around pushing kids and acting like a mad cow. I forced my way through the crowd and up to the top of the slide, where she was now standing, preparing to ride down. That's when I shoved her off the top of the slide in my first ninja attack. Not expecting to be shoved, the mad cow flew off the slide screaming as she crashed into the hard packed dirt with a loud thud. She laid there like a beached whale, trying to suck in air until someone came up to her and noticed she had a candy sticking out of her mouth. She'd lost consciousness as the candy, which was called a "slow poke," was blocking her airway. I simply slid down the slide and slipped away, pretending I'd not done anything to anyone. No one ever found out it was me who pushed the mad cow off the slide. It was my first attack upon an unknowing adversary, and served to guide me throughout my life. I was amazed no one pointed me out or said anything, as there were literally hundreds of kids on the playground. A DOEI teacher sat her up, pulled out the obstruction, and then she started to breathe again. Otherwise she might have died. I don't know if anyone ever knew I'd pushed her off. I don't remember her name, or ever seeing her again. Like so many other people, they took her to the nurse's office and she disappeared off the face of the earth. I still don't know where I got the idea to avenge my little brother. I also don't know if he did anything to provoke her, or if she just decided to pick on him. All I knew was that if someone did something to you, or your family, you had to do something to them, and right or wrong did not matter. So I did. As I said, life was tough on Main Drive. I learned to attack suddenly and quietly. My attack made me realize how to get even with someone who'd harmed, humiliated, or done me wrong in any way. I patterned my revenge attacks after that one and made sure everyone who hurt me got a surprise. It taught me that everyone keeps score, and no one forgets anything. It set the pattern for a whirlwind of revenge, getting even, keeping score, and paranoia that set the tone for the next twenty years of my life.

There was a half-crazy kid, who was supposed to have killed his brother accidentally with his father's gun. Everyone had guns, including my father, whose father (my grandfather) had allegedly taken a pistol off a dead American soldier of the 11th cavalry, who invaded México during the Revolution trying to capture Pancho Villa. According to family legend he was one of many peasants who got caught up in the fighting by being at the wrong place at the wrong time. I never believed anything my father said about anything, so it remains a mystery. I realize that anyone who killed his brother would have reason to be crazy. I never knew for sure, as rumors and gossip are as common as ignorance. The poor kid was messed up and had the survival skills of a rock. His name was Rudy Oriega, and he was famous at Andrew Jackson for getting beat up by almost everyone. I tried being his friend, but he was completely nuts and had no idea how to play, talk, or act. While I had learned to stay quiet and out of sight so as to avoid trouble, he always interrupted, argued, and capriciously decided that he wanted what he wanted when he wanted it. You know, not much unlike all average people. The poor kid had no common sense, and as a result was always in trouble. Were it not for the long and jagged scar across his face, he wouldn't have been a bad looking kid. He had a thick head of coal-black hair which covered his big round head. It was said that his father had accidently backed up into him with his car, which is allegedly how he received his scar. Of course, this was just according to rumors. All I really know for sure was that the poor guy was off his rocker, literally. The Texas educational system had nothing to offer him. Their usual solution was to paddle anyone who misbehaved, so he got a beating every time he did something wrong, which was often. The poor kid was completely disconnected from reality, and got paddled a lot more than I did. I have no idea how the school system thought whacking someone with a paddle would make them better students. Most importantly, I have no idea how they allowed him to remain in school. He was dysfunctional and completely out of it. He didn't know when to stand and fight or when to run away. In no time the bullies started in on him and he took more beatings than a punching bag. He was obviously in need of professional attention and medication, but, as usual, the Texas educational system had one care system for DOEIs and another for everyone else. They never gave a damn about anyone who wasn't a DOEI and couldn't afford to pay for special attention. I suspect the poor kid never fully recovered from shooting his brother, or whatever made him nuts. He became famous for schoolyard brawls because he'd never back down, and always took a beating. I have no idea why he didn't learn how to fight, as he certainly had lots of experience. He was a complete dumbass and would duck his head, hunch over, and start swinging his arms like two propellers. All you had to do was get in between his arms and punch or kick up, and Ka-Pow! You'd land a shot. He once hit me with a spit-wad that was aimed at someone else, so I beat him until my knuckles bled, but he wouldn't quit. This was normal on Main Drive, where fighting until you were too tired to stand was as much a part of growing up as getting pimples. I'd been fighting Beelzebub for years, and had learned how to fight, which meant I always gave better than I got. It also goes to prove that someone will brutalize another person to the same degree they were brutalized. You had to be on guard everywhere you went, not only for the guy you fought, but his relatives as well. No one forgot nothing and everyone wanted payback, so the violence continued until someone quit, died, or moved away. The trouble was no one ever quit. Things got real dicey when you had several people to look out for at the same time. I'd gotten into fights with so many people, I had no idea who was out to get me and who decided they'd had enough. After getting ambushed several times I assumed everyone wanted me dead, so I got meaner. At the time I was still too little and skinny to be of any real danger, but nevertheless, I prepared for war. I did what Sun Tzu would have done, and prayed for the best while preparing for the worst. Like Niccolò Machiavelli, I believed it was better to be too well armed than not at all. Once a fight started, being unprepared was an unpardonable sin.

The DOEI kids ignored and avoided interacting with someone like myself, who stuttered and got picked on. I was like a walking bullseye. They lived in a separate world, a separate reality, and kept their distance unless absolutely necessary. I suppose their parents warned them not to associate with "dirty Mexicans," which is what they called us. In the fourth grade I met a DOEI kid named Billy Myers, who I thought was my friend. He and I had been friends throughout the entire school year, and I thought we would be friends the following year. I learned that he had only hung around with me because he'd just moved to the area, and didn't know anyone else. I was simply the first kid who had been friendly, but once he made DOEI friends he didn't want to be seen hanging around me. To my disappointment, this has been typical of my experiences with DOEIs throughout my life, and it seems most have a different definition of the word "friend." Billy reinforced an unwritten and unspoken law when he abandoned me at the gates of a public swimming pool at West Gulf Park. We had gone together, but upon reaching the entrance the owner looked at us and said, "We don't allow Mexicans." I was shocked, but Billy simply said, "I'm not Mexican," and went inside. Billy Myers reaffirmed everything which had been drummed into my head. Learning these realities firsthand was harsh, and went against my accepting and nonjudgmental nature. I was sad I'd lost a friend. Similar experiences occurred several more times before I learned it was not sociably acceptable for DOEI kids to be friends with Tejanos. Billy was under pressure to hate us. I hadn't learned to hate DOEIs, because I couldn't see any differences between us. I never felt inferior, or less than any of them. At the same time, I never felt superior either. It was them who rejected, scorned, and attacked us. I bore witness to how ranchers and farmers exploited Tejanos as we worked for them during the summer. I heard their curses and saw their indifference to our suffering. Years later in high school Billy and I played football together, but we were never friends. He got into a fistfight once in the football locker room with Jimmy MacGregor. The fight was over a popular cheerleader named Tori Browne, who'd dated almost every football player in school. Much to everyone's surprise, her sister got pregnant and dropped out of school. Tori continued to "be popular" until eventually time stripped away her looks, along with her delusions of being discovered and living the life of a movie star in Hollywood. In the end she became just another wilted flower, discarded by all those who once sought her attention. Several years later she ended up marrying Wesley Parks. I'd known Wesley since first grade. We played football together. He was a real nice guy, who unfortunately died while crossing Highway 9 about a mile from the high school. The last time I saw Billy was in 1990 at the Holiday Inn in Corpus Christi. Unbeknownst to me, a group of former AJHS students were gathering at the hotel, where I happened to be staying. Had I known, I would have stayed elsewhere. I never wanted to see any of them ever again. Billy was disheveled, feeling sorry for himself, and drunk as usual. He'd been married, divorced, and was now working for his daddy. All his delusional dreams of grandeur, popularity, and racial superiority amounted to nothing. In the end he was just another 96er.

Sometime during the same summer Billy abandoned me at the public swimming pool he became popular, and when he returned to school he was acting like all the other DOEIs who hated Tejanos. He refused to have anything to do with me. I discovered how shallow average people are and how easily they discard others. I'd never learned to be phony, and no matter how much I tried to hide how I felt I always wore my emotions on my sleeve. This was also the year of unexplained and unsustainable burdens which squashed the innocence out of me. It was the year I discovered the complete indifference of the Texas educational school system. It did not care if Tejano children were condemned to a life of misery and poverty due to a lack of education. It taught what they considered important, which was to fit into place. In order to survive and thrive it was necessary to fit in, act right, do as they said, and kiss their asses. I discovered the unwritten and unspoken pecking order that required we humble ourselves to DOEIs. The teachers and administrators couldn't care less if you passed, failed, or dropped out. What's even more amazing is that they also saw themselves as Christians, and believed themselves to be people of God. This hypocrisy was very difficult to comprehend as a child. Contrary to what had been pounded into my head, I actually attempted to explain to myself that there must be two different gods. It seemed impossible that such blatant hypocrisy and injustice could exist while one god was protecting and loving all people. Although several DOEI ministers often spoke and prayed at school assemblies, none ever took a stance against racism and injustice. Typical of Southern Baptist religious leaders, they acted as though they spoke to God directly, and behaved in a manner which served only them and those who reflected their ideals, regardless of who they alienated. None of them realized they were being watched as they failed to recognize their own hypocrisy. Keep in mind, Southern ministers once preached that slavery was divinely approved. Andrew Jackson never taught us about the Civil War, slavery, or its inhumanities. It never taught us about deportations, gerrymandering, or racist legislation. At the time I did not realize that these alleged men of God were descendants of Confederates who fought in the Civil War to perpetuate slavery. Much like today, they demanded their rights, while refusing rights to others. Their idea of freedom included denying it to anyone they deemed unworthy. According to them, one must have political strength, weapons, and money, otherwise they don't matter. As you can imagine, this made things difficult to understand, as it seemed that even God, who was supposed to love all people, was on their side. We seemed to always be at a disadvantage and had nothing to demonstrate for all our hard work. We lived in wooden, uninsulated housing, endured swarms of mosquitoes, flies, frogs, illness, plagues, fleas, and what appeared to be God's damnation. It seemed the entire Tejano population had committed some unpardonable sin and were being punished in biblical fashion. It was no wonder so many Tejanos allowed themselves to believe they were inferior. We seemed less than, and for some unknown reason, unloved by God. The DOEIs called us "Mexicans," "wetbacks," or "greasers," and ignored and oppressed us at every opportunity. Keep in mind, in rural agricultural areas racism is cruel, overt, and equates to how you live, where you live, and whether your children suffer or not. When a DOEI rancher or farmer needed a driver, laborer, or brick layer, they always hired a DOEI as crew boss, and Tejanos to do the labor. Overt ethnic profiling was and continues to be the heart and soul of racism. In Southern Texas it was made into an art form, supported by biblical justice. Despite my naïve innocence, I began to question everything about DOEIs, similar to how a prisoner examines his captors. I remember thinking there must be a mistake, as no one else seemed to see the discrepancies. I asked myself how it was possible that Tejano parents would permit DOEIs to treat their children in such a manner. I never felt my parents could protect me, even if they'd wanted to. Even as a child I recognized the staggering hypocrisy. There were two systems for everything. One was imposed upon Tejanos and another for DOEIs. They referred to themselves as "American," or "White," which implied good, and referred to us as "Mexicans," which meant inferior and dirty. I always knew they were wrong. I knew my ancestors had lived in Tejas for generations prior to the European invasion.

I knew the European invaders had brought over syphilis, smallpox, and every other sickness foreign to this land, and wiped out millions of natives. As a teenager I spent hours reading and searching history, which taught me we were not Mexican. Although Texas had once been a part of México, it was now in the United States. We, all the native people of Texas, were Americans, not Mexicans. Although my parents spoke Spanish and had both spent years living in México, they weren't Mexican, and neither was I. Aside from a portion of her childhood, my mother only lived in México as an adult. She and my father went to live on my grandfather's ranch during the Great Depression when no work was available in Texas. This did not make them, nor myself for that matter, Mexican. My mother often spoke of life on her father's ranch with fondness. She told us wonderful stories about her brothers and parents, although this joy was never reflected in her behavior. As a child I always wondered why anyone would leave such a beautiful place in exchange for Texas. I later discovered that in typical average person fashion, she left out important details. No matter what I believed, a ten-year-old kid who stuttered was in no position to make observations on the way things were.

Texas escapee,

don Jesus M. Ramirez

Chapter Three
The Boy Who Loved Norma Jean Slaughter

"I learned about love as a child, then as an adolescent, and again as a man. I find that love does not require someone love you back. Love lives on its own, and comes as easily as breathing."

–don Jesus M. Ramirez

In the fifth grade my teachers failed me again and I was ordered to repeat the year. I never received the necessary attention to learn. As I said, it was either swim or drown. I discovered that what they called "learning" was actually just memorization of dates, names, and places. If I could keep those in my mind while I tested, I'd pass. So, I started practicing how to memorize lists of things. This did not match my idea of what an education was supposed to be, but it's what was required. I took notice of how all the recently memorized information was soon forgotten after the test, usually while "learning" something new. As I said, the DOEI teachers ignored Tejano children, especially the quiet ones, so I was a victim of their indifference. I spent the summer in silent embarrassment, dreading having to return to school to repeat the year and have people staring at me. This shame lasted until I realized that the new kids wouldn't know or care that I failed. Everyone would be too interested in their own lives to give a hoot about me. So why should I care about them. It was a lesson which has served me ever since. The truth was that aside from a few people, I didn't care what anyone else thought or said. Learning not to be concerned with people's opinions of you is a difficult challenge. We all see ourselves through the eyes of other people. Strangely, we learn to think of ourselves the way we are described by others, which is absurd, considering no one knows us like we know ourselves. I stumbled upon this puzzle as a child, and marveled at the apparent contradiction which no one could explain. I hated the way my parents looked at me, because I *saw* they didn't like me. I couldn't understand what I'd done or why, but I knew they were wrong. This is why I refused to submit to tyranny, resisting and struggling against their oppression at every opportunity, usually with very little success.

As usual I worked picking cotton during the summer, dragging a sack up and down the rows, stuffing it full to the brim. We'd drag ourselves out of bed at four in the morning, dress, eat something, drink some coffee, and wait for the trucker, known as "Tonio, el trocado," or "labor contractor." Truthfully, he was just another crook, working for the DOEI farmers who got people to pick cotton off their land. He was paid a portion of everyone's wages and cheated us on top of that. Like a vulture, he preyed upon the ignorant people of Main Drive. He picked up everyone and drove us out to the cotton fields. We'd work all day in the hot melting sun, picking cotton by hand, dragging the heavy sacks like mules until we filled them up. Then we'd carry them to the weigh station where Tonio would weigh them, deducting several pounds for the sack. We were paid one penny a pound. Imagine how much work it takes to pack enough cotton into a canvas sack so that it weighs a hundred pounds. It was a sizable accomplishment and testimony to how hard I had to work. I labored like a mule during the summers and learned the value of a dollar, especially in South Texas. As conditions got worse, the more determined I was to go to college. Like the bumble bee, I did not know I wasn't supposed to fly, and wanted to fly despite the obstacles. At the time very few Tejano kids of poor families went to college. Thank God for my innocence, as I never knew I wasn't supposed to want to go. I dreamed I could, no matter how difficult it might be. Looking back, I realize that having to work in the cotton fields and being exploited contributed to my hate of bullies. It was also another reason why my parents always said, "Never trust a gringo." For years I couldn't understand why DOEIs carried themselves as if their ancestors had behaved in an admirable manner. Then the truth hit me like a bullet. This delusional idea of ethnic superiority exists, because those who adopt it refuse to acknowledge that they are the beneficiaries of their ancestor's exploitation of native peoples. They benefited from the racist hierarchy which their ancestors instilled, nurtured, and imposed over native people from various regions. Their exalted positions have nothing to do with divine superiority, natural selection, or any other such nonsense. This racial hierarchy was built entirely upon racism, cruelty, greed, and military force. The descendants of Thomas Jefferson, George Washington, John Adams, and all those men won't acknowledge that their wealth, position, and money comes from the same people who enslaved, murdered, and exploited native populations. All such people have ancestors who never wanted their true history written, as it would expose their indebtedness to the children of former slaves. All people of color have always known such behavior is essentially nothing more than violence, exploitation, and discrimination. It's a perpetuation of the same mentality which created slavery, the Civil War, Jim Crow Laws, gerrymandering, sparked the civil rights movement, and continues to be the cause of hate crimes today.

    As a child I endured heat and physical torment. I suffered in silence, bled, cried, and repeated the endless cycle of a tortured Tejano history. Like a prisoner awaiting release from a chain gang, the summer finally ended and I happily returned to school. I proudly wore the clothes I worked to pay for with my hard earned wages. It was no small accomplishment for a child. My father earned a lot of money by Main Drive's standards, but forced us to endure terrible hardships. He took money from my wages and pretended to be proud of me for working. I certainly never felt proud of him for anything. I purchased my own clothes that summer, and bought my first transistor radio, opening the door to music, which like nothing else gave me hope. I also learned how to save and manage money. I was very proud of my accomplishments, and somewhere along the way, without knowing it, I made the passage from child to man. Around the world native cultures have rites of passage that signify a boy becoming a man. I didn't hunt and kill a lion, or go on a vision quest. I earned my own money and paid my own way. I learned independence, earned self-esteem, survived amongst thugs and thieves, and lived to tell about it.

    My plan to quietly reenter the fifth grade ended the first day of school. For no apparent reason other than to humiliate me, the DOEI teacher announced to the entire class that I'd failed. I still do not understand why an adult would take pleasure in deliberately embarrassing a child. But she did, and did so with a smile, as if she were doing me a favor. Don't ask me to explain it. I could no more do so than explain why 96ers desire to have children. To my knowledge, and up to that point, I'd never done any harm to anyone. I didn't speak to anyone for that matter, regardless of race. Not because I did not want to, but because I stuttered so much that I couldn't. I never knew I could make enemies without having to say or do a thing. Via their hostile stares, DOEIs showed me they saw me as an undesirable inferior. For many, their demonstrated hate was their only inheritance, and their sheer numbers made them powerful. Like their land-grabbing predecessors, they fought to maintain the status quo, indifferent to injustice or God. Looking back, I am amazed there weren't any school shootings. The Tejano students of the Andrew Jackson School District had many reasons to want to do so. What I still find amazing beyond description was how the teachers supported and endorsed the status quo via their statements and behavior. Those supposedly educated people encouraged the hate and worked to separate DOEIs from Tejanos. The entire school administration seemed bent on squashing any sense of pride or hope I might have had. Every year they celebrated Texas' independence from México and remembered the Battle of the Alamo. However, they deliberately excluded the truth about Mexican citizens fighting alongside DOEIs against Santa Anna's invading army. Those Mexican heroes were never mentioned as belonging to the group of men they deemed as the heroes of the Alamo. They also lied about why their heroes came to Texas soil in the first place. They deliberately omitted any details which did not support the "them and us" mentality. As I said, DOEIs saw us as a conquered people and former enemy. I cannot imagine what threat we presented. None of us wanted to fight. We just wanted to be treated fairly. I believe they fed upon their hatred willfully, because such information would have caused them to lose their sense of separateness. It also supported the Southern concept of exclusivity and racial hierarchy which evolved from slavery. They wanted the boundaries between them and us to remain clear so no one would dare cross. I grew up being hated for something I had no control over. Racism, hatred, and indifference are what I learned from attending Andrew Jackson. These lessons are burned into my very soul, and required years of self-analysis to overcome. The sense of inferiority imposed upon me by the Texas educational system required I reeducate myself about America's true history. What I found impossible to understand or forgive was that it was done simply to protect an assumed sense of superiority. It was a crime against a child.

As the year continued I felt better, having discovered a bright side in repeating the year. Once again, I made lemonade out of lemons and saw things from a different perspective. Not all of the teachers were as interested in embarrassing me as my homeroom teacher. No one else seemed to care I had "failed," as was the term back then. In truth, it was their failure, not mine, although you'll never see it recorded in that manner. As for my part, I know I tried like hell. Repeating the year had one or two perks. I was able to check out the ball quicker at recess because I knew where to go. I was assigned to clean up the blackboard, which I already knew how to do. Plus, I started doing better in class because I knew the material. I grew more confident and actually started having fun at school. All my hard work picking cotton during the summer had made me physically stronger. I had also been doing exercises and even ordered one of those *Charles Atlas, Be A Strong Man* booklets from the back of comic books. I know it sounds funny today, but I'm not kidding. As I said, I never had any role models. I learned about growing up by making mistakes and reading. You can imagine how many mistakes I made, and how many times I made the same ones repeatedly. I stumbled and fell so many times that I have as many scars on my knees as I have on my soul. Without guidance or protection, I was completely vulnerable to every temptation possible. Without proper parenting, I lacked in every area you can imagine. I literally grew like a plant in an untended garden, receiving little water now and then, but left to fend for itself.

My refusal to accept ethnic inferiority, despite years of constant humiliation, led to what I consider an intervention by the Universe. I accidentally found love. It's easy to remember your first great love. What changes is the meaning of "great" as we compare relationships through the years. I still think of her as my greatest love because of my painful discovery of what it means to love someone without hope of a response. She made me want to be a better man, even though I was just a child. Ever since, I've always told anyone who'll listen, if the person you love doesn't make you want to be a better person, then they're not the right one. Despite many troubles, and although I've never found a chest of gold, I've always considered myself one of the luckiest persons on Earth. At a very young age I found a treasure and learned the many subtleties of love.

Back then recess meant running, and I loved to run because I could do it well. I'd grown up watching my big brother Bumper run. He was on the track team. He trained and I'd watch him as he ran in a huge circle around the cotton fields that surrounded our home. As I said earlier, I once wanted to be just like him. He was my hero. Unfortunately, like most people, the more you get to know them, the less you like them. During recess the boys from the entire fifth grade went out to the playground, which was just an open field approximately the size of ten football fields. We'd play a version of football called "keep away." It was a free-for-all game of running with the ball until someone either tackled you, or you threw the ball to someone else. The whole point was to run across the entire field and try to avoid being tackled. No one wanted to be tackled because it meant everyone else would dogpile on you. A lot of kids got squashed under the dogpile. The teachers never seemed to care how many kids got hurt. I always hogged the ball whenever I got it, and only threw it away after exhausting myself by running over the field several times. One day while playing I noticed a DOEI girl amongst the boys who could run as fast as anyone. Her name was Norma Jean Slaughter. She had long brown hair which she wore in strange looking pigtails that hung out like horns from the side of her head, big brown doe eyes, a huge smile, and was red-faced from running. She was wearing a black dress and white shirt, with white stockings, and patent leather shoes. I never noticed she wasn't cute or pretty, but only that she could run fast and dodge away from the boys. I was immediately drawn to her, and threw her the ball the first chance I had, and then ran after her. Like Michael Corleone in Mario Puzo's book *The Godfather*, I was struck by a thunderbolt and fell in love instantly. Who knows, I was only a kid without the presence of mind to think and ask myself such questions. All I knew was right there, under that bright Texas midday sun, I fell in love with a DOEI girl named Norma Jean Slaughter. Her name is one of the few which I have decided not to change, in case you are interested in looking her up in the yearbook. I hope you're not expecting a great beauty, because you'll find she was not pretty or even cute. Looking back today, I wonder if I wasn't suffering from heat exhaustion or a serious blow to the head, of which I have taken many.

    My courting her took the form of my trying to play with her during recess. I'd grab the ball and run while being chased by the entire fifth grade. Then I'd make a giant circle until I found her and tossed her the ball. She'd take it and run very well, especially for a girl wearing dress shoes. Her pigtails would bounce all over the place as she ran. She'd continue until she was exhausted, and then throw the ball to someone else. I remember how she smiled as she ran, and her big brown eyes glowed with excitement. Like I said, it was pure magic for my ten-year-old mind. In my innocence, I did not comprehend that what I was doing was reason for a lynching in the South. Teachers did not like to see Tejano boys being friendly with DOEI girls. I had no idea my actions would upset so many people and bring about dire consequences. Yet, like millions of romantic fools before me, I fell head over heels in love. It was the beginning of another major life changing experience, one which is burnt into my mind and still causes me to pause in wonder and shock. I don't remember what we said to each other, or how we became friends, but we did. In my naïve innocence, I had no idea my actions would create such a problem. One particular day after an exciting game of killer dodge keep away, Norma Jean and I held hands while walking on the sidewalk together. I don't even remember why we were holding hands or for how long. What I do remember is that it only happened once, because the following moments were seared into my mind. The next few events were the first of many experiences of stolen innocence. It was also the last time Norma Jean ever spoke to me. The memory of that day is still burnt into my mind, like a branding iron of hatred on my soul. Up to that point my personal experiences with DOEIs was limited to brainwashing, Billy Myers, and what my young mind was able to comprehend. I had no idea DOEIs hated me so much. I never misbehaved in class, and I always said thank you and yes sir/ma'am. Yet none of that mattered, because my innocence was about to be smashed to smithereens.

My holding Norma Jean's hand stirred up a lot of emotion in one of the female DOEI teachers. I don't even know her name. I don't think I ever did, as not many ten-year-old Tejano kids spoke to adult DOEI women. For the most part they ignored us and we avoided them. For some reason, which only the Universe knows, she happened to be walking in the opposite direction and saw Norma Jean and I holding hands. Her expression alone told us we were doing something wrong, although I had no idea what that might be. She marched right up to us in an aggressive and hostile manner, stopped, and stared down at us. We immediately stopped holding hands. "You can't hold her hand!" she said in an angry voice. "You are a Mexican!" I had no idea what that meant. I was just me, like everyone else. I never felt ethnically inferior until the day that bigot DOEI teacher told me I wasn't good enough. I stared up at her and tried to say something, but couldn't. I don't even remember what I wanted to say. The next thing I knew she was swinging her hand back, a motion I was very familiar with, and in an instant struck me so hard the blow knocked me off my feet. It was a left hook open handed slap, and the loud crack from her blow rang in my ears as I rolled onto my back like a shot buffalo in an old Western. I slowly got up and started crying, more shocked and surprised than hurt. I just stared at her. Norma Jean just stood there, fearful and stunned silent, her big brown eyes filled with tears. The angry DOEI woman, whoever she was, grabbed her hand and said "Come with me, we are going to call your mother!" I stood there with tears running down my face, covered in dust as I watched them walk away in a hurry. I was shocked, humiliated, and embarrassed. This may give you an indication of how bad things were. No one offered condolences or comfort, and not a single adult interfered or attempted to protect a child from being slapped by an adult. I just stood there under the same Texas sun which was shining when I'd fell in love, with tears rolling down my face, paralyzed by fear. I knew I'd done something terribly wrong, but I could not understand what it might be. I knew enough not to ask. My experiences with adult DOEIs hadn't instilled any sense of confidence. Speaking my mind or asking questions was not something I often did, especially considering I was a child who stuttered. Tejanos were not encouraged to do or say anything, and certainly not in my family. The other children stared at me, but no one spoke, and then the bell rang and everyone automatically went to their classrooms. The incident simply disappeared as if it never happened, as if no one had seen it. Norma Jean's mother came to get her, and she quietly pointed me out to her when they came into the classroom. Her mother then spoke to my teacher and they both stared at me. Soon after, she took Norma Jean away. Norma Jean never spoke to me after that day. I watched and loved her from a distance without ever being able to speak to her. Imagine if you can, someone doing that to you. Then ask yourself how it might have affected you. It was one of many harsh lessons, which even now is difficult to look back upon without some emotion.

Several days past without Norma Jean coming to school, and the next time I saw her she would no longer speak to me, nor play keep away football. She even avoided looking at me and rarely made eye contact. I tried talking to her best friend, a girl named Connie Stafford, but she was a DOEI as well, and had nothing to say to me. Connie had a brother named Ross, who I thought was my friend, but soon learned I was wrong. It was one of the darkest experiences of my young life. The realization broke my heart and sadness enveloped me. I went into a silent depression, but no one noticed or cared. I don't remember how I survived. Time simply moved on and the incident was never mentioned or spoken of. It might have been during that dark period that I vowed to be a better man, even though I was only a boy. I tried to do better in everything, hoping Norma Jean would notice me, but she never did. The abusive event seemed to have been swallowed up into a dark hole, where acts of violence against children are placed in Texas. No one reported the abuse and the principal never spoke to me about being struck down by a teacher. No one made an issue of an adult woman striking a child. This is how it was in Texas, and at Andrew Jackson. DOEIs got away with such behavior, simply because no one reported it, regardless of illegality. The entire incident was pushed aside, covered up, or simply did not matter.

     Today, years later as I write about this experience, I am still stunned by the cruelty and indifference displayed by those allegedly educated individuals. I was cursed with wisdom beyond my years, and once again reminded of how I needed to get out of Texas. I continued to love Norma Jean Slaughter throughout my junior high school years. As for her part, she refused to speak with me and quickly adopted the behavior of Texas DOEIs. She even started making fun of my clothes, lunch, and the way I spoke English. Silly me, I continued to love her anyway, waiting for the return of the person I thought I knew. Norma Jean Slaughter taught me that no one ever really knows anyone, which is a valuable lesson. The sweet innocent girl I fell in love with never returned. She became one of the people my mother warned me about when she said, "Never trust a gringo." It wasn't until many years later that I learned loving her wasn't a waste, as love never is. Loving Norma Jean Slaughter made me want to be a better man. It made me try harder, work harder, and study harder. Although I knew I had absolutely no chance of winning her affection, I wanted to be better just so she could see how good I was. My loving Norma Jean Slaughter made me want to look better, read better, play harder, and generally improve myself. Norma Jean never showed an interest in me, although I caught her watching me from a distance several times. If Texas had been different she might have been my first real girlfriend. She was nevertheless the first great love of my life, and my first great heartbreak. As per her part, she never knew how much she meant to me, or how much loving her affected my life. If I had not tried so hard to impress her, I might have never played so hard at football. Nor would I have spent hours polishing my shoes and ironing my jeans and shirts. I would have never studied so hard, in hope that she would think of me as intelligent. Trying to gain her attention forced me to work on conquering my stuttering, which improved my life in general. Had she not meant so much to me, I would have never worked so hard during the summer to buy nicer clothes for the school year. Wanting to be a better man helped me establish boundaries for behaviors, as well as make me aware that someone is always watching, especially in school.

Only recently have I come to fully understand a statement I heard years ago. Until that moment her rejection had left a dark emptiness within me. "We are what we love, not what loves us." It was only after I heard this statement in reference to unrequited love that I came to comprehend its meaning. I was suddenly filled with an inner glow which continues to this moment. I realized that loving Norma Jean Slaughter empowered me. I realized that not only was I a brave child, I was a determined child, because I continued to write her during the summers, despite her mother returning my unopened letters. I still think of Norma Jean Slaughter every time I hear the song "Return to Sender," by Elvis Presley. I realized that loving her, even from a distance, gave me hope, which was something I desperately needed. I endured her rejection and continued to think of her as the same person I thought she had been. I sought understanding, and in doing so I learned all people are subject to peer group pressure. She was influenced by her parents and taught to hate by her peers. It's how hate grows and spreads, and how discrimination works. I eventually came to the realization that I never really knew her. I simply believed she was special because of how she behaved while away from her judgmental friends. When surrounded by her peers, she lost the quality I found endearing and became just as distant and cold as they were. I recognized that the qualities I initially believed she possessed were never there. Truthfully, those qualities would have never had a chance to blossom in such a racist environment. My innocence allowed me to pass her the ball, and chase her uninhibitedly while playing keep away. Yet, it simultaneously kept me from *seeing* who she really was, as well as what she thought of me. Blinded by a desperate need to be loved and have someone in my life, I also overlooked the fact that she never threw the ball back to me. This experience also taught me to never expect to be rescued. Although my discoveries left me feeling defenseless, they also improved my resilience and made me more resourceful. I've never trusted teachers or sought their guidance since. Nor have I sought their approval, understanding, or indulgence.

Today, after years of remembering how much I loved that little girl, I no longer feel sad. I know what my love for her meant to me, and that it gave me more strength than if she had acknowledged me and we'd played out our childhood puppy love. My willingness to surrender to love and struggle to gain her attention was not a hollow defeat. Now, as a Warrior *detached* from my own emotions, I feel lucky. My broken heart has healed many times over, yet the lessons I learned from Norma Jean Slaughter have been with me throughout all these years. I was faced with overwhelming racism and hatred, yet I was willing to love someone who was forbidden, while knowing I had no chance. I continued to love her in silence, suffering the pain of a child, and carrying it with me for years. What I once believed to be a burden and just another broken dream was in fact another key to my freedom. My struggles, disappointments, and defeats were the steppingstones to my freedom. The experience taught me perseverance, *forbearance*, consistency, and acceptance. I learned to lose at love and not become bitter because of it. I realized that we truly are what we love. I loved Norma Jean Slaughter, and in the end it did not matter that she didn't love me in return. Attempting to woo her in spite of insurmountable obstacles taught me many lessons about capturing a woman's attention. Most of these are subtle and almost insignificant, unless they are accompanied with perfect *timing*. Looking back, I recognize that while I did not catch the attention of the girl I wanted, I got attention from a lot of the others. Maybe this is why older women pursued and found me alluring. They perceived that I knew something about women and love. Perhaps it's a woman's intuition or ability to perceive nuances. Maybe they could tell I was in love, and fully engaged in the mechanics of its pursuit, thus making me attractive. I learned how to laugh and joke, and acted as though I were confident and happy. I pretended to be someone else until I eventually became that person. While I'll never know if Norma Jean ever noticed me, thanks to her, other girls certainly did. This is how I learned that love is never wasted. Not if it's honest and selfless. The blessings of love are that we give it, not that someone gives it in return. My wife benefits from all the lessons loving Norma Jean Slaughter taught me. I learned to love as a child, and these lessons run deep. They are instilled in the very soul of me. We are truly defined by what we love. It's amazing that Norma Jean's rejection prepared me for managing the attentions of so many others. Once again, thank you, Norma Jean Slaughter.

Texas escapee,

don Jesus M. Ramirez

Chapter Four
To All the Girls I've Known

"A Warrior's greatest strength and weakness is the same; love. His greatest gift will be to find love, and his curse will be to love an average person."
-don Jesus M. Ramirez

Loving someone who did not love me back had always been a point of frustration for me. As a kid it seemed that I always liked girls who did not like me in return. I don't even remember what it was about some of these girls that I liked. However, I do remember that for some reason the girls I didn't like, or thought of as interesting, liked me. One who comes to mind was a little girl named Gloria Vera. She just showed up in my classroom one day. She seemed too prissy, too conservative, and too confined, but she was cute. She had a dark complexion, which I did not particularly care for. As a kid I did not realize that many little boys grow up to like someone who resembles their mother. My mother had a fair complexion, and her mother (my grandmother) had green eyes and was as light-skinned as a DOEI. I learned years later she was part French. I have no idea why Gloria decided to like me, or what it was about me that she liked. What I do remember is that she sent me a note. It said, "Do you want to be my boyfriend?" On the bottom of the note were two check boxes, one with a "yes" and another with a "no." I don't remember what I did with the note. I guess I must have checked the yes box, because we started sitting together during lunch and recess. I wasn't sure what we were supposed to be doing as boyfriend and girlfriend. I don't remember if I ever liked her or not. I was just curious about what went on when you had a girlfriend, because I had no idea. We sort of just hung out together. Things went on like that for a while, until one morning when a bunch of big yellow school buses showed up to take our class on a field trip to a circus. I guess Gloria wanted to sit together and hold hands, but that didn't happen. I don't remember what I was thinking, nor do I recall specifics regarding our interaction. I just remember I didn't sit next to her, and instead stared out the school bus window during the entire ride. It was the first time I'd ever been to another part of town. I was in awe — captivated by all the new stuff. I completely forgot about Gloria, what she wanted, or that she even existed. I remember the circus, the performers, and the bus trip there and back. In truth, I have no idea what happened to Gloria. When we got back to school after the circus I went on about my business and did whatever kids do. When the day was through I gathered my things and took another yellow school bus home. The next day one of Gloria's friends told me she no longer wanted to be my girlfriend and that she'd broken up with me. I simply said, "Okay." I don't remember caring one way or the other, but she was furious at me. I think she expected me to say or do something, but I had no idea what that might be. I was bored with her anyway. All we did was hold hands, walk around the sidewalk, and sit together during lunch. I wanted to run around and play, throw the ball and tackle people. She was boring. I had no idea what little girls thought or liked. I had no idea I was expected to do and say certain things, as I'd never been taught what those things were. The whole idea seemed silly and boring. What was the point of having someone special if you couldn't share having fun. I don't remember much about her after that. I went on with my life, and life kept happening around me. At the time I was still in love with Norma Jean Slaughter, who never once showed any interest in me at all. Perhaps this is another reason why Gloria breaking up with me didn't matter.

Gloria Vera never forgave me, and I mean never. I had no idea why, and I never bothered trying to speak with her again. I didn't find her interesting, nor attractive. She had a sense of silent shame, which was common amongst Tejano girls at Andrew Jackson High School. I have no idea why she continued to hate me for so long, as I never did or said anything to her. She was still angry at me the last time I saw her, which was in the eleventh grade. I accidently bumped into her one day after she had gotten knocked up by Freddy Martinez, a loser with pepperoni-sized pimples, who I once threatened to beat up for pestering my sister. I was walking into the principal's office to get a tardy slip from Mrs. Robinson, who was the school clerk at the time. I was singing the song "Mrs. Robinson" by Simon & Garfunkel to her. Some of you may remember it from the film *The Graduate*. Suddenly, in walks Gloria Vera, dressed in her house robe, house slippers, curlers, no makeup, and to top it off, she was knocked up. She looked awful. I mean, she looked absolutely terrible. I glanced at her and smiled, but don't know why I did. I wasn't trying to be a wiseass. I thought it was funny, but I've always had an uncommon sense of humor. It seemed funny to me that the girl who'd gotten all bent out of shape because I didn't care about her, would permit me, or anyone else to see her like that. It was funny in a real twisted way, because she looked horrible. When she saw me checking her out from head to foot, she glared at me with fury in her eyes. All I could do was smile and say, "Good morning, Gloria." I hadn't known she was having sex, much less pregnant. Although I had heard she'd dropped out of school. If I'd known she was giving it up, I might have been more interested, but not really. She looked awful. There was no way in hell I'd ever permit any of my high school peers to see me like that. I never saw her again, thank God. I guess she eventually popped out her kid. Thank God it wasn't mine. Seeing her about to explode did more to teach me about self-restraint than watching all those *Red Asphalt* films during driver's education. Up to that point I had never seen a high school girl so pregnant, she was about to pop. I realized I never wanted to knock up any woman, or cause them to look like that. The fear of getting a girl pregnant was planted into my mind, and many nightmares followed. I was in an impossible situation. On one hand, free love was in the air, and there were fun and games everywhere. While at the very same time the war in Vietnam was raging, and guys were coming home in caskets. Knowing that Vietnam was where I'd more than likely end up, made the idea of not going for it seem ridiculous. However, I had no idea how I was going to have fun, get a little lovin', but not accidently knock up some poor girl. Gloria Vera will never know how much she impacted me the last time I saw her. The sight of her became the source of my nightmares. I dreamed she was carrying my baby, and I was forced to drop out of school and work in the cotton fields to feed her and the kid. I'd wake up sweating and terrified, confronted by the manifestation of my greatest fears. I dreaded the possibility of being trapped in Texas, living in a sweaty shack with a screaming kid and a fat ugly wife. When pregnant Gloria Vera stared at me with so much hatred it could have melted a flagpole, she gave me one of the greatest lessons of my life. Be very careful where you put your dick. This is a lesson I have never forgotten. Thank you, Gloria. Seeing you like that really scared the hell out of me.

Another little girl who liked me was Angelina Soto. Again, I don't know why she liked me. I had nothing in common with her. I was into reading, playing keep away killer dodge ball, reading some more, and daydreaming. Although I'd grown up less than a thousand yards from her house, I don't remember ever saying two words to her. Her sister, Sylvia Soto, would later become my little brother Punk's first second base. Angelina had a bad reputation, but I had no real idea what that meant at the time. I knew it meant having sex, but I'd never done it. I'd heard my parents having sex, but I had no idea kids my age were doing it. She had lots of pimples, and for some reason I believed she was having sex, or at least thinking nasty things. We'd been told by the nuns at church that people who had impure thoughts got pimples. I know it sounds ridiculous, but that's what they'd told us. Angelina Soto was a couple of years older, as she had been held back like me, and was more mature. She came from a very poor family, just like mine. Poverty strikes women harder. Its impact upon them seems harsher, or at least it seemed to me. One day during recess I was sitting at my desk reading a book when she came up and handed me a note. I was surprised. Again, it was one of those notes which read, "If you wanna be my boyfriend, check yes or no." It had two boxes, one with a "yes" and another with a "no." I remember sitting there, surprised. I hardly even knew she existed. I had never spoken with her or made any gesture which might have been interpreted as interest. Yet, here she was handing me a note, asking me to be her boyfriend. I wadded up the note and went out to find her. When I saw her I tossed her the note. She caught it, and I left. I have no idea what she thought or said. I never told anyone about that moment until now, and it has been a very long time. I guess I must have hurt her deeply, even though I had no intentions of doing so. Years later, she dropped out of high school, got married, and then disappeared. Before long she was back on Main Drive, only now divorced and looking for love. We talked outside of a church record hop, but I was not interested. I knew too much about her. There was no magic, no spark, and I never saw her again. Soon thereafter she moved away and got lost somewhere out there. She had several brothers, all of which were pachucos. The same guys I'd call losers today. All of them had been to jail and had blue tattoos on their arms. They wore khaki pants, tangerine-colored shoes with the huge triple soles, and were said to be tough street fighters. I had no interest in mixing with those people. I found them to be beneath anything I wanted to be a part of. I have no idea what became of her.

Another little girl who liked me was Margie Perez, and again, I have no idea why. Margie was the younger sister of the baddest, craziest, foulest creature living on Main Drive. I didn't know what his real name was and I didn't care, but everyone called him "Curly." He was several years older than me, much bigger, and was a complete psychopath. Margie decided she liked me and that I was gonna be her boyfriend. I guess she must have told Curly, because one day he randomly came up to me and told me she liked me, and he wanted me to talk with her during lunch. This scared the crap out of me, as I had never spoken to Curly or any of Margie's family before. I had no reason to. They were always getting into street brawls, raising hell, drinking, and shooting off their guns. I sure didn't want to talk with her either, but I was afraid she'd be angry at me if I ignored her, and then Curly would be pissed at me too. I was in a real jam. In true average person fashion, unable to come up with another solution, I decided to pretend it didn't happen. Well, as you can imagine, that went over like a ton of crap. The next day she tried to play with me, but I was too scared, and pretended like she wasn't there. She tried a couple more times and I continued to ignore her. You gotta keep in mind that I stuttered terribly, was as skinny as a stick, and had big ears which stood out like lampshades. I had no idea what I was supposed to say to her, or any other girl for that matter. The only reason I liked Norma Jean was because she played ball and could run fast, which at least made some sense at the time. Plus, Norma Jean seemed nice and sweet compared to Margie, who had thick black hair, dark skin, wore lots of makeup, and was tougher than I was. I couldn't relate to that. I realized I'd made a big mistake when Curly and his gang confronted me after school. He was pissed off and demanded to know if I thought I was too good for his sister. Again, I was completely at a loss. I didn't think anything like that. I just didn't like her and didn't have anything to say to her. I mean, I never knew her. I was just a stupid kid who wanted to play keep away dodge football, do his homework, and be left alone. I never thought I was better than anyone, as I couldn't even speak ten words in a row without stuttering. Before I knew what happened, Curly and his gang of thugs started picking on me without repose. Maybe they thought I was weird because I turned down Margie Perez, who was considered to be hot. Or at least that's what everyone said. I thought she was vulgar and ugly. She cursed like a guy, wore a lot of makeup, and drank beer out in the open. I'd also seen her at church dances making out with hardcore pachucos from Clarkwood, another local barrio. Even then I knew the difference between hot and burnt out. Most importantly, she reminded me of the women my father sat next to at the bars. I now realize that they weren't the problem, but back then I was just a kid who saw his mother crying and wanted help. All of Margie's friends started hating me too. I learned about a woman's scorn. She got angry at me and never talked to me again. That was fine with me, except for the spark which her hatred ignited. Things started going downhill, and didn't stop for a long time. Having my life suddenly take a turn for the worse because of a girl became a pattern. I'd never been popular before, but from that day it seems I went to number one on their shit parade. I began noticing thugs gathering into groups and staring at me. One of them would say something and the rest would laugh. I felt vulnerable and helpless, and got a small glimpse into what women must feel when a bunch of guys stare at them and laugh.

Samantha Rojas was another little girl who liked me for years. She was Jamie's sister, who would later become my little brother Punk's wife. Samantha was cute as hell, but Jamie was beautiful. Samantha and Jamie were interesting, smart as whips, and not afraid to speak their minds. Jamie was voted most beautiful in high school, not a small accomplishment considering the DOEIs never voted for Tejano girls. Punk sure screwed that up, but as they say, love is blind. He would eventually cheat on her, knock her up, break her heart, and then divorce her. To let you know how naïve I was, up to the point when Punk told me about all the stuff he'd done, I'd always considered him a good guy. I had no idea what a turd he really was. He'd been cheating on his wife from day one. During their first year of marriage, while still living in Corpus, he was banging Sylvia Soto, the same girl who was his first second base. She was married to a Marine stationed in Vietnam at the time. I had always thought Punk was a straight shooter, an upright guy, not a player who was banging anything he could get his hands on. Sleeping with another man's wife was considered reason enough to kill in those days. A man could die for doing a lot less on Main Drive. I learned he'd been fooling around on Jamie since day one, and you'd never believe who was in on it. Jamie's brother, his very own brother-in-law. Yup, Punk and his brother-in-law, a guy who I'll refer to as "Jimmy," would say they were going to go shoot pool, but would instead be out banging strange women. Talk about bad judgment. Punk's behavior made a mockery out of the entire idea of getting married. Plus, when his brother-in-law got caught, he spilled the beans. Things went from bad, to very bad. Now Punk's father-in-law, who had loved and respected him, hates him, as do all of his ex-in-laws. Punk, like most average people, was afraid of being alone. I discovered he'd cheated continuously since he'd been married. I'd been fooled and he'd been screwing around for years. When he finally got caught, it was with Sylvia, the hot little girl from Main Drive. You won't believe what he did. The dumbass took her out in Corpus to the same place where Jamie's sisters went dancing. They saw him and the shit hit the fan. In one night of foolishness he lost all credibility with his in-laws, who once believed him to be the perfect husband. When Jamie confronted him, he confessed the entire story, and the last remaining bits of hope faded into oblivion. She became a raging, vengeful woman, who should have walked out, but stayed because of their baby girl. Needless to say, things were never the same. He should have known, but like my father, he expected to continue as if nothing had happened. Sorry, no cigar. They fought like cats and dogs, and she took him to the cleaners in the divorce. In return for her vengeful behavior, he refused to visit his daughter, who suffered because of it. In the end, he was just another loser who happened to be related to me. Years later, after realizing what he'd lost, he told me about all he'd gone through, and about how much he wanted his wife back. We were sitting around a campfire behind my sister's house in Austin, Texas. I had just come back from a camping trip with a group of students, and reacted as if I had been speaking with someone who at least had an intellectual grasp on the

Warrior's discipline. I was shocked, stunned, and speechless. I was in awe of his stupidity, and before remembering he was just an average person, I asked, "What in hell did you think was going to happen?" I started laughing before I caught myself. He'd humiliated her in front of her entire family and destroyed her dreams and illusions of living happily ever after. He'd betrayed every promise he ever made and stomped on her heart, and now he was telling me how much he'd suffered. They'd been high school sweethearts and she was a virgin when they got together. He'd broken every vow and every idea of what she believed the world to be. He destroyed her life via his unfaithfulness. Of course she wouldn't forgive him, and of course she'd seek ways to make his life miserable. I laughed like a monkey until he threatened to hit me if I didn't stop laughing. I stopped laughing long enough to explain to him that he'd gotten what he deserved. As you can imagine, he didn't want to hear it. Like all average people he wanted her to overlook his mistake. He wanted his family back, and wanted to punish her desire for vengeance, while seeking a pardon for his behavior. True to form and as predicted, she made his life miserable every time she got the chance. She also took him to court for child support and still hates him today. His daughter, who is now a beautiful young woman, has him as an example of what to expect from men. Isn't that great? Punk didn't waste any time brooding or feeling remorseful. He never learned anything from all his mistakes either. You'll not be surprised to learn the dumbass married one of the women he was banging on the side. Can you imagine living with a woman who you were sleeping with, while you were married to another? Now he lives in constant fear that she's going to cheat on him, the way other women cheated with him. The Universe seeks its balance by punishing us with our mistakes, not for our mistakes. His drinking got so bad, he was walking in his sleep and pissing on the carpet. One night while on vacation, he actually walked out of their hotel room and pissed in the hallway. His drinking and etc., resulted in him being unable to get an erection. He had to have a pump implanted into his penis in order to get it hard. Now he has to pump himself up before he's able to have sex with his wife, who you can imagine is none too happy. As far as I know, he continues to do the same today. He used to be married to one woman, while banging anyone who'd let him. Lying, cheating, stealing, and excessive drinking were a few of the things he learned from our father. Bad parenting never stops hurting a person, and its effects are felt for generations. I wish him luck, better judgment, and hope that when he dies it's peacefully in his sleep. I wish he'd learn that what goes around comes around. If I could feel sad for someone, it might be for him, but he is living the consequences of his choices. He was just behaving the way he'd been taught by our father. My male siblings are chips off the old block.

Jamie's sister Samantha was very attractive. She was a bit odd, and like me, she didn't fit in. Her ideas of what was funny, cool, or interesting were very different from what was considered normal. She had big dreams, and expectations much like mine, but most of all she wanted to get the hell out of Corpus Christi. She dreamed of bigger things, travel, excitement, and of getting out from under her father's control. She had a crush on me throughout elementary and junior high school, and one summer she invited me to spend a week at her grandfather's ranch. She even paid for my bus ticket. Of course I wanted to go, not because I liked her, but because it was a chance to get the hell out of Main Drive and do something different. My father gave me permission, and then in true tyrant manner behaved passive aggressively, and took me to the bus station past the time I was supposed to be there. I missed the bus because of him. This was his style. I should have walked or had Samantha pick me up on the way to the bus station. I don't believe he wanted me to go, so he dragged his feet, making sure I missed the bus. He never apologized or said one word all the way home. I don't know why he even bothered driving into town. He could have just said no, and saved me all that frustration, and himself all that trouble. Like I said, he was a real shit. It was one of many betrayals. Samantha and I were never an item on campus, although we should have been. She was too familiar. I was interested in girls from town, not country girls who saw and did exactly the same things I did. City girls were more fun. They were more socialized, able to have conversations, laugh, and kid around. Plus, I didn't have to see them in school every day. I am not sure if she ever really liked me, or just didn't want to be alone. Life at Andrew Jackson and in Corpus was very lonely for us. Both of our parents treated us indifferently. They expected us to behave, be quiet, and stay out of sight. She was miserable in Corpus. I'm sure she was just trying to find someone to love her, just like I was. If things had been different at Andrew Jackson, and if the DOEIs had not excluded us via their indifferent racist behavior, we might have been less lonely and less desperate. She had the great misfortune of getting knocked up by a married man. She ended up dropping out of high school and disappearing. One day she was just gone. It didn't matter to me at the time. I was too busy having fun and planning on getting the hell out of there. I learned she'd fallen in love with a guy from Corpus named Hector. She innocently and stupidly got pregnant. This surprised the hell out of me. I'd always considered her smarter. The guy was married and when she told him she was having his baby, he dropped her and ran for cover. Of course his wife called her a whore and a home wrecker. He refused to have any more to do with her. He even refused to answer the phone or speak with her. I'm surprised her brothers didn't kill him, as these things got ugly in South Texas. This was shameful beyond words in the Native Tejano culture. Abortions were not available at the time, plus she had no resources. She was left in a horrible predicament. Her father must have beaten her to a pulp before he sent her to a home for fallen women in Houston. I cannot imagine the pain and suffering she must have endured. Her father disowned her, as did her brothers, at least temporarily. She had no one, and nowhere to turn. She secretly left Corpus in shame, and went to Houston to a home for unwed mothers. She had her child and never returned. I cannot blame her. She suffered terribly. Later both of her parents died and all memories of their life in Corpus vanished. Samantha and I have known each other many years and I think of her as a friend. Supposedly she married a DOEI who deals in real estate, and allegedly they travel the world together. Good for you, Samantha. You go girl! She emailed me around the time I first began writing this book. I asked her to send me any thoughts she might like to share, but she never replied. She'd told me before that Corpus held a lot of bad memories for her, and they were too painful for her to want to relive. Too bad she never learned to be a Warrior. She would have made a fine Warrior, much better than I. If only she'd learned recapitulation, recovered her lost innocence, and recaptured some of the happier times of her life. I wish her the very best, she's paid enough dues for two lifetimes. I've learned the best you can do for an average person who's suffered so much, is leave them alone. I'd only serve to remind her of her suffering. I sincerely wish her happiness.

There was a little girl named Angie Hasset whom I had a crush on in junior high school. She was Rudy Hasset's kid sister, a guy I played football with who once pulled me out of a jam. We could have been lifelong friends, but instead became enemies. He eventually joined a gang of losers on Main Drive and became another of the many thugs I fought. Angie never liked me back. However, I thought she was nice. She had a weird looking canine tooth on the upper left side of her smile that sort of popped out like a vampire. I don't remember why I thought I liked her. I do remember that she wore a plaid dress to church one Sunday, and sat behind me during mass. When I placed my hand on the backrest, she placed her hand next to mine. That was the only time I ever got close to holding her hand. As I said, the girls I liked never liked me. She ended up marrying some ignorant loser who knocked her up and then dumped her after not being able to make it. God only knows what happened to her after that. I hope she got her tooth fixed. If not, it must be awful by now.

There were others, but thank God memory fades. Like I said earlier, all the girls I liked usually liked someone else and didn't like me. It seemed I couldn't win, no matter what I did. I needed help desperately, but I had no one to speak with, learn from, or guide me. I was so damned lonely I could have died from despair. It was during this time I learned a valuable lesson, one I've repeated many times. Act the way you want to be, and soon you will be the way you act. I've learned that much of life in this superficial world is about pretending to know something you know nothing about, and acting as if you do. It doesn't matter if you are scared shitless or not. You have to step up and do it anyway. Once I learned that much of life was lying, acting, and appearing cool, confident, and a lot of bullshit, I started doing better and having fun. I actually started practicing what I was going to say to whomever I met, and it worked. I rehearsed my lines as if I were playing a part in a movie, and it worked. Wow! Was I blown away by the bullshit. I was sickened by it as well. I hated knowing there was so much dishonesty and so much bullshit. This knowledge helped me do some very gutsy things, and after a while it got easier, and I got pretty good at it. I pretended to be the kind of guy I wanted to be, and I've done things that would scare the shit out of most people. I was not surprised when I discovered don Juan taught his students the very same trick, only he called it *stalking*, not acting or bullshit, but it's the same thing. I wish I could have shared this with Samantha and my sisters, who suffered terribly. I wish I could have shown someone else how easy it was to manipulate others, but it would have backfired on me. The average person thinks such things are horrible, and by their average standards they have a point. The difference is a Warrior doesn't care. A Warrior has all he needs and more. Average people will undoubtedly misinterpret this concept completely, and use it as an excuse to misbehave. The truth is, a student of the Toltec discipline isn't interested in lording over a bunch of fools. What would be the point? When a student of this discipline reaches advanced levels they discover they have no need of average people, unless they serve a purpose in their lives. A Warrior who adheres to this discipline and lives amongst 96ers will discover that average people are necessary, as they fulfill roles required for survival in our society. Examples include fire fighters, police officers, street cleaners, waiters, and etc. However, average people make terrible friends and cannot be relied upon or trusted. The tragic reality is that a Warrior is forced to interact with them, which explains why Warriors are often thought of as sullen and very serious. The truth is that they are only misinterpreted as such because they don't share their thoughts with average idiots.

I've been many things. Such as a bodyguard, a soldier, sailor, boxer, a bull rider, a bronco buster, cowboy, hunter, investigator, a cop, and so many other things I'll not say. I've performed in front of hundreds of people as a guitarist, singer, and stand-up comedian. I've performed at the Improv Comedy Club in San Jose, California, and several other less known clubs. I've also addressed members of congress. All of it was done while pretending to be someone else, the same lesson I learned as a kid. All of it was the lessons don Juan taught of *detachment*, *stalking*, *forbearance*, and *timing*. It was learning to manage fear, control, and abandon. One of the secrets I discovered is to genuinely stop worrying about blowing it, and focus on what you want. The secret is to keep challenging yourself. It gets easier the more you do it and the less you care. Keep in mind, most 96ers are so disgusting that if you knew them better, you'd not care what they thought anyway. Don't take offense, but this is also true about yourself at this time, as well as your relatives. Titles, education, and occupation don't mean a thing. People are just people. This is why Warriors don't have heroes. I have no more respect for the President of the United States than I would for his chauffeur. I would address them both as "Sir." I am not in awe of anyone. All that ended when I began to *see*. Some might have more money, education, and etc., but that does not make them better. Being better than average has to do with behavior, not with what you own, where you live, or who your parents are. I've not known any people who are whom they say. I reject the idea that other people can dictate who I should be. I reject the idea that anyone is better than anyone else. It's easy. If they are going to die, like myself, then how are they better? Death makes all things equal and anyone who has not conquered their self-importance is average. The awful truth is all average people are shit and there are no exceptions. This includes you and everyone you know. All average people are the same, with only slight, but very predictable differences. You must learn these. Not so you can point them out in everyone else, but so you can learn to conquer them in yourself. Yeah, I know it's tough, but this is a Warrior's challenge — a nearly impossible one at that. Given the fact that 96 percent of the population are either borderline sociopaths or functioning psychotics, it's like fighting the Devil with holy water. You'll not receive applauds or recognition for being ethical, honest, fair, nonjudgmental, or kind. Even though there is a lot of lip service attached to these qualities, you'll not find them easily. Instead you'll find the opposite of all alleged Christian values. This is why people who follow this path are called Warriors. While you are struggling to offload negative behaviors and bad habits, you'll be surrounded by average people. Every new Seeker hits the same wall and asks the same questions. When confronted with overwhelming adversity, doubt will present itself, and it may seem preferable to be like everyone else. Keep in mind, the simple yet true reason not to, is because doing so is self-destructive. It eats away at your soul and leaves you void of qualities. Warriors are not living this discipline to improve the world, but their own lives. There are no altruistic reasons for adhering to such a demanding discipline. Warriors chose this path because it brings peace and freedom. The path towards knowledge is surrounded by danger and lined with 96ers, who'll ceaselessly try to dissuade you. Not because it's wrong, but because your success will amplify and expose their failure.

  The tyrants in life continuously give me motivation to keep struggling. I've defeated my greatest enemies. Only very few have gotten away, but they are not forgotten. I teach my students never to forget or forgive those who have deliberately harmed them. I am at war against those who harmed me as a child, but I no longer hate them. However, I'll not pass up an opportunity to balance the scales. I warn all my students that once the battle is engaged it continues forever, until your opponent is dead, disabled, or in prison. I am secure in the fact that if I live my life as a Warrior, power will present an opportunity to find balance. This practice of *forbearance* changes you and comes in one of many forms. My journey on the Warrior's path has shown me different versions of reality and the tremendous *focus* it takes to be vigilant of 96ers. Most importantly it has taught me to live in a constant state of war against my own weaknesses. I am by no means at the end of my development, and my struggle continues. Since discovering the Warrior's path, I've grown in ways I never dreamed possible. My journey continues to bring me joy, and the challenges in my life no longer frighten me. My ability to accept impossible challenges has opened up a varied number of opportunities. I've traveled and participated in exciting business ventures. I've witnessed phenomena and unexplainable paranormal events of tremendous consequence. The awesome nature of this knowledge and discipline continues to challenge me. I am awed by the simplistic yet frightening beauty of its nature. I know there are still many mountains to climb and indignities to endure, so I try to laugh as much as possible. I still dream of flying and I still want to see what's beyond the next mountain. Life continues to be an adventure.

Texas escapee,

don Jesus M. Ramirez

Chapter Five
Close to Hell and Far from God

"The Devil runs free in Texas and everyone knows it's true. You can see him hiding in the shadows along the highway, down empty dark streets, and in the eyes of your children. He stirs now and then to let you know he's there."

–don Jesus M. Ramirez

Everyone on Main Drive was poor as hell, and I mean poor. It always shocked me how they all had so many kids. No one could afford them, and yet every year they'd pop them out like it was a contest. None of the parents could afford health and dental insurance, or even a flu shot. Yet there were swarms of kids running around raising hell, stealing everything that wasn't bolted down, and beating each other senseless. Some were so poor they didn't even have electricity or running water in their homes. In typical Christian fashion my parents said it was their fault for not paying their bills. They accused them of spending their money on beer, clothes, and etc. I never understood how they could say one thing at church on Sunday, and then behave completely different during the week. Although we were just as poor, it was within my parent's means to give those in need a helping hand, a kind word, or even a loaf of bread, but it never happened. I learned people are punished by their sins, not for them, and everyone is living the consequences of their decisions. I also learned not to feel sorry for people and it's impossible to really help anyone. It has taken my entire life to actually put this knowledge into practice.

Summer always increased the violence, but not by much. Violence, fear, and death seemed like permanent fixtures amongst the desperately poor inhabitants of Main Drive. The summer heat brought about hordes of migrants, and like an invading army they descended upon Corpus Christi. Like locusts, gangs of thugs arrived by the truckloads, bringing with them the same insane and violent behavior already found on Main Drive. The unbearable humidity and merciless sun added to the insanity, which exploded into bloodshed. On the side of God and peace was the newly built church, Our Lady of the Rosary, the only hope left on Main Drive. On the side of Satan and his demons were the heat, poverty, racism, drugs, and alcohol. Not what you might call a fair fight.

I do not know how the idea of establishing a new church on Main Drive came about, or who was responsible, but as they say, God works in mysterious ways. Growth and change however, are rarely welcomed and do not come easily. The laws of the Universe dictate every change is always accompanied with side effects. It was no different when it came to establishing the new church on Main Drive. All the natural laws were implemented. The laws of attraction, of pull and push, and hundreds of others moved into motion. No matter how evil or divine, all earthbound ideas need fuel to operate. The burden to raise funds to build the new church was not offered up by the Pope in Rome. Instead he felt that we, a group of poverty stricken Tejanos, should be held responsible for all expenditures. Even with all their billions, the Catholic Church did not consider us to be worthy of such an investment. However, they did find it in their hearts, or should I say, their pocketbooks, to send us a priest named Father Hamilton. He was the first alleged religious leader I ever met. I thought he was scary and I didn't like him, as he looked weird all dressed up in black. He was from Ireland, and was absolutely huge. He had a giant bald pumpkin head and was as tall as a tree, with hands as big as hams and a completely pink complexion. The guy should have been a soldier, or an alligator wrestler. I'd never seen such a strange looking man in my life. I was still very young and hadn't yet discovered the world was much bigger than I ever imagined. As a child I had no idea there were so many other kinds of people. It was a real shock to discover there were actually people of different colors and sizes, who spoke different languages. I remember hearing my parents talking about "gringos, chinos, indios, and negros." Often when gringos were mentioned my mother expressed how she hated being unable to speak English. Looking back, the real shocker was why she never attempted to learn. It would have made everything a lot simpler for her. Unfortunately, she was just as stubborn as my father. In average person fashion she hated what she did not understand. She also resented feeling discriminated against by DOEIs, who never missed an opportunity to give Tejanos who didn't speak English a hard time. Average people who are given a little authority and power usually forget where they came from, and quickly morph into tyrants. The average DOEI was not only unhelpful, but unkind, unfriendly, and mean spirited. It was hard enough enduring this as a child, but much more destructive watching such individuals mistreat my mother and not being able to do anything about it. My father never seemed to care. I guess he'd developed a very thick skin, or just learned to ignore the hostile stares and angry expressions. I never did.

    Father Hamilton's arrival was accompanied by his fire and brimstone sermons. He had a terrible temper, and his dark moods seemed to dictate the terrifying themes of which he so often spoke; punishment, pain, and suffering. Not exactly what the already beaten down people of the barrio needed. Instead of hope, love, and forgiveness, he predicted damnation for failure to donate enough money to build the new church. Keep in mind, everyone on Main Drive was as poor as church mice. Yet it didn't matter to him that nobody had a pot to piss in or even enough to eat. According to him it was somehow our fault, and God didn't care how much we suffered so long as we had a new church. During one of his most impressionable sermons he raised his giant arms over his head and shouted, "God doesn't want your pennies!" He might as well have said God wants your sweaty, blood soaked dollars. This guy was as arrogant as a college professor with tenure, but we were told to respect him because he was a man of God. Today, as an adult, I'd spit in his eye and tell kids to run away from anyone wearing a dress calming to represent God. It never occurred to me at the time that the Pope in Rome could have simply written a check and paid for the entire thing. I later discovered that all churches are similar to a McDonald's franchise. They only build them in areas where they can make money. If they don't make money, they get closed, sold, or decommissioned. The same priest who was just ordering you to say six "Our Father's" and six "Hail Mary's" last week, will leave, step aside, and let the Devil have his way. Once you are out of the Church's good graces the evil bastard can bang you like a drum, and according to the Church, you'd be screwed. Sorry about that, you didn't put enough money into the collection plate, so you don't get protection from the Church. Don't worry, if you're willing to drive across town to another Church, you'll be saved. Oh, you don't have a car? Have too many children, and cannot afford to go? Oh dear, that's too bad. Well, you're still screwed.

Believe it or not we lived outside of the Church's protection and didn't even know our immortal souls were in danger. We just went on about our lives acting as if we didn't care, because we didn't. We were what the Church would call, "ignorant savages." Similar to those poor native people who the Spanish encountered wherever they landed. Apparently it was God's will that those ignorant savages be tortured, enslaved, raped, killed, and converted to Christianity. I guess it was a small price to pay, because at least their souls got to go to heaven after they were raped and murdered, right? Spanish friars allegedly brought the salvation of God's grace to the New World. According to them, native people had no concept of a divine entity that lent spiritual guidance. As per European bigotry, only their interpretation of divine mattered. Anglophiles have never admitted that these people enslaved the natives and forced them to build the missions now found throughout the Southwest. There are statues of these colonizing men, who tortured, raped, and fathered children with native women, who along with their bastard children will forever be unrecognized by the Church. All organized religions have been used as reasons for armed pacification of natives. Only those unafraid of having their fantasies destroyed can challenge history.

In an effort to raise more money to build the new church, Father Hamilton introduced the idea of the Cotton Queen Contest. It came about because most people on Main Drive picked cotton during the summer. He encouraged all the parents to enter their daughters, and no one thought to remind him how poor we all were. We didn't even have sidewalks or streetlamps. There were no gas stations or grocery stores for miles around. We lived on the frontier between Texas and México, in a Third World county within a Third World state. The DOEIs in Austin, the state capital, never gave a damn about us. None of them even bothered to try and get our vote. We were seen as a cheap source of uneducated labor, cannon fodder for wars, and candidates for the Texas prison system. Old sparky, the electric chair, got its hands on many Tejanos who made the mistake of being taken alive. Truth is it wouldn't have mattered. Father Hamilton didn't give a damn about how poor we were, he wanted a church.

At first the Cotton Queen Contest seemed like a good idea, so my sister Precious entered. However, soon thereafter the shine wore off, reality hit, and things got ugly. The parents were supposed to come up with ways of raising money, and the contestant who brought in the most money would win. My poor mother and sister got caught up in all the nastiness of dealing with average people on Main Drive, who were horrible. I remember all the trouble it caused. The fighting and yelling between my mother and father went from bad to real bad. My poor sister got caught up in the middle of it and somehow got blamed. I'm sure she would have never agreed to participate in such a contest on her own. The backstabbing and gossiping between families began immediately and started with accusations of cheating and stealing. In her own fashion, of course my mother contributed to all the ugliness. It wouldn't have been so bad if our family wasn't so completely dysfunctional. My father, whose delusional self-image and violent behavior was legendary, should have never been given a platform for attention. His self-importance, jealousy, and constant need to compare himself to others made the whole ordeal poison. The arguments and fights were unbelievable, and of course shit runs downhill, which was where I was. There was absolutely no way of helping, but I remember all the yelling. My mother cursed my sister as if it had been her fault. She cried and did as she was ordered.

I've stopped trying to excuse my mother's behavior, and now just acknowledge it for what it was. My poor sister had no more to do with the drama than I did. When things became unbearable my mother could have simply dropped out of the contest, which is what a lot of other families did, but that would have made too much sense. She was stubborn, angry, and relentless. Keep in mind, the contest had a lot of demanding requirements. They had to make a dress for my sister to wear during the coronation, and hold the dance to announce the winner. I would never have agreed to undertake such an overwhelming challenge to raise money for any religious organization. My mother should have known how much trouble it would bring, but she was determined to continue. The contest turned out to be a huge source of friction for everyone. We needed friction like we needed more kids in the family, and we continued to get both. Countless negative discoveries are amongst the many obstacles confronting Seekers. One of the most devastating is acknowledging that their relatives are the problem. It's one thing to point a finger at strangers, but it's quite another to look within our circle and recognize 96ers. Each Seeker brings unwanted changes to their circle, which always results in devastating consequences. There is no way to grow and advance on this path without changing. As a Seeker changes, they become a source of frustration for those who believe they know them. Their very presence contradicts the idea of who others believe them to be, which as a result challenges their reality. One of the many rules on this path is to never show an average person their reality. This is why Warriors distance themselves from 96ers. Once someone steps out of line, it upsets the norm and brews conflict.

  The parents of the contestants found many different ways to raise money. Some made candied apples and sold them after church or in the neighborhood. Others did the same with chocolate drinks, cake, or tamales. Somewhere along the way someone came up with the idea of holding dances in the old church hall. This may sound like a good idea until you remember that the only pastimes on Main Drive were drinking and fighting. There was absolutely nothing else to do. It's isolated in the middle of a huge field, surrounded by more fields. It was common for entire families to be involved in violent battles. The fights erupted over insults, someone's woman, or just because drunken thugs misbehave. A main reason for these battles was the lack of police protection. We lived outside the city limits and were supposed to have sheriff patrols, but the DOEIs weren't concerned with the stabbings, shootings, and insanity which took place on Main Drive. We paid taxes but lived on the edge of society without protection, yet were held accountable for actions taken in self-defense. My experiences with Texas law enforcement have been horrible and were a great reason to escape. Texas has a legendary Southern hate of Tejanos, Blacks, and anyone who does not fit into their idea of "good." I wish I could say this was only a reflection of the ignorance which was so prevalent in those times, and that now things are different, but I would be lying. Most Texas DOEIs still consider everyone not of European ancestry to be inferior. DOEIs of the United States have experienced too many generations of privilege to be willing to surrender their status. They have been brainwashed and government endorsed to believe they are the acme of superiority. A DOEI would need to be a Four Percentor in order to acknowledge, accept, and understand this brainwashing to be exactly what it is; pure fantasy and delusion. As I've said before, death makes all things equal, which makes the idea of any person believing their race grants them a level of superiority completely ridiculous. How can one biological creature be superior to another, if they are both going to die? I will say that it was worse back then, and any request for police protection was denied. Rejection for protection resulted in several men being deputized to police the dances held in the old church hall. I have no idea what the procedures were, how these adults were chosen, or what they were supposed to do in case of a fight. My father only worked as a deputy once, and things got too hot to handle. Looking back, it made no sense to intervene in a confrontation between street thugs, especially when you would also be thrown in the mix. There was a huge fight the night my father worked as a deputy, and several deputized men were injured. Mr. Rodriguez was amongst those hurt. I don't know what role my father played in the melee, but he never volunteered to police the thugs of Main Drive again. He saw no benefit in being injured or incurring the wrath of homicidal lowlifes for the Church. Unlike the crusaders sent to steal and kill in the name of God, he saw no profit in fighting to keep the peace. In 1095 Pope Urban II launched an army of knights and peasants to fight the Turks who had seized the Holy Land. Knights of the Crusades were promised riches and given absolution of all their sins. Imagine giving bloodthirsty mercenaries a chance to make war without fear of God's wrath. The alleged good men of our barrio weren't promised anything but a pat on the back. Typical of 96ers, my father never did anything unless he was paid. He hid behind a facade of respectability, yet for all his feigned machismo, he never defended his position or another person. When dealing with men he was very political, always minimizing differences and avoiding trouble. He knew that there is no upside to breaking up fights amongst thugs. Real brawls have severe consequences. Looking back, I don't know how we survived. I learned to hit the ground whenever I heard a loud bang. It might not have always been gunfire, but it was safer than standing around to see what it was. By the time I joined the military I'd already been in several gunfights and seen dead bodies. After all that trouble we had a happy ending. My sister won the contest and was escorted by her future husband, who was her boyfriend at the time. This was a big deal in those days, especially out there in the middle of nowhere, amongst the ignorant savages and migrant farm laborers. Life out there was reminiscent of a Pancho Villa movie, where a bunch of drunken tough guys shoot off their pistols, and the women all cross themselves in fear. Poverty and ignorance usually run together, both of which were abundantly present.

    Allegations of all sorts continued flying about. Instead of building unity within the community the contest further destroyed it, pitting one family against another. Father Hamilton mistakenly believed adults would behave with decorum and civility. He should have known better. The contest destroyed what little peace remained on Main Drive. There were too many hurt feelings, too many insults, and far too much damage done. People on opposite sides never spoke to each other again. Not because they didn't know one another, but because they knew one another too well. This amongst average people is like hemlock. Father Hamilton, the people, and the entire community stepped back into an ugly darkness. They damned the Church, stopped pretending to be good, and went back to partying and raising hell. I had already learned nothing would be easy if my parents were involved. My mother and father could complicate the simplest thing into a major cause of conflict, which always led to arguing, which then led to violence. It was a major heartache for my poor sister, whom I loved. She suffered tremendous humiliation at our mother's hand, which was only second to our father's abusive tongue.

Both of them inflicted emotional abuse upon her like it was a prize rather than a punishment. In truth, had it not been for church, the priest, and all the surrounding activities, my poor sister would have never had a chance to be courted by her husband. So as they say, God works in mysterious ways, his miracles to perform.

We were very short of miracles on Main Drive and I discovered that according to the Catholic Church, having God around cost money. It seems all such organized religions connect your personal assets to how much God thinks of you. According to many, the more you give to the Church, the better your chances are of getting into heaven. Once upon a time, a rich man could supposedly pay another to take his sins so he could go to heaven. Or, a rich man could pay a fee to the Church and it would grant a pardon for his sins. This might explain why gangsters, murderers, politicians, and my rich brother, Beelzebub, always make giant donations to their church. Beelzebub does this with a delusional, misguided, and completely average source of pride. He is ignorant of the contradictions within his behavior. He had no problem making substantial contributions to his church, while at the same time ignoring his sister, who spent years struggling to survive and pay medical bills for her dying baby. He saw nothing wrong with his father living out the remainder of his life in an uninsulated wooden structure in Texas, while he lives in a mansion on fifty acres, with an Olympic-sized swimming pool in his front yard. He finds nothing wrong with indulging beyond capacity, while much of his family struggles to find work, pay the rent, and simply survive. This is real Christianity.

Holidays were one of the few times my father allowed my sister's boyfriend, my future brother-in-law, who I'll refer to as "Rock," to come visit. It was all very stuffy, formal, and uncomfortable.

Thank God, he knew my mother liked music, so he'd bring his guitar and play for her. He was the guy who motivated me to want to learn how to play guitar. I am forever grateful, as my guitar has been my only companion on many lonely nights. I've spent countless nights crying in the dark, lamenting my lost childhood while holding my guitar. Music has been a source of inspiration for me. It has never abandoned or let me down. Music has accompanied me throughout my life and continues to play a major role in it today. Even now, after having lost my hearing in my right ear, I continue to play guitar, write songs, and love music. As I write this, I'm scheduled to go into the recording studio to make my first album. I don't expect to sign any major record deals, but it's a demonstration that talent is ninety percent preparation and ten percent inspiration. Perhaps the most significant song I've written to date tells the story of a kid who lives with his parents. Every Christmas his father spends all their money on booze and women. He makes a fool of himself and causes the entire family nothing but grief. It's not a happy song, so if you don't like sad songs, you're really gonna hate this one. This song won "Best Performance of the Night," when I performed it at a local song contest. Goes to show, misery loves company. I thought of sending this song to my father while he was still alive, but it wouldn't have done any good. True to character, my father kept getting worse till his very end, saying and doing things that would curl stone.

Not long after winning the Cotton Queen Contest, my sister Precious ran away with her boyfriend Rock and got married. This happened around the same time my brother Bumper married Lilith, his high school girlfriend. Later, my father would allegedly make inappropriate sexual advances towards her. I have no idea why Bumper was surprised my father would do such a thing. I would have expected it. My poor brother, who was twenty-years-old by then, should have taken a baseball bat to his head, but he didn't do anything. This was when I vowed I'd never allow my father near my wife. At the time of his death I had been married for over 25 years, and he never met her. At least Precious moved away from our father's influence. Although he never let her forget what a disappointment she was. The first time she returned to visit as a married woman, my mother, known for her sharp tongue, lit into her. I felt so sorry for Precious. I was present when my mother, who was blamed for Precious' running away, verbally attacked her. My mother, who'd ran away herself and married at the age of fifteen, said "You couldn't wait, could you?!" I never understood where she got the gall to throw morality or decorum in my sister's face, when she'd done worse herself. To call my mother a hypocrite would be like calling the Devil bad. I'm certain my father, whose mind lived in the gutter, thought Precious was pregnant, which she wasn't. I am happy my sister took matters into her own hands and ran away. I also liked the effect it had upon my father, who believed he could control his children as if they were oxen. It demonstrated just how little control either of them had, and how unpredictable things are. After of years of studying the elements of unpredictability, I recognized that there are small windows of chance where others can help or hinder us. These windows open and close randomly depending on our life experiences. Ideas, customs, and values leak into our lives via these windows, which open less often as we grow older. This explains why few people past the age of thirty develop new friends, learn to trust, or find love or happiness. My role as a mentor has given me opportunities to influence others. Much to my disappointment, I've discovered that without the aid of my energy to assist Seekers, they usually return to habitual behavioral patterns. It is the nature of 96ers to quit anything that demands change. Spiritual tourist who lack courage to face adversity quickly falter.

As a kid I remember wanting to be a pirate after watching a pirate movie. Soon after that I wanted to be a bullfighter because my mother liked them. Then after we built the new church on Main Drive, Our Lady of the Rosary, I wanted to be a priest, or at least that's what I thought. When I was eight-years-old Father Hamilton came around and asked my parents if my brother Punk and I could be altar boys. My older brother Beelzebub had been an altar boy for some time before we started. Apparently some boys had quit, and my father ordered us to fill the positions at the priest's request. What the hell was I gonna do, say no? This was all before child molesting priests hit the front page. Luckily for us, this guy wasn't a pedophile. So, I became an altar boy. Or rather I should say I was pretending to be an altar boy, as I didn't know squat about what it meant or what to do. The first Sunday we served we got to the church early. We went into the back where the priest was, and he opened the closet and got me a gown and a white shirt, or whatever they call the clothing that goes over the frock. I didn't know what the hell I was doing. I was sort of a "filler," like the people who get hired to fill in empty seats at the Academy Awards. I had no responsibilities other than to kneel and stand up along with everyone else. I had no idea what the hell was going on. It was sort of like watching a movie, only I was a part of it. I was never bored because I've always had a great imagination, and could entertain myself while staying out of trouble, unlike my older brother. The damned fool was stealing wine from the priest's bottle, and money from the collection plate. It was never very much, but I thought he was stealing from God. It never seemed to bother him any. I should have known he was just a crook. He'd take a few coins and gave me a couple as well. It's a good thing I never confessed this to the priest during confession. He never did either, which gives you an idea of what a great Catholic he was. He was a real man of God, who hasn't changed a bit. Today I recognize that a Seeker with the smallest success on this path would make a better Christian than any I've known. My ability to *see* people's energy has removed all doubt pertaining to 96ers. The fact that I continued to believe in spite of Beelzebub behaving in such a wretched manner, is a testament to the kid I was. Like I said, I believed God was going to appear, talk to me, and perhaps even take me with him. As lonely and miserable as I was, I was ready to go.

    Wearing the robe gave me special attention after mass, which was the part I liked. A lot of other kids were also volunteered by their parents, but after a few weeks they stopped coming. Not us. This was how I got the idea to become a priest. However, at the time I had no idea it meant giving up women, which was already important in my life. My wanting to be a priest was something else I never told anyone about, but I wanted to know and serve God. I hadn't yet worked out how I was going to have a girlfriend, and still be a priest though. The world all around me was such a horrible place, and I wanted it to be the kind of place it was supposed to be. Don't ask me why, but at first, I had actually wanted to join because of the uniform. After I had become familiarized with Father Hamilton's odd appearance, I began to admire his attire. In my child's mind priests were special, and I wanted so desperately to be special and gain my mother's affection. She seemed to think it was important and noteworthy to dress up, march into church, and assist the priest with the mass. Keep in mind, this was a long time ago, and things were a lot different. I guess I should say I was a lot different because I wanted to be a good boy. Once again, I was totally strange in my thinking and attitudes. I wanted to gain admiration for what I did, not for what I had, like the other kids. I had no idea my thinking was so far off track as to make me weird. I've often wondered if I wasn't born of a union between my mother and some visitor from outer space. Or perhaps it is what students of the Toltec discipline claim, and sorcerers are in fact born with knowledge of their past lives. I have no idea where or how I got these ideas. No one, and I mean no one, ever demonstrated a bit of concern or interest in helping anyone other than themselves.

While being an altar boy I acted like I knew what I was doing, while having no idea what the hell was going on. I pretended to know and people assumed I did. It was amazing. I was practicing the Warrior's discipline long before I knew such a thing existed. I was practicing abandon and control while having no idea, or fear that I might be exposed. No one ever told me to say the prayers in Latin, or asked what the words meant. Like a parrot, I just repeated what I'd heard. Don Juan would have been amazed an eight-year-old kid was doing things many of his students couldn't. I learned to move and act like an altar boy, and so I was. I eventually served during special holy masses and weddings. I still remember the first wedding I served in as an altar boy. My animal torturing brother, Beelzebub, and younger brother, Punk, also served. It was one of the first weddings in Our Lady of the Rosary Church on Main Drive, and it was a very big deal. I was supposed to carry a basket full of dimes which symbolized prosperity, wealth, and hope for the future. They were shiny and bright, and I wanted to steal them. I could have taken one or two, as I'm sure no one counted them, but back then I was too scared. I believed God, whose life-sized statue stood overlooking us, could see me. I never did anything else other than stand there holding the basket of dimes, kneeling, and standing up while the priest married the couple. I mumbled along, pretending to say the prayers in Latin, although I don't remember anyone trying to teach them to me. I was just window dressing. I don't remember who it was that got married, but I'm in their wedding pictures. I'd like to see those pictures, just to see what I looked like dressed up as an altar boy. I must have been one funny looking and very strange kid. Who would have guessed that pretending to be an altar boy would have taught me the secrets of this discipline before I'd even heard of it?

In recalling how much church meant at the time, I am reminded of the crush I developed on Sister Mary Elizabeth. She had been teaching the children how to dance, and during the demonstration I had seen the inside of her thigh. Her inner thigh was white and looked soft and desirable. I was just a child and it was all very innocent. I was attracted to her, and even though I could not talk without stuttering, I practiced and learned all the prayers I was given. This is how I became so good at memorizing things. I could repeat anything, just like a parrot, even if I didn't know what it meant. I wanted to see her and began looking forward to Sundays. I was starved for attention and sought it anywhere, and worked hard to be better. I managed to accumulate a pretty good collection of holy cards, which were given as rewards. I was on a roll, doing good and getting better. Not only was I starting to stand up for myself, but I also managed to control my stuttering a little. Things looked good for a change, but it all ended one winter, sometime before the new church had been built. Due to a major storm the mass was moved from the old damaged church to a home across the street. All the kids were herded into the kitchen and I found a spot to sit underneath the table. I was being good, you know, sitting quietly. However, the kid next to me was talking, and as it had happened before, I was blamed for doing something someone else did. Apparently in an effort to silence the person she believed was talking, Sister Mary Elizabeth reached under the table and grabbed me by my ear. She gave it a strong pull, and man, it hurt like hell. This gentle servant of God was about to rip my ear off. Feeling unjustifiably wronged, I jumped out from under the table and kicked her in the shins as hard as I could. She screamed and fell on the floor with a thud, and I flew out the back door as if the Devil were on my tail. I kept running until I had crossed the muddy fields and was standing amongst the rain soaked mesquite trees in the woods. I knew I was in trouble when I looked down at my shoes, which were now covered in mud. I knew I'd get a beating for ruining them. I spent the rest of the morning in the rain, scared and freezing my ass off alone under a mesquite tree. I finally got the courage to go home, hoping if I pretended nothing had happened, I might get away with it. I have no idea how or why, but the entire incident seemed to have fallen into some black hole. Nothing was said about it at home, and since there was so many of us, no one noticed I was already home when the rest of the family arrived. I simply used the water hose to wash the mud off of my shoes and left them under the bed to dry. I have no explanation for what happened. All I know is, I never returned to catechism, and Sister Mary Elizabeth disappeared soon thereafter. Who knows what happened to her, she might have been transferred to another diocese. I wonder if she'll ever know how much I loved her, and how much she hurt me. I never saw her again.

Not too long after that incident I experienced what I believed to be a miracle. I was alone in the church, and either because of my imagination or because it was in fact a miracle, I thought I saw a statue of Jesus Christ move. Keep in mind that Catholic Churches have dozens of statues. There was a statue of Jesus Christ standing next to the altar where I had been kneeling. I never told anyone, but I thought I saw it move. I'll never know if it did, or if it was simply my imagination. Regardless, I became convinced I was special and God had a special purpose for me. Man, was I mistaken. After sharing this with other people I've come to discover this was not a common experience. Who knows, perhaps the Universe did designate me. Perhaps I failed to see it because of all the disappointments and bitterness I experienced. I'll never know, but at that time I was convinced I'd witnessed a miracle. I gradually abandoned my plans of becoming a priest, in part because no matter what I did, my mother never acknowledged or gave me attention. The experience of seeing the statue move helped me develop an unbelievable amount of optimism, and I got the idea that I deserved better.

I don't understand why, but my father thought Beelzebub was special. Surly he valued what his eyes found pleasing, but I knew Beelzebub for who he was then, and continues to be today. He is a mean and sadistic bastard who doesn't care about anyone or anything other than himself. My father's delusional perception of him, combined with the fact that he was a good looking kid, resulted in other family members cosigning this absurdity. This only proves that 96ers are irrationally influenced by appearance, and that appearance has nothing to do with the quality of a person. As for myself, I just got pushed aside and ignored. One of the many negative behaviors and social addictions which average people suffer from is comparing everyone. In the case of my older brother and me, it was an unfair comparison. Just like so many other comparisons, there was nothing to compare. He was two years older, a foot taller, and forty pounds heavier. While he was considered a chip off the old block, I had been born sickly and premature. He'd been milk fed and powder puffed, while I was shunned and outcast. I was skinny as a stick, quiet, had big ears and freckles, and one of my eyes was cockeyed. I also had a big head and stuttered terribly. So, when the comparison contests started, I always ended up losing. It was more than just not being good enough. It was the constant hammering of the same negative beating. I learned at a very tender age that being tough meant a lot more than fighting back physically. It meant rejecting all the negative badgering and mental brainwashing. The fact that this was perpetuated by the people who were supposed to love and protect me only made it that much worse. I was supposed to be taken care of and taught how to spread my wings and fly. Instead, my parents made sure I had no wings, nor the confidence required to spread them. Some of you might be wondering how the hell I survived. Well, I guess I lived because I didn't die, although there were many times I wished I had. I don't know where I got the courage to resist, rebel, stand up for myself, and literally say, "Fuck you!" to everyone who tried to squash me. In essence I declared war upon the war. I had no weapons, no defensive knowledge, no friends, and no support. Yet I vowed to fight back until I no longer could. Resisting on all fronts is an exhausting endeavor. Those of you with romantic notions should erase them. Keep in mind that even a dying and wounded animal will fight when cornered. The objectives and purposes for choosing this path are personal, but the tactics are founded on pragmatic logic. Adopting this discipline and applying its lessons is not done for altruistic purposes. Everyone, including Warriors and wounded animals, desire to live and be free. These are the soundest reasons for doing anything. If this is what is at stake, it's less costly to fight than to submit to tyranny.

The lessons of the Toltec Warrior were not something I learned as an adult. I lived them as a child. Like a Warrior, I had no chance of winning and still chose to resist, because I could no longer go on being who I was. I had to change or die. I began to seek respite, shelter, comfort, solace, strength, and a little fun. I searched for some relief, without getting into trouble. One such example occurred while I was serving as an altar boy. I decided to pull a little prank with the wooden hammer used to whack the bell during mass. I loosened the wooden ball on the tip of the handle, and when Beelzebub tried to use it to ring the bell it went flying, bouncing all around the altar. The entire church immediately began laughing. It was a comic break which I engineered in secret, and never told a soul about until now. It was great fun watching Beelzebub trying to catch the little wooden ball, as he was in charge. Father Hamilton made sure it never happened again, and told Beelzebub to always check the ball and make sure it was tight. It was too bad, because it was great fun. It got a lot of laughs and gave me an excuse to get off my knees. It was an important event in my life, as it was the very first time anything I did got a laugh. I couldn't tell you why, but it felt great being able to make people laugh, especially those people. You've got to remember that at the time there wasn't much to laugh about. The people of Main Drive were being squashed by religion, social expectations, the weather, poverty, and racism. In addition the children were enduring injustice and pressure at school, as well as all the other difficulties which accompany growing up. For some unknown reason, despite the fact that none of these people had ever spoke to me in kindness, reached out to help me, or even knew I existed, I still wanted to make them laugh. Throughout my life I had an unexplainable desire to help people. I no longer feel this way. This passion may have died during the Persian Gulf War, perhaps the night a scud missile broke through our defenses and landed on a warehouse full of soldiers near Al-Khobar Airport. Twenty-five were killed and several hundred were wounded. Or maybe it was the racist Army Reservists from Helena, Montana, who made my serving in their unit during the war a miserable experience. Or perhaps it was the horrendous treatment I received from my boss and coworkers upon returning to my civilian job. I don't know where for sure, but the desire to help others was beaten out of me. I looked into the abyss and recognized the beauty and horror of living, understanding why total control and abandon is required during a confrontation.

As I said before, Father Hamilton had a terrible temper and often preached of fire and brimstone. His giant pink face would grow red when he delivered his sermons. He'd stand on the altar, dressed in his silk custom-made gowns, and accuse the congregation of being stingy. He demanded each family donate a tenth of their income to the Church. He claimed he often spoke to God, and said Jesus Christ was personally insulted there was not more money in the donation basket. Even as a child, when I still wanted to believe in a Christian God, I did not believe this to be true. I always questioned everything I was told, and as I grew older I gained experience by which to compare such information. I knew how hard it was to earn a dollar, and couldn't believe God needed one tenth of what I earned. I worked like a dog picking cotton to earn money, and there was no way I was going to give it to the priest. My father and mother, who were not the worst Catholics I've ever known, also disagreed. There was no way my father, who worked hauling cement and bricks for a living, was going to give away one tenth of what he earned. Keep in mind that I could buy a good pair of shoes for fourteen bucks back then. A great pair of shoes would have cost about twenty bucks. Money was worth a lot more back then, and there was no such thing as minimum wages or fair treatment laws for employees. The DOEIs controlled everything, and Tejano labor was as easy to find as injustice and booze.

Father Hamilton lived in an air conditioned house, while the rest of us suffered in the humidity and heat. He drove an air conditioned car, wore new clothes, and a servant did his laundry and cooked his meals for him. He had new shoes, money in his pocket, respect in the world, and a purpose, even if it was just to screw the rest of us. While he pointed his finger at us for being bad Catholics, the people of Main Drive survived off their manual labor jobs. As I grew older Father Hamilton's hypocrisy appeared more and more brazenly obvious. Being exposed to the contradictory nature of this well-fed and overpaid hypocrite stripped me of my naïve childhood desire to be a priest. The more I learned about priests and religion, the less I believed any of it. Instead of role modeling proper behavior he exhibited the same emotional and ego driven behavior seen in all 96ers. I never heard a word of kindness, forgiveness, or divine inspiration from his mouth. I never heard him speak of anything but damnation for the future of our souls. Instead of giving the hopeless people of the barrio inspiration, he fed their suspicions of people in authority. When I dreamed of becoming a priest, I'd hoped to become part of something bigger than myself, but all I found was more of the same garbage. This was during the time when the bishop was transferring child molesting priests to other churches, rather than turning them over to the police, and long before it was exposed by the media.

My mother thought having the priest over for coffee was a compliment. She never realized he was never interested in fellowship.

During his visits he was evaluating how much money we had in order to know how much he should expect. Who knows if he had any affairs with the women of Main Drive, or how many souls he saved from damnation. My guess would be very few. It wouldn't surprise me to learn he'd had his way with dozens of women, as he was an arrogant man. He may have convinced himself that copulation with him brought them closer to God. All the women in the barrio competed for his attention, and via his association gained social status. The competition amongst the women of Main Drive became furious, with Señora Cardenas winning the contest. I suspect it was because she had no children living at home and therefore had more time and money to spend. Her only daughter got knocked up and was sent away to live somewhere else. She disappeared and no one ever saw her again. Señora Cardenas was just another unhappy woman filled with the vanity of average people. She never gave me a kind word, or anyone I knew for that matter. I remember Señor Cardenas buying a group of kids snow cones one summer. He later died of a heart attack and she continued on as the dominant female of the church. Believe it or not, the women argued over who would wash and iron Father Hamilton's gowns. The matter was quickly solved with money. Señora Cardenas won because she had the gowns professionally cleaned. This earned her the role of "official gown and underwear cleaner." Whoopee! I have no idea what other favors she might have done for the priest, but nothing would surprise me. Knowing what I know about both 96ers and priests, I wouldn't be surprised to hear anything. Thank goodness I don't have to. You'd have thought she'd won the lotto the way she paraded around the church, as if she were personally speaking with God. Like all 96ers, the concept of good and evil was lost on her. In her mind the only important thing was that she was in charge of something everyone else wanted, which in her average mind made her better. Welcome to the Catholic Church, Our Lady of the Rosary, built on the backs of hundreds of sweaty Tejanos wanting to be saved.

A pecking order developed amongst the families of Main Drive, with Father Hamilton playing the role of king, bestowing his attentions on the miserable servants who gave him money, food, and a job. As usual, the ones with money looked down their noses at those without it. There was also a struggle amongst the men of the community for dominance within the church. I could *read* body language before I knew what it was, and learned age has nothing to do with wisdom, intelligence, or any other redeeming quality. The men of the parish were as focused on being important as the women. The only difference was the men didn't have the same role in the priest's life. Lots of the men offered their services personally, but Father Hamilton rejected them. It became apparent that he preferred the company of women. Perhaps he wasn't having affairs with them, and simply found them easier to control. He would make lists of things he needed done, and then give those lists to one of the women, who in turn would give them to the men. It was a simple system. If you wanted to be seen as important via his association, this was what you had to do. You didn't have to kiss his ass, as many tired, but only had to be willing to work for free.

My father considered himself to be the best brick layer in the barrio and wanted to show off his expertise. Perhaps like the crusaders of the eleventh century, he believed if he worked for God, he'd make up for all the harm he'd done. The problem was it involved his children, who already worked like indentured servants at home. He volunteered us to work on the church, and we were expected to do whatever he ordered with a good attitude. Lack of a good attitude or arguing was quickly corrected with a beating in front of whoever was present. He saw no contradiction in beating his children while in the service of God and the Church. You can appreciate why I don't have fond feelings towards religion. I've never known anyone who attended church worthy of the title they claimed. Case in point, my brother Beelzebub takes his blonde-haired, blue-eyed wife to church in order to show off. I still don't understand what it is about having a blonde that makes him think he's found paradise, or that anyone else should be impressed. His wife and children serve as a cover to hide his true nature. He parades them around like a farmer shows off his prized livestock. Now that his children are grown and no longer under his thumb, he must make appointments when he wants to see them. The problem is that even completely corrupted 96ers have their limits. The horrible truth is that his only relationships are with his employees and business associates. He is incapable of having genuine relationships. Those who know him as more than an acquaintance don't want anything to do with him. Although his beautiful mansion looks like a paradise from the outside, it is an abyss of despair. He roams about its halls and balconies like the Ghost of Christmas Past. One day his tombstone will read, "Here Lies Beelzebub. Who chose money over love, and died without knowing happiness."

Via my father's command we built the church's barbecue pit, along with the brick walls which lined the sidewalk leading to the front doors, both of which are no longer there. My father was rarely around during these projects, and never gave a damn about the job. Looking back, I realize he must have been seeing some woman who lived nearby. He cheated all of us and set a horrible example. I could not tolerate his behavior and rebelled, which brought about severe consequences. I believe in her book, *The Sociopath Next Door*, Martha Stout, Ph.D., got it completely wrong. She claims that most people are "normal," and only four percent are sick. I find it interesting that this is just the opposite of what I have found to be true, which is why I call average people "96ers." Even by her standards, my father would have most assuredly fallen into the category she labeled as being "sick." She also never addresses the question of malevolent inorganic entities that influence inexplicable behaviors. It is amazing how shit always comes disguised as something else. While we were ordered to work for the Church, Beelzebub was in the stage that all deluded Hollywood wannabes put themselves into. He'd convinced himself he was being mistreated, and somehow the world was responsible. He'd probably watched a movie where the handsome young rebel fights back against the wrongdoers. Unfortunately, he vented his anger upon me, and we had several fights on church property. Another great misfortune was that neither God nor his angels came to save me, even though I worked against my will in his service. Beelzebub was particularly unbearable at the time, as he'd been banging a beautiful DOEI chick who'd just moved to Texas from Virginia. He was feeling pretty special, which only served to add to the mountains of delusional crap that was his reality. I couldn't believe my eyes when I first saw her. She was gorgeous, which immediately demonstrated that she was a seriously disturbed individual. All the DOEIs were after her, yet she chose a Tejano kid from a barrio. This behavior was completely contrary to accepted regional norms. I knew it wouldn't last. The local DOEIs would inevitably show her the error of her ways. Beelzebub deluded himself into hysteria, believing he would defeat prejudice and show the rest of the world how to live. The idiot got all worked up over a chick who inexplicably went against social norms, thereby displaying a serious disconnect from reality. Something was very wrong with her. She was faced with overwhelming disapproval and social suicide, and ignored it. My predictions soon proved accurate, as she dumped Beelzebub and pretended they'd never been together. It couldn't have ended any other way. Not in Texas, baby, and certainly not in those days.

Fighting Beelzebub wasn't the only time I had to get violent in the presence of the Lord. I fought another kid on church property, whose nickname was Chamuco, which means Satan. It wasn't good versus evil. It was just two barrio kids knocking the shit out of each other over an insult. He was a tough little bastard who came and went each year with the migrant workers. During our fight the demon bit a chunk out of my forearm. He bit me so hard he tore the skin off down to the meat. Thank God I had a wooden yoyo on me, which I used to beat him with until it broke. Final score on that fight was a large scar, swollen knuckles, a cracked skull, and a broken yoyo. I'm not joking when I say I've been fighting devils all my life. Chamuco lived down the street and was the brother of a street girl named Suzy Pedarza. Suzy taught me to stay away from party girls and Chamuco taught me not to buy cheap yoyos. I have no idea what happened to either of them. They faded into one of the cracks and disappeared. One day they were simply gone, as if swallowed by the earth. Perhaps the Devil came back to claim his due.

Some of you may scoff and wonder how all this could have happened. I have no answer for that question. It may also give you the impression that there were no good people on Main Drive. Keep in mind, as a kid I was not in a position to observe or appreciate if there were. As a child, and later as an adolescent, I was focused on survival and getting the hell out of there. I remember seeing the church filled with people on Sundays, but I cannot say if they were good or bad. They were just people. The so-called good people seemed to be good because they stayed away from social events where violence erupted. The self-proclaimed good people were just as prejudice, narrow minded, and bigoted as everyone else. It would be impossible to list the residents of Main Drive under a good or bad column. I did not know any adults personally. I am relating this story from my perspective, which is as I've described; focused on survival. I am also relating this tale as an adult, looking back many years later. You may draw your own conclusions.

Texas escapee,
don Jesus M. Ramirez

Chapter Six
Bandits, Drunks, and Fools

"I would have preferred to have been raised by wolves and lived as a predator. It would have made destroying my enemies easier, and my childhood less burdensome."

–don Jesus M. Ramirez

The behavior I learned via my father's example created a formula for disaster, which brought me years of trouble and mountains of regrets. One of the many destructive habits my father taught me was to steal. He would take us out to the dump yard where he worked, a place called Pittsburgh Plate and Glass. As a child I'd be forced to spend time amongst the toxic waste, plastic containers, tarpaper, boxes, and God knows what else, allegedly searching for reusable building material. Who knows how much toxic waste I was exposed to. For years I didn't know why he brought me along, as I was just a dumb little kid. I've come to acknowledge my presence was a cover for his thieving. Having a dumb kid like me around made everything look less suspicious. I suspect he deliberately threw tools into the trash, or hid them away while working, intending to come back to get them on the weekend. This was the absence of common sense and illogical thought process which described his entire life. Most of it doesn't make any sense and is completely self-destructive. Using a child to cover up a criminal conspiracy, no matter how insignificant, is contrary to the laws of the Universe. Not to mention earthly laws. This behavior demonstrated the absence of a moral barometer, as well as irrational logic, and explains why Beelzebub is a chip off the old block.

My father made us into a gang of midnight raiders, like Ali Baba and the Forty Thieves. During the summer when the farmers planted corn and other vegetables in the fields close to Main Drive, my father took all of us out on raids. We literally raided the vegetable fields and stole hundreds of dollars in vegetables. I don't know how he arrived at the conclusion that teaching us to steal was acceptable, but he did. I have no idea how he could rationalize this behavior. I might steal to feed my children, but I would not let them see me do it. I would be ashamed to let anyone see me do such things, much less my children. I don't know what my mother said about all these midnight raids, but my father never gave it a thought. It appears she went along with the stealing, as she never said a word and put everything we stole to use. We conducted our raids like military missions. He'd drive out to the fields after dark, hand us each a burlap sack and leave. I never received any direct orders, but assumed the behavior of the eldest members of the raiding party (Bumper and Beelzebub). We would fill the burlap sacks with corn, watermelons, tomatoes, and pumpkins, and then leave the filled sacks at a prearranged spot. My father would then return about an hour later, flash his lights, stop the car, load the bags, and then take off again into the darkness. Silly me, at the time it seemed like fun. It was also scary as hell, but it made me feel like I was a part of something, and it felt good to belong, even if it was to a gang of thieves. Strangely enough we'd also been taught to believe in demons, witches, blood sucking vampires, monsters, and every other scary thought imaginable. We were forced to attend Sunday school, receive our first Holy Communion, and confess our sins, but none of this seemed important while we were out stealing from the farmers. My mother never made a fuss about our stealing. It was just considered a normal part of life. My father never took responsibility for the sins of his children. Like all 96ers, he never gave the consequences of his lessons much thought. Via his example, my brothers went on to become serial thieves, liars, womanizers, and perfect examples of average people. They have alienated their children, caused irrefutable harm, and screwed up their lives, along with the lives of any who would allow them to be near. As for myself, these night raids taught me to use darkness as my ally, with which I vented my rage and extracted vengeance upon my transgressors.

My father taught us that it was all right to steal, as long as you could get away with it. Like all 96ers, he selected which laws to obey and which to ignore, all depending on how it suited his purpose. Like all 96ers, he was a secret anarchist who pretended to be an upstanding citizen, demanding protection under the law. This is why a culture of criminality exists in this country. This is also why 96ers are the most dangerous creatures on earth. Although his behavior was troubling, I was more conflicted by my mother's blatant contradictions, and as such I questioned her. Imagine what it does to a child to hear their mother say it's all right to steal, so long as it is done with the intention of feeding one's family. Even as a kid I was stunned, and never realized that her response was defensive rationalization. Average people can rationalize and justify anything. There are no circumstances in which someone can steal. My mother was my moral barometer, and as an innocent child I looked to her for guidance. I'm lucky I didn't end up in prison after being contaminated with their example. I don't know why, but she made it sound as if it was okay in God's eyes to do something wrong, as long as you did it for the right reason. It's no wonder so many people rationalize and justify any behavior, simply by throwing God's name into the argument. Remember Robin Hood, Zorro, Kelly's Heroes, Pancho Villa, Emiliano Zapata, and a dozen others? According to this logic it's okay to steal from the rich, if you give to the poor. So it made sense, that if you're poor, it must be okay to steal from the rich, right? I'll bet the farmer who busted his ass to plant and raise those crops wouldn't agree. Nevertheless, life went on and we made raids every summer.

All this occurred while I was an altar boy, when I wanted to become a priest — a servant of God. I wanted to help people, so stealing bothered me, but it never seemed to bother anyone else. I never felt good about it, especially when they told us never to tell anyone. I was torn between what I'd been told about stealing and what my parents were doing. I knew it was wrong, and I was troubled that my father organized the events. This moral dilemma never seemed to bother Beelzebub, Bumper, or Punk. My father normalized breaking the law, along with other bizarre and self-destructive behaviors, which brought me nothing by heartache. His lack of a moral barometer affected everyone. Bad parenting never stops hurting you.

Southeast Texas has horrible hurricanes and gets huge thunderstorms. One day after a particularly bad rainstorm Bumper showed up. He was driving his work van and told Punk and I to get in. Beelzebub wasn't home at the time because he had been working as a bag boy at the HEB grocery store. Bumper, who was my role model, drove us out to a construction site in the middle of a busy intersection. He boldly parked the van next to a large water pump used to help drain the flooded intersection, and told us to put it inside the van. As soon as we did, we were gone. In less than three minutes we stole a huge gasoline powered water pump attached to a steel frame. We used it to help drain the water from our flooded backyard, and no one seemed troubled by this behavior. Not my father, mother, or anyone else. I was blown away by not only how easy it was, but by their hypocrisy. These same individuals would then tell us to pray and go to church on Sunday. I didn't understand this contradictory behavior, and still cannot comprehend the irresponsibility. Their hypocritical example demonstrated that it was all right to steal, as long as you didn't get caught.

Many years later, as a Child Protective Services (CPS) social worker, I helped put away dozens of people just like my father. It may be why I was so good at my job. My biological father was an abusive, disturbed, and violent man who molested his own daughters. He brutalized his children and pushed his sons out of the house. He was my greatest teacher and the perfect example of who not to be. Due to his horrible example I also had no guidance when it came to drinking alcohol responsibly. For instance, he once walked into our bedroom by mistake one night, thinking it was the bathroom, and pulled down his shorts as if to sit on the toilet. He was so drunk he turned to the right in the hallway, walking into our room, instead of to the left and into the bathroom. After he realized what he'd done, he tried to play it off by pretending to be looking for something in the bottom drawer of our dresser. He made a fool of himself so many times it was sickening. This is what I had as an example of how to be an adult. I promised my wife she'd never see me drunk. She never has and never will. His drinking was the cause of awful fights and why I do not believe drunks are sick, as much as they are self-indulgent and gutless. The American Medical Association managed to make Alcoholism a disease, which can now be covered by medical insurance, and it has made them wealthy. This may be a good time to point out that all professionals, such as doctors, lawyers, and etc., are in business, and business is about the money. They are not working for the good of humanity. Try getting medical treatment without money or insurance. Try getting a lawyer to take your case without money. Good Luck.

I have never made excuses for my misbehavior. I could have blamed poor behavior, genetics, alcoholism, child abuse, and etc., and I would have followed the mainstream. Don Juan would say I was lucky to have had such a perfect example of how not to be. Although every child is a victim of their upbringing, they should never have to apologize for their parents. Recognizing how badly your parents failed you is difficult. Admitting that our loved ones are bad people is the hardest thing a new Seeker will have to do. This is why erasing your past and acquiring *detachment* is essential. As I look back upon that innocent child I used to be, I am awed by how far he's come. I am amazed at how that poor stuttering abused child refused to bow to tyranny, and despite overwhelming adversity managed to survive. I am even more in awe at how that child had the courage to recognize that things would not change, unless he did. He knew that growth required separation, total abandon, and control. Like millions before, he chose the possibility of death rather than enslavement. Perhaps I was born with the knowledge of past lives, and understood that freedom was worth risking my life.

Texas escapee,

don Jesus M. Ramirez

Chapter Seven
Christmas Ghost

"Christian treachery, corruption, and dogma have caused more pain, suffering, and death than all the wars of the world combined."

 -don Jesus M. Ramirez

It's impossible to convey the sense of desperation I experienced as a young boy living on Main Drive in Corpus Christi. To understand you'd have to live the life of a Native Tejano in Texas before and during the civil rights movement. You'd have to experience the lack of opportunity, blatant hostility, and lack of political representation during that period. Imagine the Texas Rangers and local cops terrorizing strikers and community organizers. Try to picture the hopelessness and despair which came in waves of terrible weather, poverty, ignorance, and never-ending hatred by Texan DOEIs. Imagine being a child in this environment, and seeing your parents who were supposed to protect you, submit to the injustice out of fear. Try to imagine living twelve miles outside of town in the middle of a grain field, surrounded by thieves, thugs, and wild dogs. To the north is Highway 9 to San Antonio, and to the south are more open fields, as well as Texas Interstate 44 to Robertson and México. I lived on the pipeline of drugs, stolen goods, guns, and etc., coming in and out of Corpus Christi. Gun battles between rival gangs and cops along these roadways were common, with the dead and wounded piling up alongside. Added to this insanity was my ability to perceive sadness and pain, as well as *see* hatred. I *saw* that we were unwanted and despised by

DOEIs, who controlled and owned everything. The endless emptiness surrounding our barrio appeared like an insurmountable barrier. As television brought news of the Vietnam War, protest marches, and civil unrest, I was stuck on Main Drive. I dreamed of California and Europe, but without transportation it was impossible to be a part of the outside world.

    At night our barrio, and this is not a romantic description, as it really was a barrio, not just a rundown and neglected neighborhood, was surrounded by what seemed to be an ocean of darkness. Off towards the western horizon the lights of high electrical towers and oil rigs could be seen. During the day they would disappear in the glare of the Texas sun. Towards the southeast I could hear the sounds of airplanes coming from the Corpus Christi International Airport, which screamed out that freedom was possible. It signified that somewhere out there beyond all that space there was something more, something better. I still have no idea why they referred to it as being "international." In truth it was a rinky-dink little place, and it was years before it had grown enough for jets to land. As a kid I remember the fixed-winged propeller airplanes landing, which made tremendous noise. I'd sit on our front porch and spend hours watching them come in to land and then take off again. It was quite a thrill, and proof that someone was going somewhere, so I could do it too. I imagined where they were going, once again dreaming of escaping Texas. At the time I thought any place anywhere would be better.

    My earliest memories were of living in a tent, camping out beneath the stars. After that my first recollection of Main Drive is living across from Mr. and Mrs. Rodriguez, and next door to Lily Abundez. We lived in an uninsulated wooden structure that was built like a train. One room led into another, then another, and then another. The house faced west towards the street and originally only had three rooms, but my father kept adding onto it. There wasn't much going on, except for an occasional drunk roaring up and down the street, making a racket and confirming what I already knew. Main Drive was the bottom of the pit — a place where the poorest people ended up. It was isolated and had no streets lights, sidewalks, sewers, or convenient shopping areas. We, the poorest citizens of Corpus Christi, were abandoned and forgotten out there in the middle of nowhere. It was a perfect formula for disaster. There were dozens of wild, undisciplined, half-crazy kids in the street at any time of the day or night. The older teenagers were just as crazy, but ten times more cruel and violent. The lack of streetlights and dark nights made it seem even more dangerous, as someone could disappear simply by walking a few feet away. Due to the fact that there were no sidewalks, the rainstorms made it impossible not to get dirty and wet when walking anywhere. Although we had never heard of Murphy's law on Main Drive, it was most definitely in affect, and things always seemed to go from bad to worse. It wasn't long before several kids were run over by speeding cars, and families were hunting each other down seeking frontier justice. Imagine the drama and emotional rollercoaster such an event created. Everyone would empty out of their homes and surround the car, staring down at the fallen and trampled person, who was usually dead, dying, and covered with blood. Flashlights and the sounds of running feet, people screaming, stumbling, and falling would fill the air. One woman would begin to scream, cry, and pray, begging God for mercy before a dozen others joined in. Soon there'd have twenty women crying, praying, and saying the rosary while kneeling on the pavement in the middle of the night. Someone with a phone would call the police for an ambulance, which usually took an hour to get there, and even then they'd only come if escorted by a cop car. The parents and relatives of the victim would scream and curse insults at the cops and ambulance drivers for taking so long. Life and death hung by a thread and it seemed there was no way to survive. Death seemed to come out of nowhere, swooping down upon unsuspecting innocent people and suddenly take them. Most died waiting for an ambulance, staring up into the faces of their crying loved ones, not knowing why. I witnessed many tragic events while living on Main Drive, but never saw God or any of his angels intervene on behalf of a single person. This was all taking place during the Vietnam War and civil rights battles, so I guess he wasn't listening, or perhaps he was too busy. It's no wonder so many well-meaning people have left the Catholic Church. Looking back, I realize how badly it failed us, as it was the only institute that could have helped. It could have become the bridge between our existence and the rest of the outside world, simply by organizing trips into town. If Father Hamilton had had a wider vision of his role, he might have been a beacon of hope. He could have organized protests and presented our case before the city council, which at the very least would have resulted in police protection. Instead, he elected to be a tyrant, and did nothing more than condemn the wicked to hell.

  In all the years of living there I never saw or heard of anyone getting a ticket for speeding or drunken reckless driving. It was like living in the Old West, where the biggest and meanest guy made the rules, and the rest were forced to obey or face the consequences. It might compare to Belfast, Ireland, only we never had bombs going off, although an occasional oil rig would blowup now and then. We always had random gunfire at night and often heard the sound of feet on the pavement as groups of gangs chased each other down. We had jets flying so low they broke the sound barrier and shook our old wooden house. We were surrounded by danger and violence, without hope for salvation. My father's reaction was to build a bigger and taller fence, until our home looked like a concentration camp. He built a five foot fence, then added another two feet of barbed wire on top of it. He also continued adding onto our house until it almost reached the end of the lot. Our backyard bumped into a former oilfield with several wells, including large ponds of water, which smelled like sulfur and must have been a toxic waste. I was one of dozens of half-crazed, scared, lost kids who lived out there amongst the toxic oil ponds, dangerous wells, wooded pastures, and medieval mentality of the residents. That's where we lived. I wasn't surprised when I heard the open oil ponds were covered over and declared to be hazardous toxic areas. Who knows how many Main Drive kids became ill from cancer or made half-crazy by inhaling all those toxic fumes. Keep in mind, this land was sold by DOEI land developers to Native Tejanos to raise their families on. This was how little DOEIs thought we, our families, and our children were worth. We were expendable. As I stated before the opposite of love is not hate, but indifference. The actions of these individuals demonstrated complete indifference towards the health and welfare of Tejano citizens. We lived as my grandparents must have lived out on their ranch in México. We had to heat water on the stove in order to take a bath, and used an outhouse. We had to walk to and from church while trying not to get dirty, attacked by gangs or wild dogs, and maintain our sanity.

    My parents kept a large chicken coop and a pigpen in the backyard. It was like living on a farm. We were surrounded by fields, only we didn't own any of the land. My father bought a pig once a year, which we would raise and then slaughter during Christmas.

Killing the pig was a big deal. I mean, it required a lot of work, planning, and of course drinking. My father, who never had a friend that I can remember, would barrow a large black urn and dig a hole in the ground. The hole was dug in two sections so that one side was smaller than the other. It was connected via an opening, and a fire was built on both sides. When the urn blocked the air on one side, the fire could be kept burning by feeding it from the other. This is the way his primitive relatives cooked throughout frontier history, and he hadn't evolved one bit. This included his not seeing any benefit in defending or sticking up for anyone, including his children. I guess he thought one less child wouldn't make a difference.

    Killing the pig we'd raised never seemed to bother my father, which always troubled me. I still hadn't gotten used to the idea of raising pets for food. To me the acts of shooting them in the head, hanging them up, ripping out their guts, and then cooking them in a giant black pot seemed treasonous. We'd feed, bathe, and care for the pig all year, and then around December 23rd or 24th my father would take his .22 cal rifle, drag the screaming pig out of its pen, pull it towards the urn, and calmly shoot it between the eyes. The poor beast would give one short snort or grunt and then flop over. My father would then tie a rope to its hind feet, and with everyone's help, pull it up over a tree limb or a special frame built to hang the pig while he gutted it. My mother would bring large containers and place them underneath the pig, and then my father would cut the pig's throat and bleed it. Gallons of blood would pour out and into the buckets, making for a pretty awful sight. That was usually when I left. The blood didn't bother me as much as knowing that it was the same pig we'd played with and raised. My father drank beer throughout the ordeal and would continue drinking throughout the night. I'd stay up as late as I could, just sitting there in the darkness near the fire, listening to the adults talk. I don't remember anyone ever speaking to me directly. It seemed normal for adults to ignore me. To them I was just like one of the animals. I never received any attention unless I did something wrong, and then like the pig I'd get a beating that nearly killed me. When they did address me, it was only to give an order and demand that I bring them something. Rarely, if ever, was I given a chance to speak, ask questions, offer an opinion, or make a statement. Perhaps this is why I developed a speech impediment as a child. I'd sit by the giant black urn listening to old family legends, tales of adventure, and local gossip. It never occurred to me that all of the adults were simply lying to each other and pretending their mundane lives were interesting. I was an innocent kid and still had not learned to be suspicious of average people. I'd look up into the Texas night sky and admire the stars. I might have become an astrologer if someone had encouraged me to learn about them. Unfortunately, no one seemed to notice me. Aside from a word or two about the stars, my father was ignorant of the constellations. With my limitless curiosity I would have gladly learned about them, along with who knows what else. A lack of curiosity is a habit passed on to children as casually as sneezing. The problem is stupidity brought on by ignorance becomes permanent. I was fascinated by them and swore someday I'd learn more. The only star anyone seemed to know anything about was the mythical Star of Bethlehem, which supposedly led the three wise men to Bethlehem and the baby Jesus. It never occurred to me that everyone there was as ignorant as a box of nails. None of them knew anything that seemed important or worth knowing. I never questioned any of my father's ignorant statements aloud, or even said a word. It was better to keep quiet and remain alert for sudden outbursts of anger. I knew I couldn't depend on anyone to save me if he decided to beat me. It was so bad, I couldn't even run away. Where in the hell would I go? One thing I'm sure of is if any of the animals that were allegedly surrounding baby Jesus the night he was born, had been there with us, my father would have shot them in the head, and cooked them in the black urn as well.

The fire had to be fed all night, so the adults stayed up tending to it, all the while drinking and lying to each other. I'd lose interest and quietly slip away, sometimes wandering into the house where my mother was making tamales. My poor older sisters, who were treated like indentured servants, were always required to help cook the pig meat. A group of women from the neighborhood would usually be sitting in a circle, like old witches gossiping, as they'd spread uncooked dough on the corn leaves, and then add the right amount of cooked meat. The completed items were then stacked neatly and placed inside a steam pot, which was placed on the gas stove where it remained until the cooking was finished. I was always alone, even though I was surrounded by people. Living amongst so many did nothing to ease my loneliness. I have no idea where my older brothers were. They usually escaped as soon as they were able to, and never seemed to want to be burdened by the company of a sickly kid who always managed to get into trouble. Who knows what anyone else was doing at the time.

My mother would also make pinole and buñuelos. I have no idea what my poor mother was celebrating. She was miserable living under my father's tyranny. Christmas was just another excuse for him to go on a bender, crash his car, come home smelling of perfume, and cause a huge fight. I once believed that unless you've tasted these Mexican dishes, which are traditional for Christmas, you've not lived.

However, I've not felt this way for a very long time. Unfortunately, many other things which are also traditionally Mexican were implemented into our lives. As a result of ignorance, violence, and poor judgment which demanded that everything not approved of be squashed, weaknesses such as jealousy, greed, vanity, anger, pride, and shame enveloped us. My mother, who had an awful temper and could insult a saint, used shame to keep us in line. This evil tactic was used especially on my sisters. My poor sisters must have been brainwashed terribly. I feel sorry for them, and I cannot imagine how they managed to want to marry. Sex was talked about as being dirty, nasty, and disgusting. Even though my parents did it all the time, my mother never called it love making. It was never spoken of as an expression of love. As a kid I always wondered why my parents screwed like rabbits if it was so dirty. They literally made a new baby every year, which they couldn't afford. I also wondered why my father never cared if we overheard them. I cannot begin to relate how badly this affected me, and how troubling it is to treat children in this manner.

    I was warned by my parents never to bring shame upon them, but never given appropriate alternatives for solving conflicts. For example, what does a kid do when neighborhood thugs are picking on him and making his life miserable? My parents never offered to speak with the parents of these thugs, or call the police. They never went to a school parents meeting and never defended me against anyone. Any time there was a problem they behaved as if they had no part in it, and I was entirely on my own. The only method of solving anything which I learned at home was knocking the shit out of someone, or insulting them into submission. The problem was everyone in the barrio thought the same way. Adults behaved in the same manner at church dances and meetings. I still don't understand how we were expected to know how to behave, if we'd never had a lesson or an example. All I remember was being told what not to do, but never what to do, or how to think or speak. For example, we couldn't appear to be anxious or overly excited, as this was considered shameful by my mother. We weren't supposed to behave like children and act out our excitement of getting something we wanted. Doing so was said to bring shame upon us, and somehow sex was wrapped up into this ugly package. The trouble was that we all knew about sex, as we'd seen animals mate and heard my parents having sex. It was an impossible situation fueled by hormones that drove me crazy. I was sexually aroused all the time. I'd get an erection watching the teacher's bosoms wiggle and move as she wrote on the board. We were not supposed to think about sex, because we could sin in thought, word, or deed. Yet, my parents created an environment in which sex was impossible to ignore. I have no idea how my parents thought not talking about sex was better. This illogical mindset created a ton of problems for each it ignored. By this time in my life I'd seen enough to know that there was a lot going on inside of me. Imagine what raging hormones do to a young kid who wanted to be good while being told he's going to hell. My childhood innocence was shattered, and hearing my parents having sex drove me absolutely crazy. My father knew we could hear them and didn't care. Much later I realized that this was another way for him to exert dominance. It was crazy making. If there was a Christian hell, there would be a special place reserved just for him.

Maybe it was because of the sex, or maybe it was because my mother couldn't stand to see all of us together, but we were always told to go do something outside. It seemed like I was always hunting in the woods, searching ditches for bottles to sell, cloud gazing, or having a fire in the backyard. To this very day I love campfires. I love the shadows and the mysteries of the night in a wooded area. As a result I've never had a problem with being surrounded by darkness. In the Army I discovered this is very rare. During the Gulf War I was perfectly at peace standing guard after dark, while most of the boys from Helena, Montana, were shaking with fear. Those boys made up in cruelty for what they lacked in courage, as they henpecked each other into hysteria. As a child I learned where there was a fire, there would also be drinking. Amongst the Tejanos on Main Drive, if you saw a fire, you knew someone was drinking. It seemed like someone was always drinking and as a result I've never had a problem with alcohol. Even as a child I knew the Universe would provide, and therefore never felt the need to overindulge. I'd also seen drunken guys get the crap knocked out of them, and one of my biggest fears was being too drunk to fight. I always seemed to be in trouble or just getting out of it. It sucked. Main Drive was not the place to let your guard down, and always being hyper alert is exhausting. Dropping your guard around those homicidal maniacs could prove fatal, or at least embarrassing. The sick bastards who lived out there were capable of anything, including rape of other men, which they did to a poor kid named Arthur. The poor guy was the only person I knew who seemed unable to act in any other way. He was so obviously gay from the first day I saw him, and he suffered because of it. Being gay in the Sixties and Seventies was horrible, and those poor people endured terrible abuse, as did their families. What's amazing is that back then, the "fucker" did not consider himself homosexual, but only the "fuckie." The men who attacked and beat him up did not see themselves as homosexual predators, but only that "he was asking for it." I have no idea how a poor kid walking home from work at one in the morning was asking to be raped and beaten by a gang of thugs who knew him, his brothers, and his family. This event shook the community of Main Drive and exposed the thugs for what they were, but it didn't do anything for poor Arthur. Back then all the gays were moving to Houston, where there was said to be a gay neighborhood, clubs, and support groups. I have no idea if this was true, as I never cared beyond the fact that I knew those same bastards would rape and beat anyone. The trick was to carry a knife, be willing to use it, and never get caught by surprise. Today, when two men partake in homosexual intercourse, both men are considered to be homosexual. This is an enlightened thought and was not common thinking in those bad old days. As a kid I remember overhearing men brag about fucking other men. Their inflection was obscene, vulgar, and violent. Only amongst the drudges of society could this have been considered appropriate conversation. It scared the hell out of me and made me even more paranoid. I wanted more than anything to get away from everyone who lived on Main Drive.

Another thing that hit me like a ton of bricks was how I had no clue about all the sex that was going on. I don't know if it was a curse or a blessing, but it was only after looking back that I realized people were screwing like rabbits, and I had no idea. I knew my parents were doing it, because they made it so offensively obvious, and I knew all the adults were doing it, because there were so many kids running around. However, I didn't know everyone else was also doing it. I learned years later that my oldest brother, Bumper, was banging a group of sisters that lived at the end of Main Drive. It was then that I put two and two together and realized why my other older brother, Beelzebub, would walk to the end of the street at night and visit with them. I probably should have found it suspicious, as he never had any friends on Main Drive. He would invite me to take a walk with him, and I thought he just wanted to hang out. I never guessed he was afraid of walking down Main Drive alone. I never had a clue he was banging them, and he never told me. Not only was I innocent, I was stupid. I never thought a person could have such deceptive ulterior motives for saying one thing and meaning another. Silly me, I wanted to believe people were better than what they were, especially him. I was just a stupid kid and he had no qualms about using me as a decoy. I don't know where I got the idea I should, or even could help people, as nobody ever helped me. Perhaps that's the reason why I wanted to. Even prior to discovering the Toltec discipline, I knew I had to manufacture what I wanted and didn't have, and give it away in order to have it. Beelzebub never gave a damn about anyone other than himself. He used people, and continues to do so today.

The in-depth self-analysis I had to do in order to prepare for recapitulation has not only helped me reclaim lost energy, it has given me a completely different picture about my own history. It has been a harsh awakening. Not only have I come to accept how different I've always been from popular culture, I've come to understand why I never wanted to be a part of it. I used to think it was my upbringing, family, and being Tejano, but I realize it was just me that was different. Before completing the first phase of my recapitulation I believed Tejanos were different because of the way we celebrated the holidays. For example, I once believed Native Tejanos were different because we emphasized the celebration of Christmas, rather than New Year's Eve. I was told that we were celebrating the birth of Christ. Naturally, as a child it appeared we were worshiping, and must therefore believe in a different god from those who were not worshiping. As a result of this, I believed Native Tejanos were more spiritual and somehow closer to God. I believed we were better "children of God," because we were poor, like Jesus, and therefore closer to him. I had never heard of Charles Darwin, Great Britain, Nazi Germany, and other Europeans who created pseudo sciences to confirm their racist attitudes. As a child, I'd never heard of Adolf Hitler, genocide, the Holocaust, or the great American racist, Dr. Samuel George Morton, who along with his wonderful assistants, George R. Gliddon and Josiah C. Nott, believed DOEIs and Ethiopians had no species connection, and that Blacks, unlike Whites, were inherently suited for the burdens of slavery. I was an innocent child who never imagined these educated men would have murdered my entire family in a fury of ethnic cleansing, or thrown us into the ovens at Auschwitz concentration camp. Thank God I was so naïve. At the time, I believed the idea of living another year without change was depressing, and the reason why poor Tejanos didn't celebrate New Year's Eve. No one seemed to have anything better to look forward to. It was just going to be more of the same, only on a different day, in a different year. I literally never saw any improvement. The endless cycle of senseless misery went on and on, and no one learned from their mistakes. Everyone kept doing exactly the same thing, hoping for different results. More and more Christmas seemed like another excuse for people to get drunk, act stupid, shoot off their guns, and get into trouble.

During Christmas Main Drive, which was a mile long with houses on both sides, would transform into a giant display of fireworks and gunfire, much like where I live today. The displays never lasted very long, as fireworks were expensive. I rarely had a chance to light any myself, as I never had any money and my father wouldn't spend money on such things. Our crazy neighbors, who were always drinking, shot off their guns, screamed, beat cans, and made a racket.

I'd stand outside on the front porch or in the middle of the street waiting for someone to do something stupid. It was always a depressing experience. At the time I never realized the reason why I felt so sad was because I was sensing my mother's despair and my sisters' sadness. I can only imagine how lonely and depressing it must have been for my helpless, emotionally unbalanced mother, who'd go into the bedroom and cry. While I needed her comfort, she needed the comfort of someone else. All of us were alone, surrounded by the darkness and each other. I'd go out into the huge plowed over cotton fields and cry. It was very lonely and left an emptiness inside of me that may have never been filled if I had not dedicated myself to this discipline. Seekers should note that although such emptiness is not a unique aspect of life, filling it is. The secret to filling the voids in your life is to manufacturer what you want, but have never had, and then give it away. I know this sounds crazy, but only at first. If you give this concept some thought, you'll come to the same conclusion I did, and recognize the beauty of this discipline. Remember, it takes energy to comprehend. So if at first this sounds foreign and confusing, do not be discouraged. I'll admit that this concept once sounded crazy to me. It only began making sense after I surrendered to the fact that I did not know, and recognized I could not pick and choose which parts of this discipline to adopt and which to ignore. This discipline only works if you practice it as a whole. Most of you are not ready, and that's okay. We all have to begin where we are. At the moment, you are the person your mother warned you about. It's impossible to go back to that age in our life when these inner voids were created. Therefore, your only hope is to accept the Warrior's challenge to generate those ingredients in your life now. You must manufacture what you never had and then give it away. Only by giving it away will you ever come to have it. This is simply the law of attraction. You get back what you project. The simple and awesome difference is that you do it as a form of discipline and *controlled folly*.

Strange as it may sound, I never knew what Beelzebub and Punk were doing at those times. All I know is they disappeared and never invited me to go with them, and then they'd suddenly reappear before morning. It never occurred to me to ask where they went or what they did. They would have never told me the truth anyway. It only occurred to me after my recapitulation that they lived life under a different set of rules. They were looking out for themselves, no matter who got hurt, or how wrong it might have been. Meanwhile, I was trying to live in accordance with the lies of the Church and my parents, who kept telling us to be good and make things better for everybody. I never realized until recently, just how inferior Beelzebub and Punk actually were, not only as my brothers, but as human beings. Looking back, I realize I was wrong about so many things concerning them. My brothers have always been like our father, and their lives reflect it. Getting away from them was not only my ticket to freedom, it was the best thing I ever did. It's no wonder as adults we have nothing in common, only now I don't want anything to do with them. The only difference is now, even if they did ask me to visit, I'd say no thank you. I never imagined I'd feel so disgusted by their memory. Recapitulation helps you recover lost energy. It also kills any hope of reconciliation by removing the veil of innocence, and revealing reality's beauty and brutality.

As I mentioned before, Christmas was a religious event. I remember staying up until twelve o'clock to go to midnight mass, just to have something to do. The sounds of voices and footsteps filled the night air, as dozens of people made their way through the darkness towards the church. There were no streetlights or sidewalks, and because we were so far away from town there was no light pollution. We were literally surrounded by absolute blackness. Imagine being a kid, listening for signs of someone or something approaching in darkness. People usually traveled to midnight mass in groups, mostly made up of family or friends. I never had any friends, so I'd either walk alone or with Beelzebub, who never stopped being a shit, even on his way to church. I would have been safer walking alongside the Devil himself. He was always a stranger and his indifference was complete. He felt I was inferior because our parents made him responsible for me. I was naïve, meaning I didn't do anything stupid, yet at the same time, I was just a kid. My biggest problem was just trying to keep up with him and not get left behind, because things were scary as hell. The entire area was literally a killing field. Dozens of people had been murdered all around us. Every inch of road between Corpus Christi and the Mexican border is a cemetery, imprinted with the spirits of the dead.

To make things worse, in traditional superstitious Mexican custom, we'd been raised with horror stories of witches, devils, demons, vampires, and etc. Adding to the fear of the supernatural, we always had to take sticks with us to fight off dogs which people allowed to roam free. Many people had dogs, and some, like their owners, were mean as hell. Most were mad from the heat, poverty, and depression. They'd run out of the darkness unexpectedly and attack us. I once punched a large German Shepherd in the face as it charged and reared up to attack me. I got its teeth stuck into my hand. It scared the hell out of me, but like so many events of my youth, it happened without witnesses and I never told anyone. No one would have given a damn anyway. I don't know why, but even back then, having a secret seemed more powerful, so I kept things to myself. I've always been good at keeping secrets, and knew if you stuffed them, they stayed tucked away. They'll only come back to haunt you when you're alone and have not released them. I learned that what really matters is the dialogue you have with yourself, especially when you are alone in the darkness. Average people are responsible for my having to keep secrets, as they have always proven to be untrustworthy. Even as a child I knew that just because there were more of them, did not make them right. The problem is the average person wants so badly to fit in that they will never risk taking a stance against popular opinion. After placing my trust in unworthy individuals, I discovered it was better not to tell anyone anything. I had my heart broken many times before I finally accepted this horrible reality.

My parents believed we should wear our best to church, especially to twelve o'clock mass on Christmas Eve. Everyone went to church because there wasn't anywhere else to go, and absolutely nothing to do. In typical average person fashion, instead of going to find solace, peace, and compassion, people found exactly what they brought with them. Groups of women would form cliques and each would spend the rest of the night talking about other people. It seemed everyone was doing the same thing, and all of them considered themselves to be Catholic. I was dumbstruck with the obvious contradictions, but it never seemed to bother anyone else. I was just a kid, but even I knew there was a lot of unacceptable behavior taking place. The biggest topic of gossip on Sundays, or any other day for that matter, was what someone wore. For some reason everyone had something to say about this subject. Other popular topics for gossip were what people did and said. I don't know how people knew so much about what was going on in the lives of other people, but they did. I found it particularly amazing, considering I never cared how someone looked, what they wore, or what they did, as long as they left me alone. I'd already learned that pretty things did not make someone a kinder person. I'd witnessed how indifferent those who had nice things treated everyone else. I wasn't impressed. I was never greedy and never compared myself to anyone else. Nothing anyone had made a difference to me. I have no idea how I developed this way of thinking. I've never envied anyone of anything, never. The one thing I did envy was the attention some parents gave their children, as mine never seemed to know I existed. To this day, I don't associate having expensive things with being a better person. My brothers lacked this understanding. Or perhaps it was I who lacked understanding of how the world operates. This has always been a source of conflict for me. My brothers still believe money makes people better, although I still cannot see in what manner. I don't mean richer, or what money buys. I mean better. For example, somehow in their sadistic minds, they believe having money makes them integrally better than people without it. This is the common mindset of 96ers. I've not figured out this logic. It's no wonder the world is such a horrible place. The average person supports a plutocratic government and continues to provide examples of how not to be. Yet, everyone whines and complains about how unfair life is. Average people envy celebrities and want to be their friends. I'd pay someone to take them away, just so I wouldn't have to spend time with them. I had a chance to spend time with Britney Spears at her condo in Colorado Springs, Colorado, during the Sundance Film Festival. Why would I want to spend time around someone who showed the world her woo-woo. Can you imagine being stuck with her and her groupies in a condo, in the mountains, during the winter, trapped and unable to escape? Hell no. I said "No, thank you."

Walking through the completely darkened street to midnight mass on Christmas Eve was a challenge, so carrying a knife seemed like a good idea. The fact that I carried a knife into church, "God's house," to pray, never seemed like a contradiction, and still doesn't. As the National Rifle Association (NRA) says, "Guns don't kill people; people kill people." On Main Drive everything with which to kill, killed people. It was also very cold during the winters. Often people would go to church just to have a place to be warm. Midnight mass was also an excuse to stay up late. Most kids went either because there was nothing else to do, or because their parents made them. It was hypocritical as hell, and I doubt there was one religious soul in the entire building. I was probably the only person who actually wanted to be a priest, who carried a knife because I was more afraid not to. It was strange watching people come into the building, and every time someone walked in, the entire congregation would turn around to see who it was. It was hilarious, as some were clearly drunk and others were all dressed up. No one came to celebrate the birth of the Christ child, as everyone already had more kids than they could handle. No one gave a damn about another child being born. As I said, it was just something to do and an excuse to get out of the house at midnight. The larger families always made an impression. The young kids came in first with their parents who followed behind. Of course all the guys would be checking out the girls, who looked like virgins dressed in their best, with their heads covered by a veil like the Virgin Mary. In those days, before sex became so popular, most of the girls actually were virgins. I don't know if any of them ever noticed me, but I surely never took notice of them. I wasn't impressed. It was difficult to get interested. I mean, I'd known them all my life. I found them as interesting as telephone poles. Also, I always knew I would be leaving and had no interest in anyone or anything which would tie me down to that place. I hated living there and just kept my mouth shut, like a plow horse that puts his head down and just pulls the plow. It was a horrible existence, like that of a prisoner awaiting release. I dreamed of leaving Main Drive and Texas for as long as I can remember. Now, as I write, I'm even more surprised I managed to survive the entire experience. Whoever it was that made up this crap about the "good old days," wasn't a Tejano living on Main Drive, or in Corpus Christi during the Sixties and Seventies.

Christmas was one of the hardest things about being a kid. It was always difficult noticing the gifts other kids got, and comparing it to how little I received. For the most part we usually did not receive any gifts. We got clothes, because that's what we needed. The logic was simple; if you could not wear, use, or eat it, no money was spent on it. It wasn't a matter of simply being poor, as we were, but in noticing other parents going out of their way to give their kids gifts and make them happy. Compared to others on Main Drive we had a nicer home and my father drove a nicer car, but we suffered from a lack of affection. We lived in a vacuum void of affection. We were poor in ways no one but those living within our family ever knew. Christmas was frustrating and sad. Not because we suffered from poverty, but because my father was such a failure as a human being. He never behaved quite as badly as he did during the holidays. He'd come home, start a fight, and then take off again. He drank too much, stayed out too late, and caused my mother to worry. She'd worry until she got angry, and then when he finally got home, they'd argue. She would scream all sorts of horrible things at him, and he'd tell her to stop talking. As angry as she was, she never stopped. Eventually my father would grow tired of making threats, and beat her. He'd hit her with his fists, his feet, and often with a belt. It was quite a shock to see your father beating your mother, and listening to all the cursing which took place while it happened. My father would literally beat my mother until she stopped talking, and then she would stare daggers at him. He'd then tell her not to look at him, and if she didn't stop, he'd hit her again. After years of suffering and crying, surrounded by demons that danced in the darkness, I just said the hell with it. It took a long time before I actually started living with that attitude, but I discovered that hate is a great motivator. I started to hate my father and ignored my mother's complaining, curses, and criticism. I joined the ranks of angry young men who refused to surrender, and fought back despite having no chance of winning. My father gave me motivation to fight. Somehow, in the middle of that storm a light shone and showed me how to use hate to accomplish my goals. I realized that the best revenge is success. Don't ask me where I got this idea or how I managed it, but I did.

    I don't know why no one ever called the cops when my father beat my mother. Back then, there was no help for abused women, especially in Texas. Plus, we lived so far out in the middle of nowhere there were no regular patrols of police or sheriffs. To add to the misery, most of the cops were as racist as Nazis, and hated Tejanos only a little less than they hated Black folks. This was not because they considered Tejanos to be any better, but because the Black population was unfortunately at the epicenter of their hatred. Tejanos were not considered important enough to actively hate, and were viewed as being inconsequential. Growing up in Texas, I never saw a cop do anything but hurt people. It was a horrible situation, which got worse as I got older. The only time we saw the cops was when someone was arrested, murdered, having a wild party, or died. It never failed that someone would have a party and a fight would breakout. Don't ask me why or how, but for some reason there was always a fight. I don't mean a little misunderstanding between relatives or a couple of friends who just drank too much. I mean a knockdown, drag out fight between families that spilled out into the streets where blood was shed. It was brutal tribal warfare with entire families, including the women getting involved. Things got real nasty, real fast. All this was usually over an insult, as a result of too much drinking, or someone making a move on another guy's woman. Fighting over women was the number one reason for guys killing each other. I vowed never to fight over a woman, but like so many other things, that choice was taken out of my hands. Everyone who lived on Main Drive knew messing with another guy's woman was dangerous. A fight could breakout anywhere and at any time. There was no safe place and nowhere to hide. The traumatizing experience of living under a perpetual cloud of danger and impending doom haunted me all my life, until it became who I am. I've learned to manage the feeling that at any moment violence could erupt, and I have accustomed myself to be wary. It took a very long time. Also, I've learned it is impossible to teach this to another person. With the exception of cops and soldiers, no one wants to believe the reality of this existence. Contrary to what the average civilian would like to believe, soldiers and cops don't feel any safer just because they're armed. A lot of 96ers have guns, and none of them are worth the trouble you'll get into for shooting them. Average people don't recognize how vulnerable and stupid they are. They cannot accept the reality of their existence and develop a delusional sense of security out of ignorance. On Main Drive, one minute everyone would be having fun and enjoying themselves, and then Ka-Boom!

Suddenly they were trying to kill each other. It was scary as hell, causing me many moments of insecurity. Once the battle started it always escalated, as extended family members and friends got involved. The distant gunshots and explosions of these ongoing battles often lasted months, and sometimes years, because no one was willing to let anything go. It went from some stupid argument to a question of honor that never ended unless someone surrendered, died, or moved away. I witnessed countless bloody beat downs and gang street fights. I'm not talking about a couple of guys punching each other out. I'm talking about entire families going after each other with mad dog fury and murderous intentions. It happened more often during the holidays because of all the drinking. The swollen faces, open wounds, and bandages never lasted long enough for everyone to realize how precarious life on the frontier was. The violence during the holidays was only surpassed by the summer months. Every year large families of migrants showed up, set up camp on an empty lot, and sparked more family feuds. It was an endless stream of insanity. Somehow I managed to survive, and didn't die simply because I wasn't hit by a stray bullet or beaten to death.

As I said before, my father was always more trouble during the holidays, which unfortunately was the only time people ever visited our home. When anyone came to visit they would inevitably bring a bottle of booze or a six pack of beer. The very first time I drank alcohol was around the age of fourteen, sometime after we'd already moved to the Big House. One night while my parents had company, I filled a glass with premixed margarita. I drank it alone in the darkness of our bedroom. Once again, I have no idea where Beelzebub and Punk were. Like I said, I spent a lot of time alone, and they never invited me to go with them anywhere. After drinking the alcohol I remember feeling buzzed. My head started spinning, so I went to bed and fell asleep. I now realize my brothers never cared about what happened to me, or what I did, as long as I didn't interfere in their lives. I've come to accept just how distant they were from me, and how little I mattered in their lives. In their minds, in order to survive it was every man for himself. This was instinctually a foreign notion to me, and is completely contrary to the concept of family and our alleged religious values, but that's how it was. Despite the fact that I had gotten into several fights defending Punk, he felt no attachment to me. I might as well have been a guard dog who protected him when needed, but not wanted around otherwise. I don't know if that says more about his lack of morality, or my naïve desire for a family. No matter, we are the sum total of our personal inventory, and acknowledging this removes our thin veneer of innocence and fantasy. Such brutal honesty can only be shared within oneself. To attempt this level of truth with a 96er is to incur their wrath.

My parents, who were typical Catholics, never seemed to believe Christmas meant anything special. It was just another burden they endured. Just more fuss and expectations they couldn't deal with. In typical average person fashion, it was a time of reflection and self-hatred when they compared themselves to everyone else, which inevitably resulted in them hating themselves even more. My mother hated Christmas, which was just another problem because of my father. It must have been very lonely for her, stuck out there in the middle of nowhere in Texas, with her family so far away in México. My Uncles Felix and Hector, who alleged to be such good Christians, never called on Christmas, or sent gifts or letters to my mother. Her isolation, self-loathing, and despair must have driven her crazy. As for my father, he didn't care about anything. He lived his life by simple rules.

As long as he had plenty to eat, a place to sleep, and sex on demand, he was content. I don't think he gave Christmas a thought. It never mattered whether anyone was happy, other than himself. Looking back, I wonder if being such an immoral spiritual vacuum was not preferable to being so perceptive as a child. It certainly seemed that way. What good was being so perceptive? I had no power to change anything. I had no one to help me understand what I was *seeing*, or explain that I was *seeing*. I would have given anything to have a mentor, but it seems the Universe set it up this way. I was supposed to suffer alone. As much as I tried to believe otherwise, I was burdened with the awareness of the reality that we are all alone. However, the religious brainwashing I endured made such knowledge difficult to accept, as it was completely contrary to the idea of the Christian God and his alleged love for humanity. I genuinely and ceaselessly searched for this God, and wondered why I did not feel his presence. I accepted the possibility that perhaps he could not or would appear, yet wondered why he didn't send me someone to love. I was riddled with anger at my parents, my life situation, and God for abandoning me. All the while I was conflicted, because as much as I hated my father, I needed his approval. Just as I hated that the Christian God would neglect me and knowingly allow me to suffer, yet feared the idea that he did not exist. It was a horrible maze of conflicting and contradictory emotions. Knowing as much as I did, and yet being unable to do anything about it only made it worse. However, the Universe determined that I would go through it without any hope of understanding.

    Christmas was just another problem to deal with, and my parents never made it seem "special." No one made a special deal about celebrating the birth of Christ. It was just another chore and a guaranteed disappointment. Not knowing enough to know I did not know anything, I always set myself up for disappointment by expecting things to be different that year. I'm not surprised I grew so calloused and jaded, which took years to remove. By the time I discovered the Toltec discipline I was already a Warrior, without the benefit of a counselor or mentor. Average people are not aware that if we have the courage to listen and examine our lives, loneliness can be our greatest teacher. If we have the discipline to adopt *detachment*, loneliness will teach us many powerful lessons. Amongst don Juan's many lessons, this is one of the most powerful, and yet most people are unwilling to sacrifice in order to receive its benefits. Without years of loneliness, self-reflection, and *detachment*, I would never have arrived at this point in life, as I'd not yet studied the Toltec discipline.

I don't know where they disappeared off to, but Beelzebub and Punk always seemed to have somewhere to go. Despite the fact that I recognized their loneliness and invited them along whenever I had somewhere special to go, they never returned the favor. Neither of them had any nurturing or admirable qualities or characteristics. While my ability to perceive made me sensitive to the emotions of others, they were completely self-centered and indifferent. I had no one to help me understand my perceptions or how to utilize them. As teenagers, all that mattered to them was that my stuttering, social ineptitude, and ability to attract trouble made me an embarrassment. I suffered in silence and endured their rejection. The contradiction was that I never saw myself as a loser or an embarrassment. I vowed to be a better man and learned to play guitar, sing, write, and exercised fanatically. I adapted and learned to enjoy my own company. I grew apart from them as I got older and never looked back. I found a place of no self-pity and recognized that I'd have to change or die. Decades before I discovered the Toltec discipline I accepted that there was no room for timid, shy, sensitive fools who asked for permission, while everyone else was taking what they wanted. I accepted that if I couldn't be with a girl I liked, I'd be with a girl who liked me. It was preferable to being alone. My sisters and I hardly spoke, which may sound strange, but you've got to remember, there were twelve kids living in one small house. We spent most of our time trying to stay out of each other's way. Plus, we were all terrified of our father, who'd storm around the house like a medieval dictator. Sadly, instead of banding together and filling the void in our hearts, we withdrew into ourselves and rarely let our emotions show. One reason for this was our mother always made fun of everyone, demonstrating her anger disguised as humor. It was a horrible example to give your children, but she thought it was funny, so we imitated her and made fun of each other. I did not know it at the time, but such behavior would bring lots of problems. Today, I know that anger disguised as humor is still anger, and the cause of lots of suffering. My unbalanced mother had a list of problems that would have made a psychiatrist weep. She'd been abused, battered, humiliated, was raised by average people, and then married her own executioner. It's what all average people do, and explains why they seek the lowest common denominator; cruelty and sarcasm. Everything eventually comes down to money and sex.

    One of my mother's favorite distractions was to sit on the front porch and watch people as they drove or walked by. She reveled in the insults she cast towards them, which ranged from anything to how they walked, to what they wore, or how they seemed. She did not yell these insults, but only spoke them for her own amusement, loud enough for us to overhear. All of us learned this dark sense of humor. The twisted reality is that all self-indulgent, undisciplined people do this to each other. Instead of banding together against their common enemy (ignorance and poverty), they bring insults and suffering upon themselves. In this indirect fashion my mother taught us to find fault and pick on each other mercilessly. Her miserable life experience and warped sense of humor, which hid a volcano of rage, taught us that some measure of revenge may be gained by casting the proper insults, even if it's done behind the person's back. I never recognized it at the time, but today I realize my inability to stop talking while angry came from watching my mother argue with my father. Her refusal to be squashed demanded that she use her only tool to extract a measure of revenge. How many people have talked themselves into more trouble than they could handle? Learning to keep my mouth shut took so long and cost me immeasurable damage. This was completely contrary to what she said we should do, but never what she did herself. This twisted sense of humor was also how I received half a dozen nicknames.

  I know it sounds cruel, and it was, but as kids you become what your parents teach you. My father taught us violence and intolerance, and my mother taught us cruelty, mean spiritedness, and sarcasm. My father was the engineer behind this horrendous behavior, and my mother nurtured it via her rebellion against him. We were trapped and forced to endure it, suffered because of it, and perpetuated it via our own behavior. My father taught us revenge is sweeter than forgiveness for any transgression, and never to overlook an insult. He also brainwashed us to believe in demons, witches, and evil, which he personified. At night he would sit on the front porch and curse at passing shrieking owls, believing they were brujos or witches who transformed themselves in order to commit mayhem on the population. He believed people could sell their souls to the Devil and turn themselves into owls, bats, wolves, and other creepy crawlers. He also believed they'd fly around seeking to do harm to others, especially if they had been paid to do so by a person who was wronged. It's called brujerías

The concept of payment for an evil deed and act of revenge upon another is common thinking along the Rio Grande. My oldest brother, Bumper, swears his ex-wife put a curse on him that ruined his life and caused him tremendous suffering. According to him she did this because he refused to give her a divorce. She solved this problem by banging anyone she could, including people in their church congregation. When he confronted her about her infidelity, she told the minister that he was beating on her, and the minister threw them both out of the church. This is a new record, because even I haven't been thrown out of a church. I've been asked to leave dances, bars, clubs, parties, groups, and fired from my job, but I've never committed such heinous sins as to be cast out of a house of God. What's comical beyond description is that like all average people, Bumper considers himself a good person, or at least justified in his behavior. What's both amazing and hilarious is that Bumper, whom I nicknamed so because of his willingness to seek out and "bump" strange women, is a notorious womanizer. He also enjoys sharing his stories in great detail, including graphic grunts, humps, and "bumps." On several occasions I've had to ask him to stop talking because I was getting undesired images in my imagination, which works like a movie screen. I did not wish to watch such a film. I have enough ugly memories.

Like my father, who role modeled this behavior, Bumper's egotistical and delusional self-image never allowed him to see the demons and evil dark shadows that visit his house every night. Yet, I have. Average people never sense the evil energy they invite into their lives via their vile and disgusting behavior. These fools proudly repeat what they have learned from their fathers, who are just indulging in sexual gluttony. As average people like to say, "Shit rolls downhill." The problem is it gets onto everything that surrounds it. This behavior is infectious and corrupts the spirit, as it glorifies and endorses gluttony of every perversion. Imagine the seven deadly sins presented via your parent's behavior as enviable characteristics, and picture the impact it would have upon children. As in our family, which was unfortunate for the rest of us, we lived in the same house and were at the bottom of the hill. We became the unsuspecting recipients of behavior so destructive and dysfunctional, that it's a miracle none of us are in prison as serial murderers.

When my father felt angry for being tied down to a wife and twelve kids, he'd lash out at whoever was convenient. It's no coincidence that it happened to be me so many times. It's also no surprise that I've never ever felt safe anywhere, nor have I ever dropped my guard intentionally. I've developed an energy field around me like sonar, which warns me when someone is within striking distance. I can sense when I am being watched through a spyglass from a great distance. I can sense the viewer's energy upon me. For example, several years ago while in the desert with the Minuteman Project in Arizona, I felt someone watching me. I squatted and began searching the distance for someone. Sure as George W. Bush is a lying bastard, I saw a Mexican Army officer using his binoculars to watch me. I moved left and behind a mound of dirt, just in case he wanted to check to see if the scope on his rifle worked. I didn't say a word to anyone standing beside me. I figured the Mexican officer would keep searching for a target if he really wanted to shoot someone. I've had experiences with Third World military, none of which were positive. I found their sense of humor to be mixed with a degree of cruelty which would cause a saint to get pissed off. The ongoing drug war between gangs and cartels in México is fed via the pipeline into the United States. I am certain hundreds of Border Patrol officers are involved, as there is no other way to explain such massive amounts of drugs crossing the border undetected. Yeah, you'll hear about a big bust every now and again, but they use those to justify their expenditures and hiring more men. The bosses get paid twice, once for not doing their job and another for looking the other way. Like I've been saying, the Universe only recognizes energy. I spent several days on the United States-Mexican border in Arizona, sweating my butt off and keeping an eye out for Mexican drug runners. I worked alongside some very famous men who've dedicated their lives to keeping our borders safe from starving Mexican Indians. Mexican Indians who risk their lives to come work in chicken farms, slaughter houses, and tobacco fields in Virginia and Georgia, where the weather is so bad the local Klansmen won't take the jobs. The same is true about cowboys in Montana, Wyoming, and Nevada. They've all been replaced with Mexican vaqueros who work for forty dollars a day, meals, and a bed.

My father made one of the last Christmases I spent at home before leaving for the Army especially memorable. I'd spent the entire day out at Padre Island with my brother Punk and some friends. It was already dark by the time we came home, and when I drove up I was surprised to see my father come out to meet us, as he usually just ignored me. By the way, I was driving my own car, which I had bought with my own money, unlike Beelzebub who bought his car with money he'd got from our father. This may not seem like a big deal to most kids today, but having a car I'd bought with my own hard earned money was a tremendous accomplishment. Imagine living out in the middle of nowhere, surrounded by miles of fields with absolutely nothing to do. Picture hating where you lived, as well as most of those who surrounded you, and then think of that same place without a car. Yeah, it sucked. As I was getting out of my car my father approached me in a hostile manner.

"Where have you been?!" he asked.

I must have been feeling extra great, because I forgot he had the usual stick up his ass, and responded in a jovial manner.

"Oh, my friends and I went to the beach," I said.

He just stared at me with anger in his eyes.

"Who in the hell gave you permission to go to the beach?!"

His response surprised me. As I said before, he usually just ignored me and never gave a damn what I did or where I went. He never spoke to me unless he was giving an order, and I never addressed him either. I'd given up trying to talk with him. He proved to me that once an average person hates you, there is nothing you can do to change their mind. You might as well try walking on water. He replied with so much hostility, I didn't say anything. What could I have said? He on the other hand decided to fill the silence.

"If it wasn't for your mother, you wouldn't be here any longer."

"Don't worry, Dad," I replied. "I'll be gone right after I graduate."

Keep in mind, the only option I had after graduation was to join the Army, and this was during the Vietnam War.

"Good! I'm tired of putting up with you!"

Part of the reason why I remember this event so well is due to Punk's reaction. He'd witnessed everything, and was genuinely shocked by the ordeal.

"Why is Dad so mean to you?" he asked with a stunned look on his face after our father had stormed away.

I just shook my head and answered, "I don't know."

The truth was, I didn't know. Years later I learned that every dysfunctional family has a scapegoat, usually the middle child. I was not behaving the way he believed I should. I suspect my unwillingness to be a scapegoat made him angry. I have to admit, I took pleasure in screwing up his world by doing well and not getting into trouble with the cops. I had no other means of revenge, but I believed I could hurt the bastard each time I succeeded at something, and I wanted to hurt the son of a bitch badly. I took pleasure in messing up his idea of reality. Hating him gave me motivation for many of my accomplishments, until I discovered hating him was also keeping me prisoner to the memory of the torment.

When I won my first Golden Gloves I thought of him while beating the shit out of my opponents. I learned to use hate, fear, and all sorts of negative energy to accomplish what appeared to be positive goals. Yet, it was just rage disguised as sportsmanship. I guess that's why boxing was my savior, as it gave me a sociably acceptable release for the rage that burned inside. Who knows where I might be today if I'd not had the courage to step into the ring and exchange blows with whoever stood in front of me. Each bout was a blessing, and the taste of blood in my mouth was like magic. It made me want to try harder to kill my opponent. Overcoming fear was never the problem, so much as turning off and controlling my rage outside of the ring. I don't know where I got the will to enter the fray and put into practice what don Juan calls control, abandon, *detachment*, discipline, and *forbearance*. I lived these lessons like a Buddhist monk lives his discipline, which eventually broke the chains of my spiritual imprisonment. Unless Seekers become as fanatical about their freedom, it will never come to pass. Our lives amongst 96ers reinforce all that is wrong with us. Instead of recognizing this as poison, we rush to participate in our own destruction, like a herd of stampeding buffalo heading over a cliff into an abyss. The urge to give back insult or pain when received is nearly impossible to change. Seekers are warned that these knee-jerk reactions are the heart of 96ers, and the cancer that eats away at their souls. These behaviors are continuously reinforced via the constant bombardment of average behavior. The challenge of identifying our weaknesses and working to defeat them is unknown to the world. Only a fanatic who no longer wishes to be a pack member would be willing to distance themselves and begin the journey out of the mire towards freedom. The quest for spiritual enlightenment is the most difficult, yet worthwhile journey any Seeker will ever undertake. Being surrounded by packs, gangs, and herds of average people make this nearly impossible challenge that much more difficult. All Seekers will stumble, fall, and be defeated many times before they can successfully earn the discipline of a Warrior.

    I still have not been able to answer Punk's question as to why my father was so mean to me. I don't care anymore, but I have an idea. Judging by my relationship with my brothers, which is zero, and my relationship with anyone who mistreats me, I think he saw that I was not afraid of him. I also believe he knew that my willingness to rebel against his tyranny made me better than him, as he had not had the courage to do so against his abusive father. I never kissed his ass and openly hated his guts, and knew someday I'd come back to claim revenge. Unlike my brothers, I never accepted his abuse as being "normal," or just something he did. I knew, and he saw that I knew, that his behavior was a perversion and an indulgence in gluttony of emotion. He, and such individuals, choose to be who they are, and there was nothing admirable about it. There is nothing redeemable about beating your wife and children for any reason. His violence and abuse should have been stopped, by a bullet if necessary, but as a child I lacked the courage to murder him. My brothers, Bumper, Beelzebub, Punk, and "Hijacker," which is the name I use to refer to my youngest brother, never saw our father as pure evil. I admitted that things were what they were, and never sought his approval or acknowledgment. I abandoned all fantasies of having a father, and although it was an impossible challenge, I accepted my fate. He was my biological relative, but never a real father. His desire to dominate those around him made him incapable of demonstrating any emotion aside from anger, pride, and vanity. This alpha dog mentality is a common thread amongst average men. It pits one against another and nurtures hate. Instead of cooperation, the average man chooses competition. It's the reason why subordinates hate their superiors, and why they'll do anything to undermine them. Seekers are reminded that average men make terrible leaders and horrible subordinates. Riches, authority, and power corrupt 96ers completely. Never share stories of adventure or success with average people. Instead of being happy for you, they'll think you a blowhard. Their habit of comparing themselves to others engenders the seven deadly sins which feed the fires of hell.

After coming home from school one day while in the second grade, I made the mistake of showing my father the results of my spelling test. I had scored a 95 percent and was so proud of myself.

There was a list of twenty words, of which I'd spelled nineteen correctly. Yet, all he saw was the one I got wrong.

"What's the matter?" he said. "Why couldn't you spell that one right?"

That was the last time I volunteered to show him anything. I began asking my mother, who couldn't read English, to sign all my papers from school. He was so indifferent he never noticed I'd stopped asking for his approval or permission to do anything. It was better to take a beating afterwards than risk asking permission and being told no. This way I would avoid a worse beating for directly disobeying him.

Throughout history tragic world events are said to bring out the best in people, just like holidays bring out the worst in them. One year my father decided we would not have a Christmas because we had all been bad. He simply told us to forget about Christmas that year. None of us, according to him, deserved anything. His greatest quality, if it can be called that, is that he never wasted time on remorse. His statement did not come as a surprise to us, as no one expected anything from him. It was normal, and besides, by that time he'd murdered all the sentiments I might have had about the holidays. I'd bought everything I needed and could have cared less. Another detail was that none of us were bad. I mean, really, how bad could we have been? My mother was half-nuts from all the abuse, and he was as bad as the Devil himself. We were scared to death, and never would have deliberately misbehaved.

That year when Christmas was only days away, my sister Precious and her husband Rock brought us a tree as a surprise. Otherwise we would not have even had one. On Christmas night, after being out who knows where, Beelzebub came home around one in the morning. I'd been sitting in the kitchen facing the front door, along with my sisters, just talking. My father was in the living room sitting alone in the dark, and no one cared. Beelzebub comes into the house holding an unwrapped bottle of Aqua Velva aftershave lotion, which he must have received as a gift from some girl. If any of you remember that stuff, you'll also remember that it cost about 99 cents. Seeing my father sitting alone in the dark must have caught him by surprise. I overheard him from the kitchen as he went through a presentation, saying how he'd not had a chance to wrap it, but that he wanted to give him a present. My father, who was feeling sorry for himself after doing everything to distance himself from the rest of us, fell for it. He stood up and gave Beelzebub a big hug as the rest of us watched and smiled at each other. We knew exactly what he was doing. He was manipulating the great devil shamelessly without remorse, and in front of all of us. I don't believe I've ever known a bigger liar, or a better one in my entire life. I also don't believe my father really believed him, but he went along with it to show the rest of us that at least someone loved him. I found this particularly interesting because Beelzebub hadn't gotten my mother, who actually deserved something, anything. Neither of them gave a shit about the only person who suffered more and longer than any of us.

The problem with ass kissers is that they want payment for all their work. Throughout the following year Beelzebub had somehow gotten it into his head that he shouldn't pay rent, help around the house, or have to answer to our father. As a result of his refusal to pay homage, they had not been getting along. Beelzebub was a senior in high school at the time and had already joined the Army via the advanced enlistment program. The two had been fighting like cats and dogs. Playing the role of rebel without a brain, Beelzebub only came home when he had to, and even then it was only to sleep. He was going steady with a girl named Sylvia, who was thought to be quite a catch. I had to agree, she was attractive, but I'd learned after Norma Jean Slaughter that no woman was worth all that trouble. No one is. He'd spend all his time after work at her house with her family. Her parents, who didn't know him very well, thought he was going to make a great son-in-law. Trouble was he'd been partying too much and had been arrested again for drinking and driving, so things really hadn't been going well. I knew Beelzebub was working on a master plan to manipulate our father into something, and nothing was beyond him. I never learned what he was really up to, as we did not talk and I didn't care. I was happy he was leaving soon and going off to Vietnam. I hoped he'd be killed, or at least blown up so badly he'd stop being such an asshole. Like all delusional drama loving average idiots, he was going through a self-imposed exile and living a Hollywood fantasy. It was the wrong time to exert independence, as the Vietnam War was claiming hundreds of lives a week, and being drafted after high school was almost certain. There weren't any opportunities in Corpus Christi, and without an education there were absolutely no jobs worth having.

On one particular day in December, not long before Christmas that year, Beelzebub came home angry about something. I have no idea what or why. I was in the kitchen minding my own business when he started a fight with me. I was unwilling to take any more shit from him and fought back. We were engaged in a serious fight when our father showed up and started beating the hell out of him. Things had been going badly between them for quite a while. My father accused him of being an ungrateful son, etc., etc., and then fixed everything in his usual manner. He screamed, "Get the hell out of my house!" The problem was, as I mentioned before, my father had lent Beelzebub money to buy his car, which he had yet to payback. So true to his nature, he demanded the keys. Beelzebub, who thought the sun couldn't shine without him, had to hand the keys over. Poor misunderstood asshole left the house crying like a whipped dog.

That was my first real Christmas and I wish I could remember the exact date. I swear I'd make it into a national holiday. His leaving was like a ray of sunshine finally coming through after years of stormy weather. Since we'd never had any kind of relationship, the space he left was filled as quickly as a stone falling to the bottom of a lake. I discovered he'd had no friends in school. No one asked about him, no one missed him, no one mentioned him, and when they did I'd tell them the truth. He joined the Army and left, other than that I had no idea where the hell he was.

Dealing with adolescent emotions and witnessing the preferential treatment my brothers Beelzebub and Punk received was nearly impossible. It was especially difficult during birthdays and Christmases. I remember sitting outside in the backyard alone, behind our old storage shed, crying. I spent a lot of time out there, alone, looking up into the sky, asking God why he just didn't let me die. I never got an answer, and never learned why. I finally acknowledged that life was unfair and that for now things were what they were, but I also swore to escape. I knew no amount of crying, screaming, or indulging in anger was ever going to make a difference. I would never have a father like in the movies, which is the only thing I ever found myself envying. It would be impossible to say how many times I had to leave a room or turn my head, while watching a movie with a scene where a father treated his son, like a son. There are still times when I feel sorry for the kid I used to be, but thanks to the Toltec discipline, it's not often. I realize I'd never be who I am today if my life had been easier. I never would have survived all I've gone through, and I'd probably not feel as strongly as I do about this discipline. It's difficult to imagine who I might have been if I'd been treated with a little kindness, or received a little attention, guidance, and love. I think I might have become a senator or a governor.

Things got worse as my mother's illness progressed. Christmas continued to be the worst time of the year until I recognized I was keeping the pain alive by indulging in it. I acknowledged it served no purpose other than to make me miserable. What possible purpose would it serve anyone, especially me, to remain connected to such awful memories? It's the same for every person who has had abusive parents, but won't speak ill of them because of the shame attached to the abuse. Millions of innocent adults suffer from the effects of bad parenting and will never find peace. I was determined not to repeat the cycle of abuse, so I deliberately sought solitude, knowing I had many issues to resolve. This is not to say I didn't make mistakes along the way, and of course I broke hearts and promises. I've also paid enormous dues, which life extracts from everyone.

My mother's illness gradually ate away at her. Throughout the entire ordeal my father never gave her a moments rest. I have no words to convey how deeply this affected me. Today, as a Warrior, I recognize that giving these memories power serves no purpose other than to cause dissonance. These experiences validate why this discipline demands a Warrior erase his past and free himself of emotional baggage. Carrying hurt around and reliving it is a self-destructive cycle that drains precious energy. Sadness is accompanied with the process of erasing one's past, as upon reaching a place of no self-pity, a

Warrior must accept what he finds. It is the same for everyone. For instance, I had to accept the reality of what I found in my final analysis. My mother, whom I loved and needed desperately, barely acknowledged or gave me affection, and died without me ever feeling she loved me. I'll never know her. As she slowly faded away I began to accept that I was an orphan, despite having had parents and many siblings. Abandoned and ignored, I had been allowed to fall through the cracks. I didn't die simply because biology and my *will* prevented it. My mother was the sum total of her inventory, as well as her own persecutor and executioner. She lived the consequences of her decisions, and rather than be punished for her sins, she was punished by them. Her life choices brought about misery, imprisoning her in a self-made hell. In a storm of conflicting emotional upheavals, she simultaneously hated, resented, and loved her children. The Catholic Church further enslaved her with its outdated tenets against birth control. Her family, who still alleges to be Christians, neglected and abandoned her. She lived isolated, thousands of miles away from their helping hands. In the end her passing was merely an end to her suffering.

The last time I saw my mother alive was Christmas, 1979. I was living in San Jose, California, and attending college at San Jose State University on the G.I. Bill. It was an impossible challenge trying to pay rent, buy books, and survive, all while attending the University. I worked two jobs, went to school, tried to manage the demons in my head, and still pass my classes. I tried and failed so many times I cannot recall. I phoned my mother often. My poor mother never had too much to say. She had never been good at expressing herself, but she tried to make conversation. Somehow I managed to save up the money to buy a Toyota pickup with a camper shell, and during Christmas break I drove to Corpus Christi. I stopped along the way to eat, rest, and sleep. It took three days of driving almost nonstop. Pulling back into my old neighborhood after having lived in Europe, visiting the great museums and cathedrals, was an awakening. I had traveled extensively, studied at great universities, and met people of every nation and culture. It was hard to believe I'd had such humble roots. I wondered what my German karate teacher would have said, or my French girlfriend, or my Spanish bullfighting companions. I had left Main Drive a boy and had been gone for over eight years, during which I'd broken out of my shell, and like a bird, spread my wings and grown into an eagle. I was filled with conflicting emotions which continue to remain difficult to identify. Everything looked different, and yet the same. Main Drive now had streetlights, sidewalks, and gutters. The homes looked better taken care of, and the neighborhood looked altogether much improved. My mother greeted me at the door but I didn't recognize her at first. She'd lost a lot of weight, and I knew her time was near. I spent the entire duration of the trip with her, as there was no one else in Corpus who mattered. Time had covered or washed everything away. We spoke of all things, as I barely knew her like I wanted to. There were always too many people around and she was not accustomed to talking about herself. I tried to get her to tell me about her life, about her family and her childhood, but she was either unable or unwilling to open up like I'd hoped. I never got to know my mother, and she died a stranger.

During that trip I took my little brother Hijacker with me to Kingsville, Texas, to visit my oldest friend, Robert Herrera. This was before Hijacker became a thief and a con man. We ended up spending the night in Kingsville, and slept in the back of my truck, which I'd parked on the street in front of Robert's house. That night some guy slammed into the car parked right behind us, which then rear ended my truck. Apparently he was driving home from work and fell asleep at the wheel. Luckily he hit that car before it hit us, thereby slowing it down and probably saving our lives. It was loud and scared the hell out of both of us. The sudden crash immediately awoke us from a sound sleep. Robert came running out of his house, as did the rest of his family. Luckily no one was killed, but the poor bastard got a real wake up call. He had to pay for the damages to my truck, as well as to the other car he had hit. I took Robert with me to collect the money. The poor guy coughed up the cash, which he couldn't afford, at the worst time of the year.

Aside from my mother's funeral, this trip to Texas was also the last time I saw Amy Lopez, perhaps the only other person who knew me. We had been friends for years as kids. I'd met her when she was just fourteen-years-old. I can still remember exactly what she wore and how great she looked. She was a gorgeous young woman, sweet, kind, and wonderful before life did to her what it does to every average person. Her hair was long, almost down to her waist, shiny and beautiful. She was wearing a green pleated plaid shirt, white socks, black shoes, and a white blouse. She had her hair in a ponytail, and to my fifteen-year-old eyes, she was breathtaking. We became friends and remained so for many years. Then, somewhere in time we lost track of one another. Her mother, along with her brothers and sisters, were always kind to me. I think of her with fondness, especially because she and her mother came to my mother's funeral.

I'll never forget how after the service everyone came back to the Big House. The neighbors brought over tons of food. Every kind of food you can think of. We'd all gone into the backyard, as was our custom, and started a fire which we all sat around, drinking beer and talking. My father, who sets the world record for misbehavior, started hitting on Mrs. Lopez, Amy's mother. Yep, as difficult as it may be for you to believe, he was hitting on Amy's mother several hours after he buried his wife, with all his children standing alongside him. I was amused at his antics while being revolted observing his despicable behavior. My sisters were in the house crying because of his calloused indifference. His behavior nailed down the horrible fact that he had already disconnected from my mother. We had been brought up in a moral vacuum, with him as the example of how poorly a grown man can behave. His example cast a net of suspicion upon everyone who had supposedly come from the Greatest Generation, and demonstrated that age has nothing to do with wisdom, proper conduct, or knowledge. Mrs. Lopez was equally as embarrassed, as anyone witnessing this would have been disgusted. I'd gone beyond loathing him thanks to my discipline. I was now practicing *detachment*, and aware of *forbearance*. I'd already accepted him as he was; worthless with no more redeeming qualities than a stray dog. He was no more a father to me than the guy who pumped gas at the gas station. It also removed any notion which I might have had of coming from good parents or a moral upbringing. If any of his children possess good character or achieve success, it's because the individual was willing to put in the work. Our parent's examples, upbringing, and role modeling were horrible. My father would have fit in perfectly with the residents of Sodom and Gomorrah, which was destroyed for being wicked in the Old Testament of the Bible, if you can believe any of that fairytale.

    Christmas continued to be difficult for many years. However, I've managed to disconnect any of their memories from those I make with my wife. Aside from an extraordinary student which comes along very rarely, she's the only family I've known for years. Aside from my cousin, who for the remainder of this endeavor I'll refer to as "La Boca," meaning "the mouth," who betrayed me by disclosing confidential information, my wife is the only woman in my life. I've worked very hard not to be anything like my father, whom after his death means as little to me as he meant throughout his life. When I find myself acting in a similar fashion I am filled with self-revulsion. He was the most influential person in my entire life, as well as the most important. He taught me how not to be. I continue to use his life as an example of what to avoid, and never allow myself to become a part of. My escape from Texas demanded I give up thoughts of revenge, of God's justice, and of Mario Puzo's ideal of being there at the right time to witness his downfall. I'd have to kill him ten times a day, every day, for ten years in order to extract justice. Even if this fantasy came true, how would I reclaim, relive, and regain my childhood? No, it's best to let go of all that anger. I had always been confident that my energy would place me in a position to balance the scales someday, and it did. It helped me become indifferent. Via the Toltec teachings and implementation of its discipline, I was relieved of the burden of hating him. His lingering death and unrelenting poor behavior made not attending his funeral the easiest problem to resolve. Contrary to popular belief, we are all punished by our sins, not for them. Average people forget that the Universe is watching, as is everyone they've harmed. Christianity tells us we can remove the consequences of our sins by forgiving our oppressors. Popular religious philosophy claims that via forgiving another's transgressions, we will be uplifted and expunged of the effects of their blows. This is one of the biggest lies ever told. Anyone with knowledge of social work, criminal law, or medicine knows that the world is filled with suffering.

People who deliberately harmed, wrong, or humiliated you, do not deserve to be forgiven. To begin with, you are not endowed with such powers. Those who claim they've forgiven their transgressors did so at the expense of their self-esteem, and only to partake in the alleged benefits they were promised by organized religion. They agreed to wear the chains of their experiences for the rest of their lives. A Warrior would never forgive such crimes. A Warrior would seek to balance the scales, no matter how much time has gone by. To do otherwise is to condone their behavior. Most imprisoned thugs never know how much harm they've inflicted upon their victims. How can you measure the harm done to a child as they grow into adulthood? Imagine how their ability to enjoy life has been deformed. From the moment the event took place their lives changed, and will continue to be impacted by that person's actions. Not only were they robbed of their present, they were robbed of their future. The Pollyanna logic endorsed and perpetuated by Christianity is as phony as their vows of obedience. I encourage genuine Seekers to locate those who deliberately harmed them and balance the scales. This is an extremely controversial concept, which will undoubtedly be misinterpreted by many. Let me say that I do not condone, endorse, or support any behavior which places your freedom in jeopardy. The balancing of scales which I speak of can only be accomplished after a Seeker learns to *see*. Seeking balance is not revenge. The difference is in the ability to *see* and have *detachment*. There is no passion involved. It's simply a matter of finding balance. Only you can decide what measures to take. You should be fully aware of how society will view your actions. As I said, this is a sensitive issue which will be misinterpreted, and certainly used as ammunition by my critics. I am not concerned with critics. My work is an act of war by a genuine student of the Toltec discipline. I write for the benefit of my own development, and hope that it may assist other Warriors, Seekers, and Pathfinders alike. Great care and thought must be given to this matter. This cannot be overstated.

Every year the ghost of Christmas past slowly fades away. My escape from Texas demanded I work very hard to *detach* myself from all those years of misery. Every time I connect to the Universe, I disconnect from all the humiliation, rage, and desire for vengeance. Each day I feel lighter and less restrained than the day before. Every day I feel my spirit rising within me as I release the memory of the helpless, neglected, abused child I used to be. As I look out from my yard in Epitaph, California, I am fully aware that life experiences are linear, and that choice brings about consequences which demand more choices and so forth. I am now a former combat soldier, injured in the line of duty, yet still able to pursue my objectives, travel, and dedicate myself to the Warrior's discipline. I have taught my fighting students some of what I've learned. I am as impressed with the power of knowledge as they are. Each time I set pen to paper I use it to erase one layer of yesterday's weight and come up from under it, lighter and more full of life. I am preparing members of my boxing club for another event. We move towards each challenge with full knowledge of what is expected, what it demands, and what we must lay on the line in order to participate. A Warrior's life is always a challenge and an adventure.

Texas escapee,
don Jesus M. Ramirez

Chapter Eight
Visit from an Exorcised Ghost

"Where does a man go when he seeks counsel? Priests, teachers, politicians, and lawyers are hypocrites blinded by arrogance and greed. They are no better than whores, pretending to represent a discipline they neither practice nor believe. This is when the average man discovers he is alone."

-don Jesus M. Ramirez

It is December once again, and as I write this I find myself trying to re-exorcise the Christmas Ghost from my life. I find that writing about it helps tremendously. Doing so assists me in *detaching* myself and expelling the remnants of sorrow which creep into my life, haunting my dreams. It's almost impossible to believe I was once helplessly trapped in such a negative and hostile environment. Yet, as I look at my face in the mirror, which shows the scars of so much sadness, I know that it's still me. I must completely disconnect from the child I used to be, the child who is still desperately struggling to heal himself. I must consciously *detach* myself from the past, which takes tremendous discipline to stop dwelling on. This starts by *not-doing*; not talking to yourself about yourself. Secondly, it continues by not allowing yourself to reminisce with acquaintances or family, no matter what someone shares with you. You must not permit yourself to release any relevant information about your past. It has to stop someday, make that day today.

I no longer hate anyone, as no one is worthy of such powerful emotions. I refuse to expend precious energy on anything which does not serve me. I can continue to hold onto my pain, or I can choose to let it go by *detaching* myself from it. Doing so is a great struggle. I've made great accomplishments and I am no longer a helpless child yearning for my parents' affection. Nor do I seek an average person's validation. I've learned through many harsh lessons that being alone is not the worst thing in the world. I've also learned that death is preferable to a life filled with suffering and regret. I've survived sadness in the past and I'll survive it in the future. I've learned that it's up to me to monitor my thoughts and behaviors. Yes, it's a never-ending struggle, but discipline is demanded on the Warrior's path. This knowledge has given me a glimpse of what it means to be free. I am continuously at war against my weaknesses, *stalking* each of them like a hunter. I have no pity for myself and little, if any, for anyone else. Yet, I am not cold or unfeeling. As a matter of fact I am quite the opposite. I feel more connected to everyone, and it has been years since I've felt lonely.

    I only knew brief moments of happiness as a child. However, there is more to life than bliss, distractions, or what average people call happiness. My challenges became the keys to my freedom, and although I would not thank those who harmed me, without those experiences I would not be me. I've accepted the Warrior's path and know it's a matter of acceptance rather than recrimination. The price of freedom is a constant vigil over my thoughts, which are fed from self-importance. Fighting my weaknesses is my life's challenge and I acknowledge those horrible moments are the keys to my freedom. As I battle each of them, I break the chains that bind me to my past, which helps my spirit shine brighter.

    I once hoped my wife's family would accept me into theirs and allow me to be a part of their lives. It was a fantasy based upon my need to feel like I belonged. I accept that I'll never fit in amongst average people. There are too many barriers. I've discovered that even though I have advanced spiritually, people continue as they have for centuries. Led by their emotions and self-importance, they continuously compare themselves to each other. It's no wonder the world is such a mess. It's caused me moments of sad realizations when I faced the reality of my situation. I married an average woman with an average family. My wife's sisters are typical 96ers; conflicted, angry, jealous, insecure, and envious of others. As an example of dysfunctional inappropriate conduct, one of them flirted with me. Seekers should note that sibling rivalry via sexual misconduct ranks high amongst female 96ers. In this case seemingly innocent smiles and glances, accompanied with the supposed accidental brushing up against me, occurred too often to be random. Yet, she behaved as though her motives were innocent, unaware of the alleged inappropriate actions. She wears formfitting clothes, a lot of jewelry, and too much makeup, literally screaming, "Look at me!" At least until someone does. Then she behaves as if the observer is being obscene, angrily reacting with, "What the hell are you looking at?!" She deliberately emits ongoing contrasting messages and sexual energy. Seekers should note that once they begin to gather and store energy, they will attract the attention of many potential sexual partners. The average person finds a Warrior's energy tantalizing, mysterious, and highly sexual. My wife's sisters for example, are all unhappily married, and react to my energy like moths to a flame. My mother-in-law on the other hand, who may be the poster-child for enabling dysfunctional behavior, finds my energy terrifying. She recognizes the possibilities of disaster. I *saw* that I remind her of a former lover, or someone who jilted her. Her solution was to respond with random criticism and senseless conflicts. In her deluded matriarchal mind, she expected me to seek her approval and grovel at her feet. I found her expectations amusing and comical. The only conclusion possible in the world of average men was disaster. I don't understand such random and senseless hatred. Additionally, she is prejudice towards Tejanos, because according to her they are "always bragging about their ranches." Having shared stories of my poverty stricken upbringing, readers will agree that her observations are ridiculous. I explained to her how poor we were, and joked that the closest I came to owning a ranch was working on one. Of course this had no effect on her opinions. Average people don't change their minds, no matter how much evidence is presented to the contrary. After surviving tyrants and bullies, submitting to her whimsical expectations even as folly, were impossible. I simply ignored her, which for a 96er is like throwing gasoline on a fire. Average people hate being ignored as much as they hate being challenged. She is living proof that age has nothing to do with wisdom or self-restraint. All 96ers are toxic. Seekers should keep this in mind when dealing with in-laws.

I broke a very important rule when I challenged my mother-in-law, asking her to explain why my wife behaved as she did. I mistakenly hoped she would enlighten her daughter about marriage. Instead, she used our conversation to spread suspicion and hatred amongst her family. Her response was indignation, teaching me that a vital rule of marriage is to never tell your in-laws anything about your marriage. It will get out and everyone will soon hear about it. Her self-importance would not tolerate such an infraction upon her sense of superiority. She was enraged that I would ask such a question. I have no idea what her goal might have been. As I said before, amongst average people one person in the relationship must surrender their identity in order to get along. In her life, her husband has surrendered his identity. She wears the pants, makes the decisions, and he just goes along to get along. I feel sorry for him, as he's allowed himself to be dominated by her. Now she hates his guts for letting her do it. You have to fight for something, not about something. Relationships with average people will be a Warrior's greatest challenge. Students are urged to read my *Sorcerer's Secrets* book series, which speaks at great lengths about such matters. I've chosen not to respond to her anger. It has been a lesson of dealing with an average person with no boundaries, self-respect, or any idea of how little time she has left on this earth. Thinking of herself as immortal gives her the illusion that she'll have time to apologize, make amends, and connect with the people she's offended. Death will find her with many unresolved issues.

I've accepted that things are what they are amongst my sisters-in-law, who are suspicious of me. I cannot say I blame them, as average people are suspicious of everyone. As a Warrior, I already know who they are and how they think. The challenge for me is not laughing in their face and trying to appear as if I take what they say seriously. My mother-in-law wanted my wife to marry a DOEI. She falsely believed that by marrying DOEIs her daughters would find happiness. Again, she was wrong. She poisoned their minds and convinced them that Latino men were just like their father, who she apparently once despised. I don't reject her, but I also don't give her any significance. Death will bring us closer, even if it's only to say goodbye. I have no contact with her whatsoever and can only imagine what poison she speaks. I've made a Warrior's decision, which is to maintain distance, be cordial, outwardly friendly, but inwardly guarded and superficial when dealing with all of them. It's like interacting with mentally handicapped children; tiresome, and demands a lot of energy. It's a chore to force myself to do so, but after so many attempts to interact with them in real terms, this is the only safe alternative. I would prefer to avoid them completely.

I cannot begin to express my disappointment at their behavior, as I'd hoped to have a real family. Instead, what I got was a group of critics, whose only reason for interacting with me is my wife. What's the use of attempting to develop a relationship with them if their only reason for interacting with me is marriage? I've accepted that if we ever split, there would be no contact between any of them and myself. I believe I am worthy of friendship, even if my wife and I were not married, but in a society of average people, men and women cannot be friends. Sadly, my sisters-in-law, due to their upbringing, cannot have male friends or acquaintances. If I were not married to their sister, they would not give me the time of day. If for some reason we parted, I would not receive any gesture of recognition. It's another of those harsh realities that come along when dealing with average people. I've given it a lot of thought, and now that I'm on this side of it, I've decided I prefer it this way. In light of this reality, I now feel no obligation to go out of my way to acknowledge or help them if they ever need my assistance. I have no obligation to do or say anything about their misfortunes. I don't have to attend their funerals, weddings, or Christmas celebrations.

At first I could not find the words to express how sad this made me. Nor could I express how wrong I thought it was. In life's terms this meant I had no value as a person, other than what I could do for their sister. I was not worthy of any type of attention other than what I received while in the company of their sister. To me it means I am nothing more than a political relation. It means we, myself and them, have no relationship. It means we are nothing more than politically connected strangers. It means we have no affection for one another and only tolerate each other for appearances. The hypocrisy of this reality is sickening, yet the way things are.

Now, years later, I realize what a huge favor they've done for me. Via their delusional self-importance they handed me freedom from all their ugliness. I could not have tolerated being able to *see* them, knowing who they are, what they think, what they're doing to each other behind one another's backs, while pretending. Their snobbish self-delusion helped me establish boundaries in my own mind. Today, I'm past all my own delusional fantasies about having an extended family. I'm alone, but I'm not lonely. I've said goodbye to all of them in my heart and whatever the Universe sends their way, I won't intervene.

Hypocrisy has no bounds and all churchgoing, praying, good Christians commit average behavior which is not Christian. The only worse thing than having an average Christian family during Christmas, is having one consisting of political ties, wherein the phonier you behave, the easier it gets. It's pretty sickening, but there's nothing anyone can do. This is the way it is everywhere. The more you *see*, the worse it gets. It's best to avoid contact when possible. I don't visit and don't speak to them on the phone. It's best to maintain a safe distance. My wife's family has the same relationship that all average people have, which is little, none, and only evident during crisis. All average people feel alive during a time of trouble. They'll create drama just to feel alive, which is something I don't understand. I've learned via experience that all you have to do to make life interesting is walk out into a forest or deserted area at night, and make a specific sound, which I can teach you. I guarantee your life will get filled with drama immediately. They mistakenly believe we are not connected, and will therefore never have reason to interact. They don't understand that the Universe has placed us into each other's path. The best we can do is to avoid crashing into each other as we attempt to maneuver through this maze. However, for them it also means their children and I cannot be friends. At one time this troubled me, as I could have helped them. I used to blame my wife's parents for failing to instill better principles. Today, I understand that an average person claiming to have principles means only at the moment, or while in the mood. This is why a Warrior cannot connect themselves to average people, and why average people are not worthy of friendship. So, there really isn't any relationship possible, is there? What strikes me as sinful is that these people believed themselves worthy of being parents and raising children. I cannot imagine worse candidates, or the idea that these miserable creatures are perpetrating obscenity after obscenity. Their behavior is proof that a Warrior's greatest challenge is the people within their own family. The ugly reality is that average people cannot be friends. A real friendship requires boundaries, discipline, brutal honesty, and independence of thought and action. It's a sorry state of affairs and a Warrior's fate. There is no escape. The repugnant hypocrisy feels like a choking wind which blows across this great earth.

Texas escapee,

don Jesus M. Ramirez

Chapter Nine
The White Pony

"The innocence of a child is as fragile as an angel's wings, as light as a breeze, and as fleeting as a shadow."

—don Jesus M. Ramirez

I somehow managed to survive and avoid being killed by my mother's indifference, Beelzebub's cruelty, and my father's violent rage. Amidst all this cruelty and suffering I was fortunate enough to witness magic. Like all real magic it was a casual event, absent of floating angels and divine lights from the heavens. I cannot remember exactly where it took place, although I believe it might have been in the parking lot of a grocery store. A small carnival had been set up where children were able to get rides from ponies. I remember watching as parents took their children. I cannot even begin to convey how I felt towards those children, but I loved the ponies. I cannot express the sadness I felt when I compared my parents to those parents, who so lovingly placed their children on the backs of those beautiful creatures. Not only was I struck by the contrast of how my life compared, but I was dumbfounded by the happy innocence of the children, and the beauty of the ponies. I don't know how, but after that day, through my innocence I came to believe I could have had a pony of my own. I really don't know how I managed to come up with such an idea. I must have been a very innocent soul to have known so much sadness, yet still have enough hope to believe I could have had a pony. Even now, I don't know if such hope is a blessing, or just self-indulgence.

Yet, from that day forward I dreamed of having a pony. The strange thing was that I never told anyone about it. I don't recall telling my mother, Punk, Beelzebub, my sisters, or anyone else. I daydreamed of having a pony for the next several years. I'd wander around, half asleep and half awake, imagining what it would be like to have a pony. I imagined myself riding my pony across the newly plowed fields early in the morning, and coming home as the sun set. I imagined myself feeding and grooming my pony, and pictured hundreds of scenarios where we would be together.

As the years passed, the dream of having my own pony gave me hope. In the darkest and loneliest moments, when despair threatened to rob me of sanity, I kept hope alive with the idea that I might someday have a pony. Today, while writing and editing the fifth draft of this book, I've discovered that the dream of having a pony, like loving Norma Jean Slaughter, someone who would never love me back, helped make me a stronger and better person. It gave me the motivation to work towards goals which seem impossible. Only now can I truly see what don Juan meant when he said a Warrior's struggles are the keys to his freedom.

I don't remember the exact date, nor what convinced me to take a chance, but one day I decided to ask my father, who terrified me, if I could have a pony. I really cannot say how I managed to gather the courage to do so, but despite my stuttering and stammering, I did. I remember him staring at me in silence, studying me, as if he were seeing me for the first time. I have no idea what he might have thought. I have no hope of ever understanding why he did what he did. I can only say that it was the most evil thing I could imagine anyone doing. After staring at me as though he'd never seen me before, to my surprise, he said yes. I don't know if any of you can relate to this feeling, but my heart soared into the heavens with joy. I couldn't compare the happiness which I felt at that moment to anything I have experienced since. I am certain that if my heart had been a bird, it would have flown out of my body and into the sky filled with joy. I will say that it gave me hope, and hope is the most important element in anyone's life. I recently read that the most important thing a man needs in life is someone to love. Not having that, a man needs hope. Not having that, a man needs something to do. It must have been true for me, because my spirit was reborn that day. It gave my life direction, purpose, and a clear goal. I began what would be my first vision quest, with the objective of finding the right pony. Looking back, I can attribute my wanderlust to this event. It is the reason why I became a wanderer, and why I am able to take on seemingly impossible challenges and succeed. It is also the reason why I take so much time to plan, make notes, follow instructions, and talk to strangers. My not being afraid to take risks is also attributed to this experience. This seemingly impossible quest taught me lessons which I still use today. Finally, it is also the reason why I am able to keep secrets, without having a need to tell anybody, anything. I learned to be self-sufficient, self-contained, careful, and fearless. For the next year I wandered around trying to find the right pony. Don't ask me how I thought this might actually happen. When you're a kid, the unrealistic somehow seems possible. I have no idea what gave me the courage to begin my quest, but I began walking further and further away from Main Drive in search of the right pony. I had pony fever. I dreamed and thought of ponies every day of my life. I walked, and sometimes hitchhiked to places where I thought I might find a pony, where I'd seen horses, or where it looked like there might be ponies. This may not make sense to adults, but in my mind, I thought places that held horses had a certain recognizable look. It might be the same reason why I survived so many years in the military. I have always thought places that hold danger have a certain look. Sun Tzu or Napoleon Bonaparte might have called it a "soldier's eye." It may also explain why I've survived so many paranormal engagements. Places of danger are not limited to physical harm via physical threats. Just as there are places where power dwells, there are places where the energy of past events has imprinted itself on the land. Seekers should note that when such a place is identified by a Warrior, he will deliberately avoid it unless it serves him to act otherwise. If it becomes necessary to cross or enter, a Warrior will *see* why the area presents danger. Upon doing so he may come to understand how to engage it, as well as determine whether it's worth the risk. Challenging power for the sake of amusement is like playing Russian roulette. A Warrior who *sees* knows that power can *see* him as well. My experiences with such places have left negative impressions. Caution should be taken.

    A child's mind is a wonderful thing, and a child's imagination is amazing. Such a precious and innocent thing might be as rare as witnessing a miracle. That period of my childhood is filled with memories of walking alongside the road, either coming or going to wherever I thought I might find what I was looking for. I found many ponies. Every time I'd see a place set up for pony rides, which there were many at the time, I'd find a way to get back to that place. Even though I stuttered terribly, I managed to talk to the owners, and always asked them if my father might be able to buy one of their ponies. I must have seemed pretty strange to the adults I spoke with. I found that I was not afraid of other adults, as I had no reason to fear them, or at least I thought so at the time. My boldness impressed them and emboldened me. I grew more confident and with each passing moment, more certain that I would someday have a pony.

Thanks to my stubborn optimism and baseless faith in God, I somehow managed to maintain hope that I might someday succeed in my quest. Then one day I received a sign. Our neighbors across the street got a horse, which they penned in their backyard. I was sure the time was right to find my pony and tell my father where he could go buy it. I increased my searches and soon thereafter another miracle occurred. I found my pony. It was white with a brown saddle, and had been working at a pony ride. I spoke with the owner, who quoted me a price. I believe he said he wanted three hundred dollars, including the saddle. I asked him to write it down, along with his phone number, and he did, on the bottom of a brown paper bag. I don't know how I managed to find the courage to approach my father, who was usually always angry about something, but I did. Doing my best not to stutter, I managed to explain to him how I'd found the pony which he'd agreed to get for me. I handed him the brown paper bag which the owner of the pony had written his price and phone number on. My father looked down at me, as if seeing me for the first time all over again. He studied me, glaring with hatred in his eyes. Then, as if possessed by a demon he said, "Estas pendejo!" "You're stupid! I only said that so you'd shut your fucking mouth!" I felt thunderstruck. At the time I'd never imagined my father, who often said a man was only as good as his word, would do something like this. He'd gone back on his word and broken his promise. He lied to my face, just so I would stop talking to him. I must have had a stunned expression on my face as I walked back into the house, because Beelzebub saw me and began making fun of me. His cruel evil laughter continued, as he found great pleasure in my suffering. I've concluded that he must have been listening and watching while I approached my father. He overheard the entire thing. I remember the great pleasure he took in laughing at me. I still cannot understand what kind of joy he could receive in seeing another human being suffer. I can still see his face, as he laughed at my sorrow. His evil laughter echoed while he stood there pointing at me. I was completely shocked and out of breath from the sheer cruelty of my father's actions. As I said earlier, Beelzebub's cruel laughter has accompanied my darkest moments. Seekers are reminded that taking pleasure in another's pain is standard behavior for 96ers. Attempting to understand why they behave so wretchedly is pointless. It's simply their nature, and demonstrates why average people can never be trusted or allowed to know your inner thoughts. Deliberate actions to avoid interacting with such individuals will not be easy, as they are everywhere.

Years later as an adult, while making an emergency trip to Texas for my nephew's funeral, I made the mistake of sharing the fact that I was unemployed. I'd planned to ask Beelzebub to share his connections, so I might be able to find a job in Texas. Instead of helping me via his alleged many connections, he pretended as though he'd never offered to help, when in fact he had. He then suggested that I learn to drive a semi-trailer truck. I told him I did not want to be a truck driver, as I did not want to be away from my wife. We had only recently gotten married at the time. Plus, I was having problems with post-traumatic stress disorder (PTSD) after having returned from the Persian Gulf War. After hearing my reply, he suggested I bring her along, because according to him a husband and wife could make a lot of money as team operators. He found my situation hilarious and again burst out with his evil laughter. While watching him laugh I was reminded of the discovery I'd made years ago as a child; never give an average person the benefit of a doubt. I made the same mistake I'd made a dozen times before. I gave him the benefit of a doubt, and hoped he'd changed. After all, he had offered to help me find work during a phone conversation. I could have kicked myself for making the same mistake with him that I'd made with my father. The years I had spent away from them had cast a fog over our experiences, and I'd almost allowed myself to forget just how inhumane and cruel they truly were. It was the same realization I'd had about Beelzebub many times throughout my life. I had to accept the fact that I had once again made myself vulnerable to his cruelty. Being the sadistic bastard that he is, he jumped at the opportunity to humiliate me once again. I learned that unilateral forgiveness is like trying to put out a fire by throwing gasoline on it. After all these years I have still been unable to comprehend his sadistic nature. I've surrendered the quest for an explanation or form of understanding, and have arrived at the conclusion that acceptance is much more important. I now accept the fact that he is a disturbed, evil bastard, and nothing anyone can do will ever change that. I wonder if he and I were not mortal enemies in a past life. I imagine I must have caused him tremendous shame in that life, because he seemed determined to humiliate me in this one.

My fantasy of having a pony was ended that day. My father's cruelty, followed by Beelzebub's laughter, was all that remained of my hopes. It's difficult to explain how much this event changed my life. Aside from breaking my heart, it ended my childhood. The betrayal laid bitter seeds of anger which festered like an open wound for the next ten years. My father's calculated and malicious cruelty is still beyond my understanding. I cannot begin to understand why an adult, supposedly my own father, would execute such an evil plan. What could have been the purpose of this behavior? Why not just say no, and be done with it. Why pretend? Why betray? Why? To this day

I have no idea. I went through the darkest phase of my young existence. I surrendered to my rage, resentment, and feelings of injustice. I never spoke to my father again, except to say yes or no. I hated him with an anger that turned into motivation to push my limits, and I swore vengeance. I regret to admit my own anger blinded and chained me to that hate, which connected me to him and Beelzebub. I now understand that those horrible moments were the keys to my freedom. I would have never worked so hard or fought so long to become mentally and physically stronger. I would have never had the passion and desire to begin boxing, refuse to be squashed by bullies, or reject the notion of giving up on my dreams. Without their constant cruelty I would have never had the courage to leave home only four days after graduation, and join the military during the Vietnam War. I would have never had the strength to undertake seemingly impossible challenges and succeed. Now as an adult, I've wandered over mountains and crossed mighty oceans. I work to remove all the pain and humiliations of my childhood. I work to erase the hate and not waste any more energy on either of them. I refuse to surrender to anger and hate. I knowingly reject any thought, image, or feelings which drains my energy. I refuse to associate with anyone who demonstrates cruelty, arrogance, or intolerance. I know that anyone who'll be cruel towards someone else will not hesitate to do the same to me. Seekers are warned that those who discriminate are displaying the ultimate form of self-importance. Such individuals are ticking time bombs of conflicting emotions, which will eventually go off without notice. Caution should be taken to avoid them.

Not knowing how to cope with the heartache and humiliation, I sought refuge in the only place I knew. I walked into the woods in search of solace. In my solitude, I never spoke of that incident again. The humiliation and shame I felt remained locked within my heart. I hated myself for believing my father and having counted on him. I swore I'd never give him another opportunity to disappoint me again. I never expected anything, or ever asked him for anything ever again. I hated being dependent on him, and he never missed an opportunity to remind me of what a useless burden I was. I learned I was alone, and always have been. I was on the Warrior's path even before I knew it existed. I wandered through the woods in my self-imposed isolation, until one day while hunting I had a significant experience. As I laid upon a blanket, resting my head on my backpack, I looked up into the sky and amongst the clouds stood a white pony. The blue Texas sky surrounded it, as I watched it move, flowing in the wind. It was the white pony I would never have. Tears filled my eyes and ran down my face, and I continued staring until its image disappeared. Then as if by magic, just like my innocence, it was gone forever. The loss of innocence cannot be measured by any known means. It can however be observed in the eyes of children who have known catastrophic events and poverty. The loss of security robs a person of hope and the spiritual substance needed to empathize with others. It forms callouses around your heart and sucks the very brightness from the sky. While we agree that man must eventually leave fantasies behind, we also know that a child must have them in order to desire life.

Just as I'd learned by loving Norma Jean Slaughter, love is never a mistake. My search for the pony grew into a love affair with horses. Amongst the many adventures I experienced were trail rides across Yosemite's wilderness on horseback. Traveling the John Muir Trail, I witnessed the indescribable beauty of infamous sites, such as the Golden Staircase. I also spent much time tracking lost tourists in

Apache Junction, Arizona. I was told by an alleged witch that my spirit would be taken to heaven on horseback. I have no idea what to make of that statement, but I felt it was worth including in this work. I have always loved horses. Later in life, while living in San Jose, California, after my first tour of duty around 1980, I bought a horse. I named him Smokey. Looking back, I realize it was a poorly thought-out decision. I learned how expensive horses are, but I loved Smokey. It was around the same time John Travolta made the movie, *Urban Cowboy*. I'd dreamed of having a horse all my life, so after giving it almost no thought at all, I bought one. I couldn't afford him, nor did I have a place to keep him, but I wanted him so badly. Throwing caution to the wind, I decided to live my dream. I had Smokey for a little over two years. I almost went broke, but I loved that horse and cared for him as best as I could. However, due to my upbringing, countless mistakes, and broken relationships, I was forced to sell him. Now all that remains are several photographs and memories. I hope whoever bought Smokey cared for him as well as I did, and loved him at least half as much.

As I write and edit this book for the fifth time, I know I've continued to grow. Today, before I make a decision of what to buy, I asked myself three questions: "What do you want? What do you need? What can you afford?" Had I followed this decision making formula I would have taken emotion out of the equation and acknowledged I could not afford Smokey. I did not need him, and was only living out a childhood fantasy. It's amazing how long it took for me to arrive at this seemingly simple formula. What an advantage I would have had if I'd had someone advise me along the way. The impact of bad parenting has continued to be a major setback throughout my life, as it will be for all those who have suffered similar experiences. Past behavior is the best indicator of future behavior, and the effects of bad parenting last forever.

The same old woman who told me my spirit would be taken up to heaven on horseback, also told me a horse was my spirit guide. I believe she was just blowing smoke up my whazoo. I have no idea what she really wanted, or thought she'd get if she lied enough. The strange thing is I don't believe in heaven, at least not the one I was taught to believe in as a child. Although, I wish I could believe. Who knows what she really meant. It would be great to be able to afford to own a horse and land near a national park, and have endless trails to ride. Yet, those are just more fantasies. As a child I wanted a pony more than anything in the world. I believe it would have made me a different person. The same way my father's betrayal and blatant cruelty welded the hate I felt towards him to the core of my soul. I've worked for decades to remove it. I may never own another horse, but I will always love them.

The white pony still wanders through the clear blue skies of my mind. I think of it and of how much I learned during my search for him. I know my dream helped me accomplish much more than I ever believed possible. I discovered the world held hope and not everyone was as cruel or evil as Beelzebub and my father. I realized I had to escape from Texas and get away from them. Looking back on those horrible moments with *detachment* is like watching a movie about a poor kid who gets the stuffing beat out of him by two villains. I now know that my realizations were those of a naïve child. At the time I sincerely believed it was possible to escape vile individuals. My innocence led me to believe I might one day find a place of peace on this earth. Today, after having followed the Warrior's path for over forty years, I recognize that 96ers exist everywhere. They cannot be avoided, only managed. Seekers should keep in mind that although there are certain geographic areas which have customs and characteristics that should be forsaken, all changes, no matter how insignificant, begin with you. Before you can impact those around you, you must first conquer your own weaknesses. This is why those who follow this path are called Warriors.

When I first wrote about my quest to find the white pony, I would often fantasize about what I would do if I had millions of dollars. It always included a beautiful home on a hill, surrounded by a park-like setting of green pastures, and a herd of white ponies. I envisioned children playing and my wife smiling while I happily hold her hand. I'd always said that if I won the lotto, I'd adopt a dozen kids and buy each of them a horse. Now, maybe I'll buy a dozen horses, and adopt one kid. What I know for sure is if I ever adopted a child or a horse, they'd never have reason to doubt I loved them. Today, eight years after writing the first draft of this book, I'm not sure I'd want to adopt any children, although I'd still want a horse. Kids are too much work, too much of a burden, and unless I could isolate them from the rest of society, I'm afraid they'd be just as distorted as all the kids I see on the streets every day. It is frightening how poorly raised these kids are, which validates my statements concerning unresolved childhood issues. I find I don't fantasize about having millions of dollars anymore. Perhaps I've given up the idea that I ever will. Either way, I know death is stalking me, and I don't have time to waste daydreaming of what might have been. Instead of dreaming of having money, I'm working on winning my freedom and accomplishing tangible goals. Oh yea, I still fantasize, but it's no longer about what would have been. I've won my battle with the tyrants in my life. I never killed them or had them punished, but instead did what I suggest everyone do with people who've hurt them; get the hell away from them, no matter who they are. Average people don't change, don't admit their wrongdoings, and will never ask for or deserve forgiveness. My father's cruelty never squashed me because I simply refused to submit to his authority. I've met dozens of individuals who hate their parents, but continue to endure their abuse, simply because they want what daddy can give them. They surrender their souls whenever daddy threatens to write them out of his will, submitting to his tyranny. Never trade your soul for money. Doing so makes you the same as all those people you pointed to and laughed at.

Today, as an adult looking back at the beaten and neglected child I once was, I am amazed at his strength. I cannot explain where or how I developed such character and resilience. I won more than a battle, I won a war over countless attempts to brainwash me into becoming like my oppressors. The battle for my spirit continues as I feel dark forces around me. Seekers should recognize that this is not a battle between good and evil. It is a fight between imprisonment and freedom. During the moments when I am tempted to react in an average manner, I sometimes feel Beelzebub's dark spirit and my father's hatred have combined to form a cloud which looms over me. There have been times during the night when I've sensed their evil presence around my home. While traveling through Texas I've often felt Beelzebub's spirit become aware of my passing. My sense's warned me that their spirits are united in effort to infect the world with cruelty. I do what every Warrior must do. I *ground* myself, connecting my spirit with the Universe, shut off my *internal dialogue*, and push away the remnants of their association. I used to believe our paths would cross again. Today, more experienced and more secure, I realize that it wouldn't matter. I don't fear such an encounter, as I've earned my freedom. I need to believe the Universe will grant me the opportunity to balance the scales and wash away the hate, resentment, and desire for vengeance. I have worked to remove any remnants of anger and unburden any baggage which I might still carry. I don't want to hate them. I don't want to be angry at anyone, as energy is too precious to waste. I once believed karma had to run its course. Today, I no longer feel this way. I live as a Warrior, fortifying my *will*, and sharpening my spirit as I would a sword. I need to believe the Universe will place me in an advantageous position. No combat veteran would willingly seek a confrontation with overwhelming forces. A Warrior who places himself in a strategic position will never have to. I've learned to go around obstacles, not try to knock them down, or force anyone to submit to my commands. Warriors know they must be prepared to meet life's challenges and that each might be his last. I believe the Universe will put me in the right place at the correct time, and I will not be surprised when I come across any person who has wronged me. This is true about everyone I've met over my entire life, regardless of whether our interaction was positive, negative, or indifferent, as our paths have been joined by powers beyond my understanding. I would not be surprised to find Beelzebub around the next corner. He and my father's memory has haunted me throughout my life, and I have sought refuge in many places. I've filled the void within my soul in every imaginable way. Even as I write this, all these years later, I cannot yet claim complete success. I have learned that there is no replacement for a loving family, only adequate substitutes. This truth was dramatically demonstrated by the rejection from my wife's family. My in-laws proved that the same spirit which existed within my father is a contagious and deadly disease, which exists everywhere. Like Beelzebub, my mother-in-law's materialistic view of the world convinced her that a person is what they own, and a person can fill the emptiness in their soul with things. Yet, despite many expensive objects that surround them, it is all pretend. There is nothing one can buy or steal which will ever replace passion, affection, and genuine emotions. Just like I know there is no form of revenge which could extract payment for the wrongs they've done. It is also true that seeking revenge for those wrongs is pointless. It is up to me via *intent* to present a solution, solve the equation, recognize it when it happens, and then move on, and far away.

Like all average people, after years of being pushed away I lashed out in anger. I mistakenly believed I was simply not permitting anyone to mistreat me. This behavior brought me innumerable problems, and I paid horrible consequences. I suffered terrible losses, hurt wonderful people, and broke many hearts. I've stopped lamenting these losses and have determined not to repeat these mistakes. I've learned you cannot make someone love you, but you surly can make them hate you and not want to be around you. I've learned to accept people as they are and stop hoping they will change. They will never know me nor be able to utilize my knowledge when they face life's challenges. I am under no obligation to offer assistance. I've elected to stand aside and let life takes its course. Death gives no one time to waste trying to gain approval. Instead of trying to fill the emptiness, I simply stopped indulging, as it's no longer important. I've found peace and dignity in my solitude, and find that being alone is not the worst thing in the world. Changes come quickly and unexpectedly.

Texas escapee,

don Jesus M. Ramirez

Chapter Ten
The Moon Watcher

"Asking why is as pointless as pondering the reasons for being born."
-don Jesus M. Ramirez

I have been looking up into the night sky all my life, and have literally spent hours staring up at the moon, trying to understand its secrets. The moon has helped guide me across oceans, deserts, and mountain ranges, and has brought me back from war. I have watched it from mountains in Switzerland, Germany, Austria, France, Spain, Iran, Iraq, Pakistan, and dozens of other countries. During the Persian Gulf War I spent moonlit nights searching the desert for movement. My most wonderful experiences have been accompanied by a full moon, as have my most dangerous. I watched as one of Saddam's scud missiles streaked towards our position on a full moon night, and blew the hell out of everything around us.

The moon has witnessed my sadness, joy, and despair, and has heard my wishes more than once. I have been captivated and mesmerized by its beauty all my life. Ever since I can remember I have bathed in its light and asked for its blessing. All this thanks to my mother. She, more than anyone, influenced me to become a lover of the moon. I have loved it during all the pain and loneliness I've experienced, and in doing so I was never alone. I've always had the moon. Although this may sound of little comfort, it is the same moon which my mother and I sat under together. It is the same moon that witnessed the few moments I was able to spend alone with her. This may not sound like much to those who knew their mothers, but I never did. It might not be important to those who never wondered what kind of person their mother was, as I have. I've often wondered if I might have made better decisions under happier circumstances if she'd lived. I remind my students that life is about choices, and the tougher ones bring important changes in life. Few people have the courage and discipline to identify their shortcomings, make the necessary changes, and become the people they want to be. This is the challenge of a Warrior and why they are always at war against their own weaknesses. A Warrior battles their weaknesses daily, and even though they know they may not win, they struggle because surrender is not in their character.

Texas has great full moon nights, out there in the middle of all those huge cotton fields. Surrounded by darkness, the moon brought magic to my life. I may have been answering the same call to bathe in its light as ancient natives did for hundreds of years, long before Europeans invaded these shores. I understand why ancient cultures worshiped the moon as a goddess, believing it to hold special powers. It was one of my mother's greatest pleasures to sit on the front porch and bask in its light. The moonlight lessened the burden of her suffering and lifted the weight of her unhappiness. Momentarily the moon restored her vigor, and in rare moments she would share stories of her childhood. Many of her memories were sad, but sometimes, under the moonlight, she'd recall happier times and we'd laugh. She would tell the story of her parents, who fought alongside Pancho Villa in the Mexican Revolution. I learned about my Grandfather, who was a documented, certified, and verified hero and officer in the famous División del Norte. She spoke of the storming of Torreón, one of the biggest battles of the war. She told how under the leadership of General Pancho Villa, the rebels, along with some 16,000 poorly armed and poorly equipped revolutionaries, charged across the desert towards the fortified city of Torreón, Coahuila, México. My grandmother, along with 2000 other women, was among those who stormed the walls of Torreón on foot, which was defended by 10,000 federal troops.

At other times my mother softly rocked in her rocking chair as she hummed Mexican love songs. Once she called me to her side and asked me to kneel at her feet. She then held my face and spoke gently. I don't remember what she said, but she tenderly placed my head down on her lap and caressed me like I was her child. It was the only time I felt she loved me, and for years I treasured this memory as my favorite. It may not seem like much to others, but to me, it was the sweetest memory I had of my mother. I now understand she was just indulging in her own fantasy about her mother and the love she missed, but at the time her attention meant the world. Unless you've grown up in a large family with everyone placing demands on your mother, you have no idea what this means. I would have given anything just to be able to spend more time with her, and have gotten to know her as a person. Like all average people who were abused and neglected by their parents, sadness creeps up on me.

For many years I felt I would have been a much better person if I'd only had caring parents. Knowing this caused me much sadness. Like a sentimental fool I would sit outside alone in the darkness under the moon, sending out prayers for my mother's spirit. I now realize the power to be or not be who I want is within me, and not determined by who loved or didn't love me as a child. This is 96er behavior. All those moments were not wasted, and as I searched through these painful memories I discovered that she taught me an important lesson. No matter how much you love someone, you cannot love them any more than you love yourself. My mother is the perfect example of children having children and hating them, while trying to love them, having never known love themselves. She above all others serves as a testimony of what awaits 96ers who expect children to fill the voids in their lives. She helped instill the knowledge that life is suffering, and the less you want the better off you will be. I knew these lessons decades before I ever heard of Buddha, don Juan, or the Toltecs.

Texas escapee,

don Jesus M. Ramirez

Chapter Eleven
A Tejano Greek Tragedy

"My mother's ghost haunts the empty house we once lived in. Her heartbroken spirit moves about, searching for her children, her childhood, and the love she dreamed of. The only tale more unfortunate than a Greek tragedy is a Tejano one. There is no lesson to be learned, no wisdom to impart, and in the end all we have is sobering sadness."

-don Jesus M. Ramirez

My mother's death caused a lot of friction, which is common for dysfunctional families. Any situation involving a bunch of messed up people will never have a shortage of conflict. Each person has their own reality and remembers the same events differently. It's no wonder that amongst average people family reunions are just excuses to vent, say horrible things, and vow never to see each other again. As a family, my siblings and I are as close as we are ever going to be. Unfortunately, in life there are no happy magic endings, but only a struggle and an acknowledgment of just how alone each of us are. For many years I blamed my father for my mother's illness. Rather than holding on to hatred and resentment, I should have *detached* myself from my painful memories and offloaded the baggage. I've had to work hard at not having my father and brothers in my life. What I find amazing is that I have to consciously and continuously work at it, which is why I know recapitulation is a process, and not a one-time event. I've learned, as will all who persevere, that there is no safe place or haven from our own past. Without the *detachment* of a Warrior, a

Seeker will never get this far. They will give up in frustration and rejoin the mindless masses. As a genuine Seeker wishing to succeed, you must learn to find interest in your mistakes. Every stumble and fall must be viewed as an entertaining process. Not in the sense that you enjoy failing, but that you know becoming a Warrior is a lifelong endeavor. You must plan, knowing you will fall and hurt yourself, and yet remember that this is what is supposed to happen. You are supposed to stumble, say stupid things, and make horrible mistakes. Yet, instead of hating yourself for failing, learn to say, "That's one mistake I will never make again," and then allow yourself to move forward.

As a Seeker you must learn to call things what they are, and not what you'd like them to be. You must begin by using correct language and descriptive words, without attaching emotional baggage to them. This is very difficult. However, it is essential that you only describe events as they occurred, without adding romanticized self-description or make-believe Hollywood endings. My father's story is as common as rain, just as you'll find your story will be. Don't allow yourself to get caught up in a web of self-pity and romanticized bullshit. There will be plenty of stranger than fiction stories in your life, and in those of the people you love. If you don't die, you'll live, and it's amazing what the body is capable of doing on automatic. Looking back, the entire experience seems to have happened to someone else. I wish it had.

We buried my mother in an open field. I was one of her pallbearers, as were my brothers and father, including Hijacker, even though he was still a little kid at the time. After the service I stood at her gravesite, staring down into the hole, knowing she was not in the coffin. I hoped she was in a better place and was no longer suffering. Such experiences make it clear to see why the Toltecs sought an alternative ending to their lives. Standing there I felt the beginnings of a seemingly never-ending journey of heartache envelop me. I would never know her, and we would never spend time, just by ourselves. I knew that no matter what else happened, I was an orphan. All of my siblings were, and still are emotionally crippled. We had been raised to compete, not to nurture each other. One of the many harsh realizations a Warrior must eventually confront is that people who once mattered, will not only stop being important, but eventually drift out of their lives. It is an unavoidable fact which those on this path will face. In truth, those people were never as important, wise, or good as you once believed. It was your need and self-imposed blindness that assigned them qualities they never possessed. They continue to remain the same. The problem is you've changed. While change is a Warrior's characteristic, tool, and major asset, it is a monster that upsets the reality of average men. The distance between a Warrior and the average man is never greater than at the point of this realization. Every accomplished Warrior has traversed the same path and come upon the same sadness. This is the aloneness of a Warrior.

I have no relationship with Punk, who has not spoken to me in years. He is just like our father, and I don't enjoy his company. I never understood how he could change his position, color, and mood, depending on what he wanted and who was winning. Perhaps more disturbing is that he never found anything wrong with our father's behavior. On several occasions I literally risked my life to save him, and although I never expected anything in return for doing so, his behavior disappointed me tremendously. As an example I will share the reason why Punk decided to stop speaking to me. Several years ago Punk's wife, who I'll refer to as "Cockroach," came to San Francisco for a work related conference. I volunteered to show her the city, as I lived nearby and have been there hundreds of times. We had a lot of fun, and I assumed everything was fine. Soon thereafter, during a telephone conversation with Bumper, he asked me if I had made a pass at her. I laughed aloud, asking him what in the world he was talking about. He then informed me that Punk had told him that Cockroach said I had made a pass at her. I was completely shocked, as I was never more than courteous towards her. I continued laughing and called my wife into the room to tell her what Bumper had just said. What's especially disturbing is that she had given her approval for me to spend the night in San Francisco during Cockroach's visit. She didn't want me to have to drive over the pass after dark on my way home, so I stayed in a nearby hotel, away from Cockroach. I have no idea where Cockroach got this ridiculous notion, but I suspect it was the way she was viewing me, not the other way around. She must have been having sexual fantasies, and out of shame and fear, twisted it to relieve her guilt. At the time I wondered why she would even say such things to my brother, knowing how he'd react. I was disappointed with Punk, who never asked me what happened, but simply decided to stop speaking to me. Without hearing what I had to say he told Bumper, as if Cockroach's allegations were fact. If my wife told me something like that, I'd make a special effort to ask what happened, not just stop speaking to the accused.

On a good day my youngest brother, Hijacker, is a moral vacuum who finds humor in the pain of others. For some reason he believes he is getting away with something. In typical 96er fashion he believed I was as morally corrupt as he. His street values reflected his thoughts that anyone who does another a kindness is demonstrating weakness. Several years ago his wife tossed him out of their home after he was caught screwing around. He moved into a trailer park but was unable to make the rent. I loaned him money I didn't have, and expressed how important it was that he pay me back, but he still thought he could play me like a punk. His behavior is common amongst street people. It's best to keep a distance from such individuals, as they will only drag you down into the mire. He has no loyalty, honor, or self-respect, and does not value anyone beyond what he can get from them. I've had many disappointments throughout my life, but the only emotion I've had towards him in years is disgust. Anyone who knows him would probably say the same thing. My description might sound judgmental, but it is also accurate. As of today it has been close to twenty years since I loaned him the money. I have no use for anyone who would behave in such a manner. I think what bothers me the most is his lack of respect for our relationship, which he sold for one hundred dollars. I spoke to him once, when I called Bumper to say hello. He got on the phone, but I had nothing to say to him other than how he was a disappointment. I saw no point in reminding him he still owed me money. I can only imagine all the despicable behavior he's continued to display. Strangely, I once thought of him as a prince. You know, like in the movies, he would have the best of all of us. Yet he turned out to reflect the worst of what it means to be a man on this great earth. For years I felt a deep sadness that he turned out so badly, because my mother died as a result of giving him life, and she loved him so much. Yet, at the same time I know it was my own self-indulgence that caused me to feel so. As a Warrior, I have far more to think about and strive towards. He is just another one of the millions of average people out there, who upon an undesired interaction are hardly worthy of the time it takes to say, "Excuse me," or "Have a nice day," and then leave. He has no more value in my life than the last guy who cut me off while driving, or the last person who said, "Good morning." It's pointless to wonder why, as there are no answers to any such question. There is no why. There is just reality.

I've spent years and much time indulging in sadness, self-pity, and anger. I've cried so many times I might have filled a river, all in a storm of self-pity and indulgence. I've even sensed what I believed to be my mother's spirit several times. It may have actually been her, if only to tell me to stop indulging. Looking back, it's amazing just how far our self-indulgence goes. The last time I permitted myself to dwell in misery was in August of 2004, while I was planning a trip to Texas. I was sitting alone in our living room, playing an old Mexican song which my mother used to like, when I sensed her presence. I looked up and saw her spirit standing before me. She was smiling down at me, with her hands folded in front of her. I cried. What's amazing is I've learned all I have to do to see her, is silence my *internal dialogue*, and call her. I know I can call her whenever I want, but why would I do so? Wouldn't it just be more self-indulgence? A Warrior has no use for such sentimentality. It serves no purpose and only burdens him, thereby deplenishing his energy.

For many years I believed my mother to be my first hero. I now know this belief stemmed from my describing her as I wished she had been, rather than how she truly was. As a child she filled my head with romantic notions of what it means to be a man. She lied about her childhood, the same way so many 96ers do, which caused me more harm than if she'd fed me a spoonful of poison. However, in her mythological story telling she somehow managed to instill a love of music and film within me. I find it interesting that regardless of how delusional or imaginary the basis of my beliefs may have been, they have produced substance as real as the earth itself. My love for music and film not only continues today, but has exceeded my wildest expectations. Music has become another tool which helps me fight against the onslaught of negativity. Learning to master the guitar and sing has been a constant source of inspiration. Although I've not found fortune or fame, writing songs about my experiences has helped unburden me of self-indulgence. Via my songs I have successfully accomplished what 96ers hope to do by sharing their inner most personal secrets. I refuse to compromise my standards in exchange for company. My guitar and songs have filled the void of being unable to express sorrow, tell my stories, and simply be creative. Many 96ers claim to love music, yet use it as a flag of rebellion and indulgences. They behave horribly, and wear costumes with outrageous hair colors and styles, all in a pathetic attempt to fit in while claiming to be individualistic. Ignorant of history and lacking *detachment*, none of them realize it has all been done before. There is nothing unique about them. Instead of seeing music as a tool to fly above average men, they use it as a highway to destruction. Throughout my years on this path I've never met a 96er who drew strength and solace from music. Only a Warrior could do so.

  My oldest brother, Bumper, was my second hero. He demonstrated how dangerous the world is by making me an accomplice in a knife fight at the tender age of eight. We were standing at the school bus stop when six thugs approached us in an aggressive and hostile manner. Without saying a word my brother calmly handed me his books and a cross which he wore around his neck. I stood there holding his belongings, looking up at him. In the next instant I was caught up in a whirlwind of violence. Knives flashed and fists struck bone, as the grunts and moans of the fallen filled the air. All this occurred before my innocent eyes, leaving an impression of cruelty and harshness, which tore innocence from me in a fury of blood and violence. Bumper taught me to stand up against bullies and thugs, even when outnumbered. He also motivated me to take up running. As I said before, he was on the track team. He trained and I'd watch him as he ran in a huge circle around the cotton fields that surrounded our home. Learning to love long-distance running was a lifesaver. At the time it was considered insanity, completely unheard of on Main Drive. No one would willingly subject themselves to run, unless they were running away from someone or something. Running helped me clear my head via endorphins which are released through exercise. It also releases rage and pent-up sexual frustration, of which I had a lot of. More importantly, it put me in touch with my Warrior spirit. It helped cleanse me of doubt and strengthened my resolve to fight relentlessly until I won, or died. I knew I was in a life and death situation, as there was absolutely no hope on Main Drive. You could literally feel the desperation in the air, and see proof of how it sucked the life out of people and stole their chance for happiness. I'd see guys I'd gone to school with drop out, get married, and move two houses down from their parents, continuing the cycle of misery. It was horrible to witness the same ignorance continuing via another generation of desperate people. It scared the hell out of me. I knew I had to get away from Beelzebub, my father, Main Drive, and Texas.

Bumper's story is a perfect example of the desperate cycle which existed on Main Drive. He was handsome enough to be in the movies, but due to my father's treatment and emotional handicap, he dropped out of high school and married Lilith, a spoiled girl from Main Drive. Their marriage was rocky from the beginning and got worse as his womanizing increased. Bumper seemed to have no boundaries, and once while I was a teenager he used me to cover up his infidelities. He asked me to accompany him on a trip where he planned to meet up with his mistress. Soon thereafter, Lilith phoned me and demanded I tell her what she wanted to know. I was surprised she thought she could order me around and talk to me in such a manner. I had no idea she thought so little of me and so much of herself. Like all average people, she misinterpreted silence and politeness as weakness. This is how delusional and out of touch 96ers are. In her most indignant and self-righteous tone, she demanded I tell her what was really going on with Bumper. I found this disturbing, because I hated bullies. Also, there was no way I was going to rat on my brother, no matter what he'd done. By this stage in my life I'd learned to hate tyrants of any gender. Plus, it didn't help that at the time I was catching hell from other women in positions of authority. The last thing I needed was my sister-in-law giving me shit. As you might suspect, I was less than submissive or cooperative. By this point in my development I had earned tremendous self-esteem via boxing, and I would not permit anyone to push me around. I made it a point of honor to stand up for myself, even if it meant an ass whipping. When my sister-in-law attempted to roll over me, she chose the wrong method of approach. I told her to go ask Bumper, and never to ask me such questions about him again. I let her know she had the wrong idea about herself, as I did not see her as anyone who had authority over me. I was firm and remained polite out of respect for my brother, otherwise I'd have given her a different response. I never told Bumper what she asked me, and I also never allowed him to talk me into going anywhere with him again. What really blew me away was that he assumed I would cosign his lies and unfaithfulness. I was stunned that he would risk his marriage and daughter for casual sex. I was equally as disappointed with his second base. She was supposed to come from a religious family, and her father was allegedly an elder in the church. I was so disappointed in him, especially considering all the harm done to our mother because of our father's womanizing.

Bumper's wife was beautiful and smart. She might have been a tremendous asset to him if he'd known how to appreciate her talents, rather than feeling threatened by them. His entire life might have been different if he had not been such a womanizer. He saw his banging strange women as something to be proud of, not something to hide and keep secret. He learned all this behavior from our father, but rather than rejecting it as aberrant, he endorsed it. At the time I was insulted that he assumed I'd be a part of his cheating. Tragically, his behavior went from bad to worse. Lilith had every right to be angry, as she deserved not to be lied to. All of my brothers have developed an average person's ability to rationalize and justify whatever they do. They have no inner barometer or self-monitoring guide helping them stay within the boundaries. I am shocked and amazed they have managed to make such a mess of their lives. They exemplify the term "average," and serve as my examples of what not to do. Bumper and his wife divorced after years of turmoil, which left both of them devastated. Rather than gathering himself and learning from his mistakes, what do you think Bumper did? He jumped from one bed into another, and married the girl he was banging on the side, who I'll refer to as "Lucy." I felt so sorry for this poor girl. She deserved better. Lucy was still in high school and didn't deserve to have her fantasy of happiness dumped on. I honestly don't believe Bumper loved her, or even wanted to be with her. I think he married her because he was afraid of being alone. His habit of chasing skirts continues today, validating that no one changes unless they have to.

Bumper made the ultimate mistake anyone who cheats on

their partner can make. He married his mistress. What's even more amazing is that Punk did the same thing. A blind man could have foreseen the future and known this wouldn't work. Soon after Bumper and Lucy married he started cheating again. Allegedly, Lucy repaid him in aces and started screwing strangers she met on the street, along with someone she worked with. The problem was that both she and Bumper worked at the same correctional facility. According to Bumper, he brought a knife to work with plans of scaring her lover. However, Lucy was aware of his intentions and warned the authorities. Bumper's locker was searched and the knife was found. This was a major violation of security, and he was in line to be fired. However, before he was, he took it upon himself to go over the warden's head, contacting the attorney general, who conducted an investigation, exposing information the warden should have been aware of. It turned out that Lucy had married her lover in secret while still being married to Bumper. In typical 96er fashion, the warden fired him as revenge for going over his head and exposing his incompetence. Once again, Bumper demonstrated a fact about 96ers. They will kill themselves if it also destroys their enemy. These words of caution should be taken to heart, as Warriors must at some point interact with 96ers, and there will be conflict. After this discovery Lucy was transferred out of state, while her new husband had to stay working in Texas for twenty years. The rest of the story would curl cement, but there's no point in going into it. It's normal behavior for average people and should serve as a warning. Anyone else would have learned their lesson, but not Bumper. More bad karma and an endless cycle of cheating, divorce, and remarrying followed. He remarried, divorced, remarried, divorced, and then remarried and divorced again. He did this five times. I'll bet a hundred bucks to your dime he's never been faithful to anyone, and considers cheating an integral part of marriage. In the old days, if he were a woman, he would be called a whore, but because he's a man he's called a player. The average man's sins against women are too many to address. They believe in the delusional concept of throw away people who can easily be replaced. Average people are always looking to trade up. They are never satisfied with what they have. They feign respectability because it serves their purpose, but it's all a lie. Gluttony, greed, and vanity demands they have more and better. Without self-restraint the average man has no chance of avoiding the destruction of himself and those around him.

  My brother Beelzebub was, and still is a coward, a phony, and a ridiculous fool. He is the classic example of auto-discrimination. He felt inferior and hated being Tejano, along with everything associated to it. He looked down upon his family roots. He sought to belong to the in-group of DOEIs at school, but of course they quickly rejected him. He responded by adopting their manner of speech and refusing to associate with anyone or anything connecting him to what he believed to be inferior. He made a feeble attempt to play football, but lacked courage. He tried, failed, and then dropped out. He bullied me around at home when I was younger, but when it came to stepping up, when it mattered, he was nowhere to be found. His biggest thrill was getting DOEI girls, and for some reason it was a big deal to him. I never had any interest in anything he said, but I listened when he bragged. I knew he wanted to get the hell out of there as badly as I did, and couldn't understand why he made a fuss over his alleged sexual conquests. Don't ask me to explain that one. He is a textbook example of those who suffer from self-loathing. For some reason he saw DOEI girls as forbidden fruit, and as such he believed them more worthy. As for myself, I never made a big deal about who

I had sex with. I never believed it was anyone's business, and wouldn't have bragged about it anyway. It was stupid to do so. Once a girl heard you were bragging about having sex with her, she'd drop you, and then her brothers would want to kick your ass. What sense did that make? It was better to keep quiet and get a little lovin' now and then. Everyone needs a little affection, and secrets make better friends. The ability to maintain trust demands that no part of anything be repeated to anyone. This is not an accepted idea amongst 96ers, which is why trust is as difficult to find as Jesus Christ. The only way for three 96ers to keep a secret, is for two of them to die. Caution should be exercised any time you have dealings with 96ers. I guarantee everything you do or say will be repeated without your knowledge or approval. Seekers hoping to rise above the masses must recognize keeping secrets as an aspect of discipline.

After graduation Beelzebub wasted no time in distancing himself from the rest of us. He joined the Army under horrible circumstances and disappeared. He alleges to have served in Vietnam, but I cannot honestly say he did. Knowing what a manipulator he is and how much he likes attention, he may have forged his release papers. I never cared either way. I know he was stationed in San Antonio, Texas, where he remained after being discharged. He'd come to Main Drive and spend all his time making fun of everyone he saw. Actually, all of us looked down upon the people we grew up with. I don't know why we thought we were better or different. Perhaps it was our mother's example. She instilled suspicion of everyone, which she disguised as higher standards. She taught us to believe we were better and different, but it was all based upon self-delusion. No one is different or better, everyone is average. My mother forbade us to associate with the people from Main Drive, who were typically underachievers, high school dropouts, unemployed, uneducated, married with children, and drunks. It was easy for me, as I wasn't wanted around, even by the losers. Every time I tried to fit in with the thugs on Main Drive, I was rejected. Looking back, I should be grateful. I might have ended up being one of them. I know now there was no way I would have fit in anywhere. Not after my experiences seeing demons, hearing voices, listening to my parents having sex, and getting the shit beat out of me almost every day. It's no wonder I never had any friends. With the exception of one or two people, I've never sought contact with anyone from my old barrio. My isolation was complete. The trouble was I never had a choice. I couldn't fit in even with other people who didn't fit in. It would have been great to have a bunch of other people as friends who also saw demons, heard voices, and liked to spend their days stomping around the woods. It would have been great to hang out with people as weird as me, but I was alone. I grew up alone in an overcrowded house, surrounded by people I'd known my entire life, but my paranormal experiences caused me to be isolated. It is common for children of abusive parents to not only feel alone, but to expect that bad things are going to happen. Lacking confidence and strength of character, innocent children believe they are the problem, not their parents. Millions of 96ers rob their children of the ability to receive or express love. This causes immeasurable harm that will damage every relationship they will ever have. Many average people believe that being psychic is a gift, yet their belief is born out of ignorance, as they cannot *see* and have never experienced the sadness I describe. Those who doubt me need only look into the eyes of an abused child.

Beelzebub still doesn't have blue eyes, but now wears blue contact lenses and has changed his last name. He married and divorced twice before he finally married a blonde-haired, blue-eyed DOEI woman. The trouble is he's too much like our father and cannot stop fooling around. Poor woman, she's paying in aces for whatever he's buying her. While I was stationed at Fort Sam Houston, in San Antonio, Beelzebub suggested we hit the town. We had a few drinks, and then I realized he was using me as a cover. He wanted to see a woman he was trying to bang, which was why he'd invited me out. Just like Bumper, I was his excuse for being out of the house. He told his wife he was taking his little brother out on the town for a drink. I should have told her, but it seemed a cruel thing to do in front of their children. I wasn't surprised he had a possible love connection waiting for him. Keep in mind, at the time he'd just recently married, and allegedly found the love of his life. Yea, right. His behavior was beneath me. If I invited my younger brother out I would role model proper behavior, not demonstrate such conduct. I do not find cheating on your wife, lying, and breaking your promises to be acceptable behavior. I am not casting stones, nor am I claiming to be without fault. As a matter of fact, my second longest relationship ended because I did everything wrong, twice, and then did it again. After that I knew myself well enough to know I was not ready to get married. I knew I would have possibly done the same thing, which is why I didn't get married. If I was going to mess around, I certainly would not let my younger brother witness it. Nor would I flaunt it in such a blatant manner.

After returning from the Persian Gulf War, while suffering from PTSD, I asked Beelzebub for help. He said he'd call me back, but he never did. He taught me a valuable lesson, which would have made don Juan laugh. Be very careful who you ask for help, and even more careful whom you refuse to help after they've asked. I've learned you can hurt someone as much by simply doing nothing, as you can by deliberately harming them. I don't hold his refusal against him, as everyone has the right to say no. However, refusing to help after you've offered also has consequences. I am not one to turn the other cheek or forgive deliberate maliciousness. I cannot think of any reason for us to address one another again, except perhaps at a funeral. I didn't attend my biological father's funeral, so I may never see him again, which would be all right. The Universe made us brothers and placed us here for a reason, but he chose to make us enemies. In truth, instead of growing closer as death approaches, we've cemented our distance. I know death is stalking us and time is running out. We were once miserable souls trapped under the same roof, controlled by an evil tyrant who somehow taught him the same cruelty. The Universe put us in conflict and in the same struggle. This is what we have in common. I can only imagine how messed up his kids are. I imagine a kid torturing small animals, starting fires, and abusing smaller children, just the way he did. I feel sorry for anyone who crosses his path. I hope his kids haven't inherited his flavor for cruelty or his sadistic sense of humor. During the rainy season Beelzebub would capture toads and stick a wire through their mouths, forcing it through until it emerged out their rectum, bringing with it their intestines. He thought this was funny and got a kick out of it. He would also capture stray cats during the day and keep them captive until after dark. Then he would soak them in lighter fluid and set them on fire, just so he could watch the poor animal run away, screaming in pain, dying a horrible death. I foresee terrible things for his children. If you've ever wondered where serial killers come from, look no further. I wouldn't be surprised to learn he has bodies buried under his home or somewhere on his property. Keep in mind, he lives in a mansion on fifty acres of land in Texas.

Amazingly, the Universe set it up so I would work with abused children. I'm still in awe of how the Universe moves and places you in positions to grow and develop, or surrender to your weaknesses. I *saw* it in Beelzebub. It made him rich, thereby giving him the opportunity to do good, or surrender to his demons. I already know which he chose. My time as a social worker taught me about being a child and put me in touch with the child I was never allowed to be. I doubt his work experiences have had a similar affect upon him. The last time I saw Beelzebub was when I returned to Texas for my nephew's funeral. The poor misguided kid, who'd recently married, supposedly shot himself by accident and died instantly. The dumb kid actually shot himself in the eye by looking down the barrel of a gun, which had a bullet lodged in the chamber. The gun accidentally discharged and the bullet passed through his eye and out the back of his head. Of course, this experience traumatized my sister and her husband terribly. I could not begin to imagine what such an event might cause a parent to do. It was a horribly tragic incident. While I was in Texas, Beelzebub had the opportunity to demonstrate kindness, which as usual he failed to do. Instead, he chose to laugh at me. I grew up hearing his laughter during the most painful and humiliating moments of my life, which is why I hate bullies. Once again, Beelzebub didn't pass up an opportunity to demonstrate his cruelty, which was only surpassed by his indifference, just like our father. I've not spoken to him since, and I would not willingly subject myself to his company. All I can say is that I feel sorry for his kids, wife, employees, and anyone else who allows themselves to be deceived by him. I doubt he'll ever wish to speak to me again either, especially after this book hits the streets. I suspect he will distance himself further, as code names only do so much to disguise a person's identity. Either that, or send someone to beat or kill me. If his wife is smart, she'll use this book as an excuse to leave, take her children, and begin the slow process towards healing, but I doubt it. She's not very smart and has already signed off on trading her happiness for money.

I've always held my father, Beelzebub, Punk, Bumper, and Hijacker as examples of the person I would most not want to be. I tell my students that it's easy to teach absolutes, and I would absolutely not want to interact with any of them by choice. As a matter of fact, I'd rather walk through a storm than have to sit in a car with any one of them. So much of the sadness of Christmas is wrapped up with one or more of these individuals. In spite of how much I dislike my father and brothers, I don't wish them harm. I've learned negativity seeks its own and that we are punished by our sins, not for our sins. The Universe will seek its balance. I cannot imagine a greater sin than the deliberate and intentional humiliation of another human being, especially a child. This goes ten times for finding humor in someone else's suffering. Instead of helping others, for some reason average people in positions to help usually use those positions to hurt. There must be a specific definition for such behavior, one which extends beyond simply "dysfunctional." I've coined a new phrase, "Inter-generational Habitual Dysfunction Syndrome," (IHDS). It might be the only way to describe such a thing without referring to several degrees of sick behavior. Were it not for the Toltec discipline I might have been just another average person. The difference is I found this discipline and grabbed onto it for dear life. I became a fanatic, and refused to let the world squash me. I rose above every challenge and beat them by not surrendering to my own hatred, or to a sense of righteous indignation that goes along with self-indulgence. I beat their predictions. I am a self-manufactured person and who I want to be. I selected characteristics and values from books, movies, or anywhere else I could find hope. I should add that there were many times when finding hope seemed impossible. Don't believe I've been untouched by all this insanity. Imagine if you can, growing up in such an environment with these individuals as your relatives. Of course I've behaved poorly, many times. I cannot blame all of this on my father's miserable example, or my brothers' shameful role modeling. At some point in everyone's life they must step up and accept the consequences for their conduct without blaming anyone else. Unless a person does so they will never distance themselves from their childhood, when they were victims of their parents and environment. I am a winner, not because I've won, but because the struggle continues and I've chosen to battle rather than surrender.

    I have to say, I did not look forward to my father's death, when I might feel obliged to return to the scene of so much misery. When it finally arrived I simply chose not to. I did not attend his funeral, nor did I go to see him during his final days. There really wasn't much reason for me to have done so, as there will never be closure. How can any of us have closure? None of us will ever have a father or ever know our mother. None of us will ever be closer to each other than we are right now. An average man might say this is sad, but for a Warrior, it is what it is. I will not allow myself to indulge in sadness or anger, as doing so would waste energy and serve no purpose. With the exception of a very few, I do not look forward to seeing any of my siblings. We have lost the small connection we once had. My family continues to suffer from the curse of bad parenting. The gap which it creates continues to affect a person throughout their lives, and is especially evident during times of crisis.

At home my closest sister was "Nugget," whom I loved very much. This is of course not her real name, but out of love and respect for her privacy, this is how I will refer to her throughout this work. Unfortunately, even my connection with her is one which I've created via deliberate effort. She and her husband lost their firstborn son to a brain tumor. The poor kid suffered for fourteen years. Much of his life was lived in a vegetative state before biology finally took its toll. Her suffering, average mentality, and lack of spiritual grounding caused her as much trouble as her son's illness. She lost her balance and connection to the Universe and sort of went nuts. It was around this time that she told me not to call her anymore. She simply said that she was "too busy to talk on the phone." It was sad. I've learned you cannot make a person be someone who they're not, and you cannot make someone love you, no matter how much you want or need them. In typical average person fashion, she now hates everything that reminds her of her loss. She will not let him go and has suffered ever since. I do not claim to understand or know how she feels, as I've never had a son, much less lost one. I know several people who have lost children, and none of them have ever been the same since. She blames the people who never offered support, guidance, or solace, and feels justified in doing so. Tragically, it also chains her to her misery, reinforces her self-indulgence, and further compounds the ugliness that is average behavior. Her obsession now focuses upon her daughter, who by my own observation is suffering the effects of being micro-parented.

My sister Nugget was once the closest person in my life. Growing up, I did what I could to protect her, but for the most part the best way to do that was to stay away from her. When I could I'd buy her sodas at school during lunch, and sit with her. She'd sit alone on the benches in the student quad reading books. She was just like a sweet little bird, deserving much better than she received. I wish I could have done more for her. I loved her and gladly pounded the hell out of several scumbags who attempted to inappropriately hit on her. I once stuffed a thug who had disrespected her into a trashcan and rolled him down the stairs. I even punched out several thug girls who jumped her in the girl's bathroom. I felt no remorse for nailing those girls with as powerful a right hand shot as I would a guy. Although I was doing the right thing by rescuing my sister, I still had to fight all their brothers, cousins, uncles, and friends for months afterwards.

    I was speechless when she said she was just too busy to spend time talking with me on the phone. The gap she left was especially felt during my first Christmas without her. I missed her, but the Universe seemed clear. I never forced my attention upon her, or anyone. You cannot make someone love you. I never expected an apology, as that would require she admit she was wrong, and average people do not admit such truths. I acknowledge that life gave her a tough hand to play, and I cannot say I would have done any better. I can say she has chosen to indulge in her misery and extend her suffering. Like all average people, she wants everyone to set aside their lives and feel her pain to the same degree. She expects everyone to demonstrate the same sense of loss, which will never happen. She'd like to have a monument built in her son's honor, and wants validation for her decision to keep him alive as a vegetable in order to give her solace. Even though allowing him to pass would have been the Christian thing to do. Instead, her and her husband nearly lost their home, went into debt beyond recovery, and endangered their relationship. I'll bet she has not shared an intimate moment with her husband in years. She has isolated herself from him and everyone else. There's a good possibility that he's not known a tender moment or had sexual contact with anyone for the same amount of time. There is also a good possibility he's either found, or is seeking physical contact with another woman. If this is the case, my sister, in typical average person fashion, will never understand or forgive him. Were it not for their daughter, I do not see many reasons for them to continue living together. In her self-indulgence she never gave a thought to what was going to happen after the storm passed. She never considered how those who tried to help her through the crisis might react to her behavior. She is now suffering the same self-inflicted pain all average people suffer from after experiencing such a loss. They rationalize and justify everything they do and say, claiming it to be "a mother's right after the loss of a child." She believes anyone who has suffered a loss has the right to act out any way they choose, which is how all average people justify their behavior.

Much to my surprise, when my sister deliberately cut all ties to me it improved my life. I no longer had to hear, know about, or deal with any of the drama that went on in her life, which is considerable. Life seems to be getting stranger and stranger, and I never imagined things would get this far out of whack, but they have. I'm happy I live so far away and do not have to be a part of all the insanity.

Several years ago I received a letter from Nugget saying she wanted to reconnect. I guess it seems acceptable for her to reject someone, throw them out of her life, and then say, "Oops, I didn't mean it." I've discovered that time builds walls of distance, and all those years without contact kill sentimentality. All the warm fuzzy feelings I once had for her are gone. I've given up trying to explain people's behavior and my dysfunctional family. I've learned that all

96ers come with a lot of baggage and are more trouble than they are worth. It's impossible to make sense of average people's behavior. There are many things you cannot come back from, such as making accusations of sexual misconduct, cheating on a spouse, or lying and stealing from your relatives. She was once special to me and I loved her very much, but she massacred my feelings. In the end, her neurotic behavior eventually forced the removal of the rose-colored glasses I once wore when viewing her. She was just another 96er, unworthy of my affection. I've recognized that I assigned qualities to her which she did not possess. I made excuses and rationalized her decisions and behavior. Her rejection forced me to view her without the benefit of my need for affection. Time, distance, and spiritual growth altered my view of all my siblings. It was an awakening. This is why a Warrior can never go home again. Not because home is no longer there, but because he is no longer the same.

  I am grateful my sister Nugget and I were able to share as much as we did as kids. I understand the loss of her son impacted her profoundly, but I cannot claim to truly understand. I also do not understand the need or desire to have children. I don't understand the obsession to keep a child who is sick to that degree, with no hope for the future, alive. I don't understand the martyrdom role she demanded to play, or the expectation for public mourning. I never considered myself so wonderful that I wanted to reproduce myself. I chose not to have children and thank the Universe for giving me this knowledge. I've never regretted it. This is largely due to my experiences as a child. I cannot imagine why anyone who grew up as poor and abused would want to have children. I cannot imagine how anyone who grew up neglected could really believe they are qualified to be parents. Yet, this is common amongst 96ers. They yearn for someone to love them, but most importantly they desire a sense of belonging and being connected to something larger than themselves, never realizing that they always have been. They've never learned that all of us are connected to everything around us. We are the people we hate and love the most. We are those people who everyone points a finger at and uses as examples of how not to be. We are the people our mother's warned us about. My parents were not wonderful people, and they most definitely were not who I'd have chosen as parents, yet they reproduced twelve children. None of us are the products of great genetics, which makes the desire to reproduce even more absurd. Add this to the fact that aside from being comfortable, my wife and I wouldn't have anything to leave our children. Considering how much energy children take, and how expensive things are, you've got to be nuts to deliberately bring a child into this world. Every parent I've ever known wants to give their kids everything they never had, which is utterly and completely self-absorbed. They continuously give their kids the things they always wanted, but forget that the wanting was what made them struggle to succeed. By handing their kids easy access to wealth, they've removed the desire and struggle to obtain it. They've also removed the thousands of lessons learned along the way, and the discipline required to do so. Then they wonder why their children are such lazy, pitiful losers, unable to cope with life or make simple decisions. Their daughters get pregnant at fifteen and their sons become junkies. Their kids never accomplish anything and spend their adult lives waiting for their parents to die just so they can spend their inheritance. No thanks, I'll pass.

  Added to this awful reality is the aspect of sex for sport. I've told my students countless times, biology will always win. This is why priests, ministers, and nuns are constantly being exposed as fornicators. Biology and the natural desire for sex will never end, and will continue to be a source of turmoil. For example, I recently received news of my sister Nugget's husband, my brother-in-law, having a sexual liaison with a barfly in Houston. I predicted this as a possibility when I originally wrote this section of the book, and have therefore elected to post an update. I got this information from my brother Bumper, who enjoys spreading gossip and flaunting inside knowledge of unhappiness. This is due to his average person's obsession with comparing himself to others. The reason why this is a point of irritation for him is that he has been accused of being a shameless womanizer by our sisters. When he heard one of their husbands was fooling around, he actually smiled and laughed. Instead of being concerned for their marriage and happiness, he elected to spread the news. Explain that for me. It's typical average person behavior. This is another of the many habits and customs we inherited from our parents. They taught us repeatedly via countless examples to take pleasure in another person's misery. No matter who that person is. He shared this bit of awful news with me and laughed disrespectfully. I cannot imagine how he could find humor in this, but he did. Please note that these are average behaviors and not anything out of the ordinary. The ability to find joy in another person's suffering is a common trait amongst 96ers, especially if they have history with that person. It is anger disguised as humor. It's the same negative energy that exists within all average people. It's the heart and soul of all family reunions, which is a great reason to avoid them.

    I hope my brother-in-law is not fooling around. Not because I judge him, but because it would send my sister over the edge. She's a difficult person to get along with, famous for her temper and foul mouth. I doubt he'd seek an alternative sexual partner if my sister had not abandoned that aspect from their lives. He also grew up on Main Drive. We went to school together, played on the same football team, worked in the same cotton fields, and endured the same racism. He is a perfect 96er. After all these years he still harbors adolescent jealousies, resenting me for the chances I took while in high school. I nearly fell off my chair laughing when my sister told me he was still jealous, as according to him "I had lots of girlfriends in high school." His statements validate that 96ers will never stop hating, comparing, and rationalizing their indulgences. Like all average people, he compared himself to others, hating those who had what he wanted. When he looked at me he saw me through his average eyes. To him I appeared to be without a care in the world, just fooling around, having fun, and loving life. Like all 96ers, he recognized his own suffering, but never that of anyone else. He had the same opportunity to emulate admirable behavior or create his own, but instead chose to dwell in his misery. He hated me for having the courage to break out of the mold, never realizing that I was just as scared and nervous as he was. I just got tired of feeling like a fool, and took my chances despite the potential consequences of failure. He continues to criticize me today, describing me as arrogant, which is the ultimate testimony of a 96er's circle of self-imposed misery. Like all average people, he hates the person he envies. As I've said before, there is no way to help an average person, and trying to understand them is a waste of time. As usual, the best solution is the easiest. Treat them as though they are mentally handicapped children, never trusting or depending on them. Never be honest, share sincere thoughts, or reveal an indiscretion. It's best to use an alternative history filled with sunny afternoons and blue skies. Never reveal a weakness, a past mistake, a hidden desire, or a violation of ethical conduct. All average people are your potential executioners and will happily betray you. If the rumors of my brother-in-law stepping out are false, I'm happy. If they are true, I fear the day it's discovered, because of the explosion that is sure to follow. If I learned about it all the way out here in California, I can imagine what's going on closer to home. At least he had the forethought not to fool around near home, something I cannot say for my father and brothers.

Texas escapee,

don Jesus M. Ramirez

Intermission
Standing at the Edge of the Precipice

"Some say the secret of life is faith. I say it's finding freedom."

-don Jesus M. Ramirez

The tale of my escape from Texas continues in the second installment of this series: *Escape from Texas, Book 2: Journey out of the Abyss.* In the course of my journey, the lessons of the Toltec discipline have clearly demonstrated power, effectiveness, practicality, and necessity for anyone seeking spiritual freedom on this plane. This truth also extends to anyone disillusioned with today's watered-down versions of religion, or those sickened by our political, criminal justice, educational, and medical and mental health systems. Those who have always wanted to belong to something bigger than themselves, but have never found anything worthy of their mettle, are now called to action. Those seeking to grow, expand their minds, and unburden themselves of yesterday's pain, must answer the challenge. Are you ready to change? Do you no longer wish to be who you are? Are you tired of living the mundane existence of the average person? You'll have many opponents to such a decision. However, keep in mind that of all your challengers, no one and nothing is offering anything more than the same shallow, meaningless life you've always known. They'll point out the many complex concepts and criticize, but again, not be able to offer solutions. These are the average fools who take up your time and waste your energy.

I see my challenge as the implementation of a program in

which Seekers who wish to continue on the Warrior's path can find assistance in unraveling its mysteries. I invite interested individuals to contact me through Toltec Institute. Be forewarned, I have no patience for liars, cowards, frauds, or fools. I seek honest, hardworking, disciplined individuals who are sincere in their desire for spiritual freedom. My program is available to anyone who is willing to dedicate themselves, do the work, stay the course, and forge ahead. Newcomers are urged to remember that nothing worth doing is easy. I strongly advise taking a serious look at yourself before seeking my guidance. Everyone is encouraged to live their lives to the fullest, fight their fears, push their personal boundaries, and challenge what they believe. Each Seeker must determine whether to accept reality as they perceive it, or adopt another's. There are millions of 96ers who deliberately live in denial of their paranormal experiences. There are millions more who because of their lack of energy have never, and will never experience the wonderment of this precious existence. No one is required or requested to adopt another's worldview or perspective. As in death, we are all alone. Each Seeker must make their own way, as there is no single manner in which to approach knowledge. Seekers are reminded that every endeavor should be approached with caution, fully aware of the consequences and prepared to manage the possibilities. No promises are made, guaranteed, implied, or offered. I encourage you to sing louder, dance more, love, run, and play. Stop being shy and surrender to the idea that you are going to die. You have no time to waste being timid. Whether you attempt to free your spirit or not, you're going to die regardless. Those who enter these dark waters will have come to know themselves before they die. Those who don't, will die ignorant of the power they've allowed to slip through their grasp. Death is stalking all of us. This cannot be overstated. We have no guarantees. There is no assurance that tomorrow will come, and if it does, that it will be the same as today.

I'll be expecting you.

Texas escapee,

don Jesus M. Ramirez

Essential Concepts and Vocabulary

"No one will ever know you as well as you should know yourself. Until this challenge is accomplished, peace will forever be elusive and personal power a mystery."

-don Jesus M. Ramirez

Newly arriving Seekers should expect to spend as much as two or more years getting to know themselves well enough to start. A commonly overlooked rule of the Universe is that everyone must start where they are. You must begin wherever you find yourself, no matter where that is. You could be homeless and living on the streets, a prisoner in a cell, a multimillionaire in a mansion on top of a hill, or just another ordinary, timid, and scared individual. No matter, self-importance is the best and worst part of us. It is what drives us towards excellence, yet simultaneously causes the average man's destruction. The overwhelming impact self-importance has on our lives demands that this concept be addressed repeatedly throughout this work. This is a point of significance, as repetition is intentional. My objective is to illustrate the many forms in which self-importance attacks, as well as how it manipulates us to act against own higher knowledge. Those upon this journey must have an understanding of its impact before starting. To defeat self-importance one must follow directions without self-pity, as if removing a cancer. This is essential and must not be overlooked. Do not jump ahead without understanding this concept.

Countless self-proclaimed masters of the Toltec discipline

have wrongfully minimized the concept of self-importance, making it appear as though it were just a bump in the road on the path towards knowledge. Conveying the near impossible task of defeating self-importance in such a manner makes this discipline appear accessible to the masses. This is a perfect example of watering-down a discipline beyond resemblance of truth in order to make it more marketable. This is a betrayal and deliberate misrepresentation based on the desire to make a dollar. Without conquering self-importance, advancement towards power is impossible. I have met alleged Buddhist masters and leaders of religious cults who claim spiritual enlightenment, yet have no understanding of this concept. I make this a point of consequence for those who believe themselves innately advanced and beyond the average person. I have taken great care to convey this concept using many different illustrations, which will be helpful to genuine Seekers willing to set aside their egos and study them. My comprehension of this enemy came at the cost of many years of steadfast dedication, as I had no help in gaining an understanding. Consequently, it took me much longer than it will take you, because you will have a guide. It would have been impossible had I not become fanatical about it. Even so, it required years of experimentation, failure, and experience to draw from.

    Self-importance is one of the most difficult concepts to grasp, as well as one of the greatest obstacles to identify in our lives. It has always been and continues to be an extremely difficult lesson to convey to prospective students, as it goes against the grain of the average person. The near impossible task of defeating this enemy challenges what society has consistently drummed into them. Experiencing the resistance to change, along with continuous refusal to examine this aspect of their character, has caused many promising Seekers to surrender. I have watched many would-be Warriors leave in confusion, only to stumble and crash into themselves as a result of indulgence in self-importance. I do not expect many to grasp how destructive this enemy is, nor will I hold it against you when you don't. I expect you to fail. I expect you to throw this book across the room in revulsion, as it would not be average if you didn't. However, I hope that as time and life repeatedly beats you down, you, and all of those who left, will return. A wonderful aspect of this discipline is that no one is punished for being average. Averageness is the curse of being born. Keep in mind that a commonly overlooked universal rule is that no one changes because they want to. People change because they have to. As a Seeker or Pathfinder, you are fortunate, as I am also on this path. I understand how difficult it is to rein in behavior which you were told demonstrates confidence. I know how difficult it is to live like a Warrior amongst millions of lost, violent, lying, cheating, untrustworthy average people. These mindless drones will antagonize and frustrate you with their self-centered behavior. This applies tenfold to those of you who are married, have children, or are attempting to change while surrounded by a herd of average people.

Relationships are impossible with average people. This will be by far and without exception the best relationship book you will ever read. Why, you ask? Because this book teaches you how to manage your partner, while at the same time managing yourself. It teaches you to overlook most behaviors, and yet does not hold you responsible for anyone but yourself. It will teach you to *see* people as energy and determine whether you should or shouldn't interact with them. It teaches how to recognize deception and gives you the strength to cut anyone or anything from your life in an instant. You'll be amazed to discover the power you've always had, but never knew how to use. None of this is guaranteed, and no one will do it in a short while. The journey never ends, and will take the rest of your life.

The need for affection, relatives, and occupation are some of the many obstacles a Seeker faces upon their path towards knowledge. You will stumble, fall, suffer, and agonize many times throughout your life. You will be betrayed, disappointed, and lied to, and you'll make many poor decisions, as we all do. Yet, you will also see how these same events will destroy others, but not you. This discipline will give you the tools and strength of heart to continue to struggle, which is all that life will ever be. I have had to battle the same demons you'll face. I have had to learn to silence my *internal dialogue* and control my reactions. I had to train myself to respond to the message, and not the messenger or their words. I have trained myself to recognize and *read* human emotion, via learning to recognize my own. Another commonly unknown universal rule is that only those who are constantly at war against their weaknesses find peace.

I have no master other than myself. I claim no supernatural powers or knowledge. Although I have acquired much education in the academic sense, there are no titles, certificates, or degrees that matter. I do not claim to have known or met any alleged famous shaman or teacher. Anyone who bases their supposed knowledge on such claims or believes such things matter disqualifies themselves. Such an individual has not conquered their self-importance and does not understand the meaning of *detachment*, both of which are essential to this discipline. Such individuals are driven by a need for recognition, and I would not trust their quality or interpretations. There is no need to name those whom I am describing. It does however bring to mind those who have started their own churches and given themselves a title. It's amusing, pitiful, and amazing that they can find such large flocks of sheep to fleece so easily. I am as equally amused by gurus who bequeath their flocks of sheep to their children. There can be no better example of average behavior than a person wanting to make their child successful, instead of requiring them to achieve success for themselves. Why not just call them divine and be done with it. It is ridicules. I hold myself to strict universal standards because I am in this for my own benefit. Death is stalking me. I have felt it brush past me and experienced its presence. These are not just words on page for me. I choose to gather and store energy in order to fight for my own life and keep death at a distance for as long as possible. I am not in competition for recognition or public endorsement. I am not motivated by greed or pride. Death has shown me how truly worthless the trophies of average men are. As I lay dying, death showed me how meaningless everything and everyone is. Titles, money in the bank, cars, women, and positions of power mean nothing when you are dying. It is the loneliest experience one will ever know. The challenge is to face death sincerely, with the knowledge that you have lived like a Warrior and fought the best fight you could.

Another commonly unknown universal rule is that regardless of position, appearance, or social station, comparing yourself to another will only lead to strife. This is an extremely difficult concept. By not comparing yourself to other people, you are never less or more than anyone. This stores and saves an amazing amount of energy. I have provided many illustrations and relevant examples in hopes that genuine Seekers will begin to understand. There is so much to learn, but for now I will focus on man's greatest enemy; self-importance. Please note that my use of the words "man, him, himself, his, and etc." is in reference to "mankind," and not the male gender/sex. Students of this discipline already know that women make dangerous and lethal adversaries, as well as great allies. Great caution should be taken if you have made a female enemy. You are advised to remember another universal rule; no one forgets nothing.

Before we begin the journey into ourselves, it is necessary that essential concepts and vocabulary be identified, explained, and defined. Firstly, I would like to give you a picture of who "those" average people who drive you crazy are. The average man is a gigantic vulgar conglomeration of ideas and behaviors, which create an unbelievably difficult problem for themselves and the world. These contradicting and mutually exclusive ideas and behaviors are what average people consider to be special and unique about themselves. This is one of the many lies and uncorrectable mistakes the average parent makes when socializing their child. All children within our society have been lied to from birth, being told they were wonderful and unique, but in reality they are as common as rocks, and just as uninteresting. The average man's view of the world, along with his opinions of himself, is twisted. His reality is based on lies and half-truths. His views and interactions with the world are nothing more than an expression of self-promoting desires and delusions. He spends his entire life wanting more, as it has become his nature to do so. He is driven by these cravings and the feelings that he believes their fruition will bring. This self-centeredness manufactures a completely delusional self-concept that demands it be catered to, nurtured, comforted, and stroked like a mother would a neurotic baby. The need for the average man to have his narcissism fed is based on a desperate neverending need for validation. His self-deception and desires feed and validate his prejudices. This is what average people call, normal. The average man wants what he wants and will use religion, the law, violence, and any other advantage or accessible resource to gain it. He makes no apology for his vanity, pride, or greed. This applies to land, property, titles, money, power, or other people. The Southern plantation slave masters proved that greed, fed by fraudulent claims of divine rights, can lead a nation to war.

According to an independent study, the primary reason why small businesses fail is due to employee theft and fraud. The consensus is that the average employee will either create or take advantage of an opportunity to steal.

- Twenty percent of employees deliberately plan to steal from their employers, and will create an opportunity to do so.

- Forty percent of employees will occasionally give into temptation to steal if the opportunity arises.

- Twelve percent of employees will commit fraud regardless of circumstance.

- Twenty-four percent of employees will commit fraud if they have the need, opportunity, and believe they can rationalize their behavior.

Statistics concerning the behavior of individuals employed in larger companies is said to be remarkably similar. The primary difference is that smaller businesses are incapable of withstanding the financial losses accompanied with such behavior. Although the intention of this study was to investigate the source of small business failure, it succeeded in exposing the nature of the average person, as the general population and that of the workforce are one and the same. According to this study, 96 percent of the workforce are compromised and fall into one of the 4 categories listed above. It is for this reason that I have coined the term "96er," which is just another name for average people. This same study also unintentionally revealed that only four percent of people will not steal or commit fraud, regardless of need, opportunity, temptation, circumstance, ability to rationalize, and etc. I refer to these individuals as "Four Percentors."

Average people, or 96ers, are unashamedly unethical in every aspect of their lives. It is indeed the trademark of a 96er to be randomly cruel, kind, loving, or hateful. They justify and rationalize every act and every thought, no matter how bizarre, because it's what they want, or worse, how they feel at the time. In their minds there is no need for explanation or reason, other than their own personal desire. Their narrow-mindedness, prejudices, and ignorance is easily justified and rationalized. An average person can justify stealing from their family as easily as they can rationalize cheating on their spouse. Furthermore, average people can do so, so effectively, as to completely wipe away guilt and remorse. They are ethical vacuums without a moral barometer. They have taken the shamelessly hedonistic marketing catchphrase, "What happens in Vegas, stays in Vegas," to the extreme. Such hedonism rapidly leads to self-destruction. The truth, as everyone knows, is that there are consequences for such behaviors. In addition to this is the universal rule that no one forgets nothing. This is especially true with law enforcement.

The recent reports of young American soldiers killing innocent Iraqi men, women, and children demonstrate and validate how under the right circumstances, average people can justify and rationalize any action. The average person staggers and stuns the world with acts of premeditated cruelty. It is mindboggling for many to understand how allegedly "good" young American soldiers, become dehumanized in such a short time, as to commit these hideous crimes while serving their country. The average person manufactures within themselves limitless inconsistencies and contradictions, and then rationalizes and justifies them. No matter what the problem or how unethical their solution, their self-deception is equally as bizarre. The average man, fueled by self-importance, is a walking and talking contradiction. He operates and is governed by emotions in his endless search and hunger for validation.

These unpleasant and disgusting tendencies are not limited to the poor uneducated masses, but are equally as noticeable amongst the so-called "enlightened" population. Race, ethnicity, social and economic status, job title, position, religious background, education level, gender, family connections, and etc., have no relevance in any regards to the quality or inferiority of a person's character. In addition, they have no positive effect on the average man's ability to deceive himself.

Man's destructive self-importance, which is constantly reinforced, is a Warrior's greatest enemy. This is so because it exists within himself. It will attack him in so many ways that it's impossible to identify them all. A Seeker will be bombarded and machine-gunned relentlessly by his own weaknesses (biases, insecurities, stereotypes, and etc.), which I refer to as "personal demons." Simultaneously he will be attacked by average people, who use what they consider to be "common sense," to rationalize and justify their behavior. The new and untrained Seeker will want to give as good as he got, earn respect, and get some payback. The urge to, do as the Romans do, when in Rome, will be difficult to resist, yet that is the challenge. Indeed, a new Seeker will have to battle himself, while battling the average person. This will be a difficult period, as readjustment without constant reinforcement is nearly impossible. The truth is that the only real way to learn this discipline is to live it. In order to live it, one must have an example and constant reinforcement of this discipline's many facets. A Seeker needs his teacher's energy in order to grasp and see the discipline applied in normal life situations. There are no shortcuts and those who truly wish to live as Warriors need continuous reinforcement. This extreme difficulty is why those who elect to undertake such a challenge are called Warriors. As Warriors they must go to war against the socialization that has kept them bound, and continues to bind the rest of the world. The challenge seems nearly impossible, as those who dare to accept it are also products of this twisted society. As such they must constantly battle the brainwashing and propaganda they endured, as well as the ever-present pressure to assimilate. One of the most seemingly insurmountable obstacles one on this path must face is that of unresolved childhood issues. The heart wrenching and painful discoveries hidden within the souls of many Seekers are often devastating. Another unknown universal rule is that acceptance is much more important than understanding. Therefore, the challenge for all new Seekers is to identify these unresolved childhood issues and document events in as much detail as possible. They must include every detail, including time, place, what they felt, what they saw, and etc. One of the most important aspects of this task will be to recall those involved, noting what role they played, who helped, who refused to help, and etc. It is paramount that a Seeker does this knowing that they do not need to understand, but only document. You should not attempt this unless you are under the guidance of a genuine Warrior. Social workers, counselors, therapists, and psychiatrists are frauds. Stay away from these average people if at all possible. They hide behind alleged qualifications earned via intellectualization in academia, rather than real-life experience. This cannot be overstated and must not be attempted unless you have a solid support system. I suggest you avail yourself of groups such as Hospice, Alcoholics Anonymous (AA), Narcotics Anonymous (NA), Veterans Affairs (VA), and other survivors and support groups, including those of elderly and widowed individuals, and etc.

As a new Seeker, interacting with 96ers will undoubtedly be your greatest challenge. For this reason I have dedicated much of this work to their fundamental management and defeat. I suggest thinking of the average person as being mentally deficient or mentally handicapped, as mentally and emotionally inept is an accurate description. In addition to this, interacting with them from this perspective will assist in eliminating any expectations you might have had of them. Never share personal experiences, mistakes, or flaws of character with 96ers. If you must talk to someone, travel out of town, find a social gathering place, and speak with a stranger. Never reveal your indiscretions, accidents, or fantasies with anyone who is part of your daily existence. All 96ers are your competitors and willing executioners.

All average people hate being challenged, questioned, or contradicted. They demand everyone support their pompous and delusional concepts, no matter how false. They seek clear and easy answers to any question, no matter how complex the issue. They want simple instructions which they can agree with, but also does not challenge their concept of reality. They hate to be embarrassed or shown up, and always see themselves as being good, while seeing others as being bad. They demand immediate justice and punishment when it comes to others, but kindness and understanding when it comes to themselves or their loved ones. Average parents will condone murder, theft, assault, molestation, or rape by their children, but will not tolerate any infraction of rules by anyone else. They desire fame and public recognition, but refuse to offer congratulations, even when it's obviously due. They crave power, authority, and lordship over the masses, while longing to be flattered and have their asses kissed to the point of religious idolatry.

Self-importance is the best and worst part of us. It is what drives us towards excellence, yet simultaneously causes the average man's destruction. The average man who is seen as successful has learned to use these weaknesses to manipulate, control, and direct others. These are the so-called leaders of society, and they have learned via older manipulators how to use the average man's weaknesses against him. These individuals have developed the use of language, and adopted the right image in order to position themselves in authority. However, they are essentially and fundamentally the same creature they despise. They are extremely dangerous and personify self-importance. These individuals will not be found at antiwar demonstrations or working towards social justice. Not only do they not have such feelings, but they are aware that behaving in such a manner would not serve them. It would be impossible to manipulate the rich masses if they gave the impression of having different values and beliefs. These powerful 96ers hide behind masks of respectability and call themselves "conservatives."

A new Seeker must accept that interacting honestly with average people is hopeless, impossible, and pointless, yet that is whom he must share the world with. This is why the Toltec discipline and the Warrior's path is applicable, empowering, and enriching. Exploring your own self-importance will take years, countless battles, victories, and defeats. It is why I call myself and anyone upon this path, a Warrior.

Self-importance

Self-importance comes at you in many shapes and disguised in many forms. Let's examine this complex challenge, starting with a definition. Keep in mind that self-importance is the best and worst of us. It is what drives us towards excellence, yet simultaneously causes the average man's destruction. It is also the main cause of energy drainage, and the very heart of a 96er. This concept is not easy to understand, nor is the subtleness of its destructive potential. As in all disciplines, the journey is what makes the experience so valuable and inspiring. You will have to unravel many challenging ideas to answer your own questions, just as I did. Those of you who read this material will have an edge, but only if you apply the discipline. These concepts are extremely difficult to grasp. There are no shortcuts, and you must learn them via steadfast discipline while engaging in a never-ending struggle.

I suggest every Seeker begin by gaining an understanding of *detachment*, *forbearance*, *timing*, *inner silence*, and *will*. Without these basic and essential tools you will never discover how to defeat self-importance. You must be in touch with the reality of your impending death, knowing that you have no time to waste indulging in excesses or deprivation of pleasures. I urge every Seeker to volunteer at Hospice and visit VA hospitals via their ongoing volunteer programs. This must be done consistently for at least a year. However, Seekers must be aware that dealing with someone else's death is in no way comparable to dealing with your own. These experiences simply assist in the development of understanding and learning *detachment*. There is no other way to attain an understanding of death, other than to face your own and temporarily win. Those who have, know the horrible and tremendous impact which such an experience has upon one's development. This is why learning *detachment* is essential. This cannot be overstated.

Detachment is a difficult concept for new Seekers to understand, as they often confuse it with an average person's disconnect and calloused indifference, learned via brutalization. To develop an understanding of this concept I would suggest considering the act of judging others, which is a major component in energy drainage. If you make a critical judgment of a person or situation, you are not *detached*. If you feel insulted or angered when someone makes fun of you, you are suffering from injured pride, and expect others to see you as you see yourself. You are not *detached* and are "expecting," thus setting yourself up for disappointment. You should have nothing to defend; no pride, no ego, no nation, no creed, and no one other than yourself. There should be no one important enough to make you feel insulted or complimented. As long as no one physically harms you or someone you love, you have nothing to defend. If this happens, then you are now on a completely different level, and should defend yourself enthusiastically. Yes, there are many exceptions, and as in all things regarding this discipline, there are no black and white answers. You can decide how far to take it from there. Remember, you must survive on this plane, and if you harm, cripple, or kill someone, there will be consequences. No matter what you do, you must do it to your advantage. It must serve you. It cannot come from anger or a need for revenge. Study the laws of self-defense. This must be considered carefully. Also, note that when I say, "someone you love" I am referring to a husband defending his wife, or a parent their child, and etc. This does not apply to loudmouth average fools of any gender or relation who instigate altercations, regardless of whether or not they claim the title of "friend."

If you are going to do anything outside of the law, you must do it alone, and be prepared to live with it for the rest of your life in secret. You must also be fully prepared to live with the consequences. It won't be easy. Prisons are filled with allegedly "good" individuals, who lost it during a moment of anger and killed or crippled someone. If you are involved in a physical altercation, you must never lose your judgment, and always manage your emotions. It will be the clear thinker who wins the battles, and sometimes the war. Remember, Warriors do not always win. Do not expect justice. Cops are dangerous average people with a lot of authority. Never give a cop a personal reason to see you jailed.

If you find yourself feeling sorry for someone, you are indulging in self-importance, and are not *detached*. This behavior is a reflection of your desire for others to feel sorry for you, or to be like you. While an average man sees someone and feels sorry for their position or circumstance, a Warrior only *sees* a person who is engaged in the consequences of their decisions, and therefore does not feel sorry for them. If you feel sorry for someone because they appear ignorant, you are indulging in self-importance. This is a reflection of your desire for an individual who you see as being ignorant to be more like you. You are setting yourself up as the example or standard of how everyone should be. A Warrior will discover the many forms of self-importance as he comes across the subtle and varied manners in which this enemy presents itself. It is a never-ending struggle which never gives respite.

One of the many benefits of this discipline is the ability to *read* others. The ability to do so, and do so correctly, will make you feel powerful. As much as feeling powerful helps, it can also hurt you if you permit yourself to be deceived by it.

After examining some common aspects of self-importance, it

is not difficult to see how defeating it is a near impossible challenge. The many disguises and forms in which it presents itself in our lives are overwhelming. Keep in mind that although absolutes are much easier to understand, this is not how life presents itself. The test is in monitoring yourself. Defeating self-importance is not a game, and you must become deadly serious about doing so. Developing a guardian who will help, watch over, and protect you is essential. You must become your own guardian and best friend. Of all the people in the world, you must learn to love yourself the most, but never allow yourself to indulge in self-destructive, egotistical thinking or behavior. Great care must be taken in the development of your guardian, less it becomes a guard. There are essential differences between the two that a Seeker must grasp and fully understand. This is another difficult concept, and will require great study.

The challenge of defeating self-importance is never-ending and will be very difficult. It is for this reason that I have incorporated the use of the "seven deadly sins," or the "cardinal sins." These seven sins have been used since early Christian times by religious leaders to educate and assist people in monitoring and managing their behavior. I have adopted their use for the same reasons. However, I place no religious value in any of them. Sin is merely another word for failing to hit the mark or perform to your own standards. The objective is to save energy via avoiding the consequences of self-destructive behaviors. I have no belief in a religious God, and I don't believe there is a paradise where I will be safe, protected, and never suffer. After many years of experience, I have discovered that the seven deadly sins serve as an excellent foundation, with which a Seeker can grasp hold of self-importance. They assist in a basic categorization of the innumerable forms in which self-importance presents itself. Readers are advised that although I place no religious value in any of these "sins," society and the law have similar ideas of morality, crime, and punishment. You should remember that no one forgets nothing, and no one forgives anything. If you've wronged someone, you should expect consequences. Don't expect forgiveness, and don't forget those you've wronged. I can assure you that they will not forget you. Once the fight begins, it won't matter who threw the first punch or fired the first shot. Violence is a normal part of existence in the United States. We are a hostile and bigoted country. I will not paint romanticized pictures for you, nor will I attempt to comfort you by adding to your delusions. If you've harmed, wronged, or betrayed another human being, you must remain alert for the rest of your life, or theirs. There is no such thing as real forgiveness amongst average people. If you are a parent who has molested, abused, or neglected your child, be prepared to face them as they grow stronger, older, and bolder. The effects of child abuse last forever. The effects of bad parenting never stop hurting a person and continue for the rest of their lives. It will not be pleasant. I suggest everyone read the book *Toxic Parents* by Susan Forward. It's filled with great information and illustrations. It is not a nice book, but it may help you manage your demons.

Seven Deadly Sins

Seekers are encouraged to examine the following sins for ways to choose less energy draining responses to situations. The objective is to store and maintain energy so as to better face the powers of the Universe.

- Pride
- Greed
- Envy
- Wrath
- Lust
- Gluttony
- Sloth

Pride

Definition:

1. A high or inordinate opinion of one's own dignity, importance, merit, or superiority, whether as cherished in the mind or as displayed in bearing, conduct, etc.

2. The state or feeling of being proud.

3. A becoming or dignified sense of what is due to oneself or one's position or character; self-respect; self-esteem.

4. Pleasure or satisfaction taken in something done by or belonging to oneself or believed to reflect credit upon oneself.

5. Something that causes a person or persons to be proud.

Synonyms: Arrogance, conceit, haughtiness, loftiness, pomposity, pretension, superciliousness, vanity, dignity, ego, honor, pleasure, satisfaction, self-confidence, self-respect, egoism, egotism, gratification, pridefulness, self-love, self-regard, self-satisfaction, self-sufficiency, self-worth, amour-propre, ego trip, self-admiration, self-glorification, self-trust.

Antonyms: Depression, gloom, melancholy, misery, pain, sadness, sorrow, trouble, unhappiness, woe, disgrace, humility, modesty, shyness, timidity, meekness, reserve.

Pride comes disguised in many forms. It is the reason why 96ers react to insults and perceived threats. Average people are very sensitive about many things, but no one knows for sure what those things will be at any given moment. They themselves do not know how they will react to anything, as they always react according to how they feel at the moment. They live their lives led by their emotions. You must *read* whomever you are speaking with, as well as everyone around them. Whenever you come across arrogant loudmouths, remember that they are not really proud, just stupid. Avoid stupid people of all ethnicities, genders, ages, and social and economic levels. If you must interact, do so without drinking. Don't go any place they might wish to show off, as they may decide to use you as their scapegoat.

Early Christian leaders have identified humility as being the opposite of pride. I discard religious views on most matters. Organized religion is a business designed to keep average people obedient and fill the pockets of church leaders, while simultaneously perpetuating government and society. In prewar Germany religion was used to motivate women into having more children, so as to fill military ranks. I've known many priests, pastors, ministers, and etc., and none have impressed me. A Warrior could only be humble with and amongst other Warriors. Having to operate on this plane, it would not serve him to appear humble amongst average people, as they would interpret his humility as weakness, and respond with insult or assault. In the world of average men it is better to appear competent, mysterious, and potentially dangerous. The only instance in which it would serve a Warrior to appear humble is if he were practicing *stalking*, and wished to present himself as such. A Warrior must be able to camouflage himself and become whoever he wishes. The key is to behave or act in a humble manner. Doing so is nothing as nonsensical as sincerely feeling humble. It's a Warrior's strategy to do what serves him, when it serves him. The key element in his strategy is *detachment* from what 96ers think or say. A *detached* Warrior has the potential to be an extremely dangerous adversary. As a Seeker working to attain understanding of a Warrior's strategies, you should always keep in mind the manipulative nature of 96ers. Those in authority have a great dexterity for manipulating others via fine words, such as honor and duty. Do not allow yourself to be fooled. Old men send young men to war in order to get richer and guarantee that their children won't have to fight the wars they've started and perpetuated. It's the history of every nation. Most politicians have never fired a shot in defense of themselves or anyone else. These individuals are perfect examples of average people.

I believe the opposite of pride is loneliness, emptiness, hopelessness, despair, and mourning. A lack of self-esteem is a multifaceted issue, which is why it's almost impossible to help someone find it. I believe the best way to teach someone self-esteem is to give them responsibility. Only through learning how to manage an assigned task and being accountable for it will they learn self-esteem. There must also be an element of danger and serious consequences for failing. Otherwise the experience will be meaningless. The essence of self-esteem is autonomy, which can only be learned via responsibility.

Despite what the average person would like to believe, the only way to learn anything is through action. There are thousands of recently graduated psychiatrists, psychologists, therapists, counselors, social workers, and etc., who believe their education fully qualifies them to offer advice to their clients. In truth, the most difficult challenge many have ever faced themselves was leaving home and getting daddy to pay for their education. I've known many such individuals who consider themselves professionals, when in reality they are simply frauds taking money under false pretenses. They repeat what others have told them is true, and most of those people have learned what they claim to know via reading about it in a book. They never experienced it themselves, nor do they know their alleged truth to be real. Their words are mere transference of misinformation, which no one ever bothered to verify. Such behavior is dishonest, fraudulent, and a violation of universal laws. Higher education generates thousands of deluded average people, pretending to be something they're not. Therapists, counselors, social workers, and alleged mental health experts of all sorts should rarely be trusted. Priests and nuns who counsel about sexual matters should be laughed at.

Greed

Definition:

1. Excessive or rapacious desire, especially for wealth or possessions.

Synonyms: Avarice, grasping, grudging, illiberal, mercenary, miserly, parsimonious, selfish, devouring, gluttonous, ravenous, stingy, excess, gluttony, hunger, longing, selfishness, acquisitiveness, avidity, covetousness, craving, cupidity, eagerness, edacity, esurience, indulgence, intemperance, piggishness, rapacity, ravenousness, voracity.

Antonyms: Apathy, charitable, generosity, munificent, philanthropy, sharing, full, satisfied, dislike, distaste, indifference, benevolence.

I find greed to be the major motivator with all 96ers, which makes it the easiest tool to use against them. Greed can be used to move mountains amongst average people. It can be used to start wars, make peace, build bridges, and establish elaborate schemes which could serve a Warrior greatly. The key is to remember that a Warrior must be able to live amongst 96ers, but never be one of them. A Warrior in the process of executing a plan must be able to exhibit all the symptoms of a greedy individual, without feeling them. He is able to do so because he knows that in the end it doesn't matter. He knows the Universe will provide him with prosperity if that is what he desires. The difference is that he will never be a slave to it, or to what it brings. *Detachment* is the key to his freedom and peace of mind. As mentioned before, the concept of *detachment* requires great effort to understand and implement. This is where having a teacher helps. If a Warrior chooses, he can involve himself in projects of any nature. It must be done with complete awareness and acceptance of the consequences. He must have an ace up his sleeve and an alternative plan in the event one is necessary. He must also be wary of betrayal, knowing that greed is a 96er's greatest weakness, as well as justification for horrible actions. New Seekers are reminded that betrayal always comes from within the group.

Early Christian leaders have identified charity as being the opposite of greed. I disagree. For a Warrior, giving things away has nothing to do with being charitable. It is once again based upon pleasure, indifference, or deliberate manipulation of a situation or a person. When a Warrior gives something, he does so for completely different reasons than an average person. I often direct my students to give things away to strangers, knowing they'll never see them again nor receive anything in exchange. This helps new Seekers learn to squash their self-importance and develop *detachment*. I suggest approaching this exercise deliberately with the intention of giving away your greed. This teaches new Seekers to place less value on money, and focus on the knowledge of how easily 96ers can be manipulated. It also feeds into a 96er's fantasies of magic and the goodness of people. Seekers are reminded to be wary of generous 96ers. Money in this society comes with a lot of strings. Once you discover what a 96er wants, you've got a direct line into their mind. Next to greed, pride is a 96er's greatest enemy. Remember the adage from the Sixties, "Cash, grass, or ass, nobody rides for free." Throughout history sex has often been used as currency, typically by women. Seekers are reminded to be wary of women who ply them with sexual favors. I repeatedly warn my male students that women do not offer sex without strings. Even those who don't want marriage will ask for something. Society has conditioned women to view sex differently than men. I warn my female students that if they bed an average man, he will typically consider them to be his property. This never has pleasant results.

Envy

Definition:

1. A feeling of discontent or covetousness with regard to another's advantages, success, possessions, etc.

2. The feeling of antagonism towards someone because of some good which they enjoy but which one does not have oneself.

3. An object of envious feeling.

Synonyms: Hatred, ill will, malice, prejudice, resentment, rivalry, backbiting, coveting, covetousness, enviousness, grudge, grudging, lusting, malevolence, maliciousness, malignity, opposition, spite, evil eye, green-eyed monster, grudgingness, invidiousness, jaundiced, resentfulness.

Antonyms: Friendliness, like, liking, love, loving, comfort, confidence, contentedness, good will, kindness, pleasure, indifference.

The envy of an average person is intermingled with pride and greed. It is a black potion of veil low frequency emotion that provides the justification for many of the world's evils. It attacks 96ers like water carries wetness. It is almost impossible to distinguish one of these weaknesses from other average behavior.

Early Christian leaders have identified love as being the opposite of envy. I don't agree with this analogy. Nor do I agree with the common belief that hate is the opposite of love. I don't believe love is the opposite of anything. It is unique in its qualities and just as difficult to find. Within the context of this common belief I find indifference to be a more suitable opposite to love. Any person who has experienced indifference can attest to the difficulty of both facing and accepting it. Think of all those good Southern descendant of European immigrant (DOEI) Christians throughout history, who stood by watching while thousands of people of color were beaten, jailed, and murdered. It was their indifference that condemned thousands to suffer and die under the yoke of racism, poverty, and government oppression. This example should serve as a warning to all genuine Seekers. Religious beliefs have never overpowered bigotry, nor have they instilled physical courage.

    I believe the opposite of envy is sincere joy for someone else's success or happiness. Such joy can only be experienced by a Warrior who has steadfastly followed this path for at least five to six years. This is the approximate time required to develop the necessary *detachment* from your own weaknesses. During this stage a Seeker also bridges their disconnection and sheds the layers of calloused indifference created via a lifetime of brutalization. Envy has many layers, but its basic form is easy to identify in your behavior. If you are not genuinely happy for another's success because you feel you deserve it, or because you feel you're better, more gifted, or superior in anyway, then you are enslaved by envy. None of these concepts are black and white, nor are they easy to identify. Each of these very common weaknesses requires tremendous concentration and fanatical attention.

Wrath

Definition:

1. Strong, stern, or fierce anger; deeply resentful indignation; ire.

2. Vengeance or punishment as the consequence of anger.

Synonyms: Acrimony, asperity, conniption, dander, displeasure, exasperation, flare-up, fury, hate, hatefulness, huff, indignation, ire, irritation, madness, offense, passion, rage, resentment, rise, stew, storm, temper, vengeance.

Antonyms: Calm, calmness, delight, ease, glee, happiness, kindness, liking, love, peace, pleasure.

Great care should be given to this emotion. However, it is important to note that not all anger is destructive. Anger can serve to assist you in times of crisis. A Warrior can learn to use it to help shut off his *internal dialogue* and hide his energy. When a Warrior learns to manage his anger, it becomes fury, and *focused* fury is a powerful and very useful weapon against the *unknowable* entities that cross our path unexpectedly. Anger becomes a weakness and is self-destructive when we engage it in response to feelings of indignation, self-righteousness, pride, greed, or envy.

Early Christian leaders have identified patience as being the opposite of wrath. I disagree with this analogy intensely. I believe the opposite of wrath is indifference. If a Warrior feels indifference when faced with the *unknowable*, then he is ready to manage himself in such a manner as to be able to survive the confrontation. When he can experience indifference intermixed with controlled fury, then he may not only survive, but win. Japanese martial artists refer to this state of mind as Mushin, which translates to "no mind." It is achieved during combat when a Warrior is only in the moment, not thinking about reacting or about what to do next. The actions of his opponent dictate and direct his responses, so no thought is required. I teach my students to respond from a position of no thought, in which there is no distance in time from the moment one sees an opening to the point one takes a counter shot. Much concentration must be given to questions regarding this concept. Years and many tests may be required to master this challenge.

Lust

Definition:

1. Intense sexual desire or appetite without idealized or spiritual feelings.

2. Uncontrolled or illicit sexual desire or appetite; lecherousness.

3. A passionate or overmastering desire or craving.

4. A lust for power of pleasure.

5. Ardent enthusiasm; zest; relish.

Synonyms: Craving, desire, excitement, fervor, greed, hunger, libido, longing, yearning, sensuality, thirst, animalism, aphrodisia, appetence, avidity, carnality, concupiscence, covetousness, cupidity, eroticism, itch, lasciviousness, lechery, lewdness, licentiousness, prurience, salaciousness, salacity, sensualism, urge, wantonness, weakness.

Antonyms: Apathy, dislike, distaste, hate, hatred, chastity, purity, restraint, aversion, disenchantment, disgust, loathing.

I have a problem classifying lust as a weakness in the context of average people. Thoughts of sexual conquests are fed into our minds on a continuous basis via our eyes. These images are then transferred into how women dress and display their bodies. I cannot find fault in a young man wanting to bed every young girl that via her manner of dress and behavior is suggesting a possible liaison. I have no religious ax to grind, and I do not believe sex is sinful or wrong. However, there are certain boundaries and practical questions we must consider. Before I embark on this discussion I want to remind readers that I do not have "value judgment" on women or men who have multiple sex partners. Powerful men and women throughout history have considered bedding multiple partners a part of being in power. But, as I said, there are boundaries. I teach my students not to lie to potential partners in order to facilitate sexual relations. I instruct them to be honest. Yet at the same time, I also instruct them to offer an alternative personal history and disconnect from their past. To an average person or newly arrived Seeker this may seem contradictory. A Warrior however, knows that this is strategy and deliberate action with the intention of expending the least amount of energy. Always keep in mind that the overall objective is to gather and store energy. I advise my students that to lie to someone who has genuine feelings towards them, while they do not reciprocate those feelings, is wrong. It is also unnecessary in today's society. For example, most young people who desire sex will not hesitate or give morality a second thought. Most of those who do hesitate only do so out of fear of the potential consequences. I also advise my students to be direct about what they do and do not want. If a person is not prepared to enter a relationship, then I suggest they say so. If they do not want to have an exclusive relationship, then I suggest they be upfront about this. If by doing so, the individual who they are pursuing refuses to engage them sexually, then so be it. At least that person will have the opportunity to move on, knowing their situation. If they choose to stay, which I believe most will, they will do so with a clear understanding of what is real. Regardless of behavior or action, a genuine student of this discipline would neither suffer remorse or guilt. Therefore, these suggestions are not based upon morality, but strategy with the intention of expending the least amount of energy. It is not strategic to create enemies via sexual conquests under false pretenses. My students are obligated to remember that everyone is responsible for their conduct. Precautions should be taken to avoid transmitting sexual illnesses.

Serial womanizers, or "players," are untrustworthy. I would never trust anyone who habitually lies to women in order to bed them. Nor would I be willing to continue an association with such an individual on any level. My reason for doing so is simple; I could not trust them to be honest with me, and I do not suffer cowards, liars, or fools. The world of a Warrior must be compact, disciplined, and clear of emotional baggage. Every individual already has plenty of baggage to deal with, without bringing more into their lives by lying to their sex partner.

Another important point in regards to this subject is that women become energetically connected to the men they bed. I will not go into detail at this time, as it is lengthy. However, let it suffice to say that a female interested in bedding a potential partner must ensure the person is worthy. In all likelihood, they will be connected to that person for the rest of their lives. I am not suggesting women should be celibate or remain virgins. I am however suggesting caution and a high level of selectivity about whom they choose to bed. I know it has become more sociably acceptable to have multiple partners. This will change, just as other customs have throughout history. It is also a matter of quality verses quantity. Sexual relations with someone whom you have genuine feelings for is a spiritually uplifting experience, whereas random and casual sex becomes something to hide. The objective is to not add unnecessary baggage to your life. This can potentially become very troublesome in the future. If her past is well-known, a woman will be stuck with the history of her behavior, as will her husband. Women should realize that the average man's ego cannot withstand such a blow. Female Seekers are forewarned. If you've had multiple partners and your husband knows about these experiences, problems will occur. This is one of the best arguments for erasing your past. Do not make your husband your social worker or counselor, it won't work. Keep your sexual history secret and out of areas of discussion. As an illustration, I made a rule with my wife to never share details, names, places, and etc., about our prior relationships. I simply stated that I did not want to know how many lovers she had before I met her. Any time this topic comes up I always repeat the same thing, "I don't want to know. That was before I met you, and it has nothing to do with our relationship." This eliminates hours of arguing and saves tons of potentially wasted energy. Today, after over 25 years of marriage, it has become one of the good habits we've developed. When she behaves in a jealous manner or wants to know one of my ex-girlfriend's names, I say in a lighthearted manner, "I've been married so long I can't remember anyone else's name but yours." It always eases the tension and gets her to smile, because she knows I'm kidding. Seekers who haven't been in relationships for as long need only change the words to utilize this tactic. For example, "The first time I saw you, I fell so in love I forgot everyone's name but yours." The objective is to keep the peace and save energy. In an average relationship, one of the couple must surrender their ego in order to keep the marriage from blowing up. As much as everyone says they want honesty, they cannot handle it. This often happens with women who were popular in their youth. Jealously becomes a major and never-ending problem in relationships. I advise everyone who wishes to be happily married to move away from their hometown into another state. This is especially significant if you partied a lot in your youth and had multiple sex partners. No man wants a woman who has slept with men they know. It creates endless problems of jealously and may be the cause of a breakup. During the settlement of the West it was common practice for lonely men to marry "working girls." Many lonely men married women who worked in brothels and saloons. However, those were very different times and circumstances. Today, this leads to angry and jealous outbursts of violence. Another point to consider is that a woman will not want her children to know her past. Average people make terrible parents. They talk about everyone they know, and will either tell their children directly, or their children will overhear them. The next thing you know it will be going around in school, and then your kids will hear about it. It will be the cause of many very embarrassing and humiliating problems. It's best to think long-term and be very selective about whom you bed. Anyone who has been the subject of gossip will understand how damaging and painful it is. Many people are in jail or in the ground because someone repeated something they heard about someone they didn't know, and then did so at the wrong time and place.

There have been thousands of people who've been undone as a result of their involvement in inappropriate or illegal sexual liaisons. We've seen church ministers, politicians, celebrities, doctors, lawyers, and etc., caught with someone other than their spouse. I will not point fingers or pass judgment, as doing so would serve no purpose. I will only say that those who follow this path, regardless of gender or sexual preference, will attract many possible suitors. Individuals with an excess of energy are very alluring, and as such, you will have many opportunities to engage in new relationships, as well as play outside of existing ones. If you decide to cheat I advise caution, discretion, and complete secrecy. Never have an accomplice cover or lie for you, and always let your partner know that you are cheating and the consequences would be severe if exposed. I would suggest restraint rather than a foolproof plan.

For female Seekers I suggest finding a male counselor/adviser, not another woman. Yes, it's true that you'll want to feel safe, secure, and be able to relate to your counselor. However, you must ask yourself whether you want a friend or someone who will be honest with you. Do you want someone to cosign your misery, problems, and experiences, or would you prefer someone who can actually enlighten you and help you understand men? Every woman in the entire world has been conditioned to respond to men via their upbringing and experiences with their father. All women are conditioned to nurture, revere, and subject themselves to men. This is not an attack, just a description. All women, depending on their upbringing and religious background, have baggage regarding men to some degree or another. A woman who has been married will not be as able to assist you with your relationship as a man who has been married. Yes, it's true that it will be uncomfortable and difficult to find someone to talk with, which is why you can contact me. However, it is important to keep in mind that talking about sex, relationships, mistakes, and etc., should be difficult. It should be a growing experience. Keep in mind that no one changes because they want to. They change because they have to. Average people don't ever really change. They just run out of gas. If you are uncomfortable, then you are in the right place. However, for your protection, establish boundaries and stay *grounded*. Students should be wary of transferring their emotions to their counselor. Sexual transgressions are serious violations of ethics. Serious consequences can be expected when the Universe seeks its balance.

Early Christian leaders have listed chastity as being the opposite of lust. I believe an absence of sexual desire is as negative as an absence of any other natural instinct. Such matters are too complex to give simple suggestions or directions. Much will have to be considered, as well as many points and situations examined. I would suggest continued study and analysis.

Gluttony

Definition:

1. Excessive eating and drinking.

2. To endure or perform a task of a specific nature.

Synonyms: Craving, demand, fondness, greed, hunger, overeat, overfeed, overstock, oversupply, flood, gorge, cram, stuff, inclination, longing, lust, passion, penchant, propensity, stomach, taste, thirst, weakness, willingness, yearning, zeal, zest, appetence, appetency, itch, liking, proclivity, ravenousness, relish, urge, voracity.

Antonyms: Apathy, disinclination, dislike, hate, hatred, indifference, lethargy, antipathy, aversion, abstain, curb, disgust, distaste, loathing, repulsion, revulsion.

Individuals who excessively overeat have emotional issues. They have become habituated to behaving in certain manners, and do so without thinking. A Warrior does not feel the need to overeat or horde anything. He knows the Universe will reward him with more food, opportunity, and etc. A Warrior is generous towards those within his circle. There is no sense of desperation — no need to cling or squeeze the life and love out of anything or anyone. A Warrior touches the world gently, with care and the assurance that there is plenty more to enjoy. He applies this confidence to everything in his relationships, or his eating for that matter. He monitors and manages his desires, knowing the real joys of life come in small packages and quantities.

Early Christian leaders have identified temperance as being

the opposite of gluttony. For the average person, moderation of an indulgence may suffice as an inverse. A Warrior however, is absent of the need to horde or overindulge. He knows his personal power will provide him with all he desires and more. The endless yearning to have more is an integral, innate aspect of 96ers. This characteristic is one of the many horrors that poison them. They are infected with pride, greed, envy, wrath, and lust. These weaknesses become so entangled with gluttony, they are impossible to separate. The endless indulgence of the average person gives way to enumerable problems. In their compulsive quest for more, they indulge in comparisons, which only lead to more destructive behavior. It is a never-ending cycle of misery. Much to the world's chagrin, this inevitably leads to spiritual decay, which spreads like a lethal virus. This includes criminal and anti-social behaviors, ranging from gossip to murder. According to research, the major cause of crime occurs when people compare what they want to what others have. Outwardly this appears to be a battle between the haves and have nots. In reality, it's the manifestation of the unceasing, yet normal indulgences of average people. Those who believe they deserve what others have, simply because they've worked all their lives to achieve a 96er's concept of success, have created our culture of criminality. A Warrior who has experienced recapitulation no longer envies anyone, and acknowledges that everyone lives the results of where they invest their energy. For instance, if a farmer desires corn, he cannot plant cotton seeds. As a Warrior, if you desire material riches, by all means go after it. There is no universal law against wealth, only in how you obtain it. While it is true that unfair laws, social injustices, wars, and other manmade disasters play a part, a Warrior never knocks down obstacles, but instead goes around them. Racism plays a major role in how people develop, where they live, and how they live. In our society, above all other random events in our lives, the color we are born is the most significant. This, along with a desire to gain wealth without struggle, creates monsters who die young and harm many while they live. As it is with most illnesses of the spirit, it begins with self-importance. It is not self-destructive to want to live better. However, it is self-destructive to believe that others don't deserve what you desire as much as you. While it's not wrong to want to win, it is disadvantageous to believe you deserve to, simply because you want to. In the end, you only get what you've earned.

Sloth

Definition:

1. Habitual disinclination to exertion; indolence; laziness.

2. Spiritual apathy.

3. Failure to pursue virtue.

Synonyms: Idleness, inactivity, indolence, inertia, laxness, lethargy, listlessness, slackness, slothfulness, slowness, sluggishness, do-nothingness, lackadaisicalness, languidness, supineness.

Antonyms: Activity, busyness, energy, life, liveliness, vigor.

A Seeker will never succeed if they possess the characteristics associated with this weakness. A Warrior must work nonstop to achieve even a small expertise in any aspect of the lessons upon this path. He must study, read, examine, travel, and challenge his body and his mind relentlessly. He must experience and fail, then get up and do it again. There are no shortcuts and no translators or helpers. Unless you are fortunate enough to have found a teacher, you will be on your own. There will be no one to guide you. You may have to give up your old thinking patterns and agree that you need someone like me in your life. I wish I'd had a mentor like myself to help me along the way. My life would have been very different. Without a mentor, guardian, or guide, you will use this book and the books of others, but ultimately it will be up to you to either continue or surrender. I would never consider a lazy person for a potential position within my program. Anyone who does not have the strength of discipline to have discovered this knowledge is half-dead already. I will not consider anyone who portrays the slightest degree of laziness or cowardice. My experience is that lazy people are scared to try. Their sensitive nature has made them incapable of withstanding the realities of their surroundings. They have surrendered. I would advise anyone who has surrendered to consider the fact that all of us have been pushed against the wall many times. Struggling is the nature of our existence, and so is being alone. Yes, this is harsh, but no harsher than the millions of lazy individuals who burden their parents for the rest of their lives, with their inadequate conduct and below standard behavior. I am not a Christian. I do not believe anyone deserves forgiveness or a second chance. A Warrior is always pragmatic about his choices. He uses simple logic with immediate results. On a combat patrol inside enemy territory, a leader would eliminate anyone who jeopardized or endangered his men. The Spartans went as far as discarding infants who were born deformed or sickly. It was not done with malice or evil intent, but for the protection and perpetuation of their society. Today, movies are made of their culture and they are considered heroes. During the Battle of Thermopylae, "The Hot Gates," a student of the Toltec discipline would have fought a guerrilla war, attacking the Persian's supply lines, not throw lives away in some foolish last stand. As a Warrior, I suggest letting another fool die for his country. You live for yourself. Let the wannabe heroes and medal winners die if they choose. I will live for me and my freedom, and continue on the path with heart. I speak from hindsight after serving in the United States Army for over 23 years.

  Early Christian leaders have identified diligence as being the opposite of sloth. Of all the opposites provided, I would have to say that I agree with this one the most. The use of the word diligence, which is defined as constant and earnest effort to accomplish what is undertaken, assists new Seekers with attaining an understanding. However, this does not come close to describing the true ruthlessness and discipline of a Warrior. Years of fanatical dedication to this discipline is required to gain such an understanding. For this purpose, and for the sake of assisting new Seekers with comprehension, this example will suffice as an opposite. Wealth dictates which doors are opened and which are closed. Sloth is an equal opportunity success killer. As poor, but ambitious individuals, watch the parade of wealthy kids obtain what they cannot, it may appear as though trying is useless. Average people raise their children to believe that no matter what they do, things will always be the same. It is then no wonder so many choose crime instead of an education. Learning a trade or skill is valuable in any culture. Wealthy people may have further to fall before they hit rock-bottom, but they will eventually hit harder. Poor people have little room for indulgence and must quickly acquire discipline or die. Although there are no easy answers, the competition is not that tough. Warriors know that 96ers operate on less than fifty percent or their capacity. This is especially true for children of wealthy parents. These individuals have little or no discipline, have never faced adversity, and lack physical and spiritual courage. A Warrior, regardless of ethnic background, has learned to squash his self-importance, and knows it is not necessary to be first. He knows it's not always the fastest runner who wins the race. A Warrior knows that material possession is not a sign of quality or intelligence. Things never give a person value, just as a lack of them does not infer inferiority. Real intelligence can be better measured in how one makes decisions, as well as how much discipline one demonstrates while doing so. Our educational system is based on intellectual analysis, repeated dogma, and memorization. Good grades in class are not a sign of superiority or superior intelligence, but rather training and practice. Most people could do equally as well in class, if they'd received the same training and attention. To succeed in our educational system one must have staying power. One must have the willingness to endure and push through the challenges, distractions, and temptations of life. Wealth alone does not bring happiness or guarantee a long life. Without wisdom and a spiritual foundation, riches will always bring about destruction. On a darker side, laziness becomes a habit, which then becomes a pattern, which leads to a tragic ending. Anyone who desires the strength and wisdom of a Warrior must ask themselves whether they possess the fortitude to stay the course. Unbeknownst to 96ers, once an individual makes contact with power, there is no turning back. Power will not release or forget those who have challenged it. This is not mere dramatization, but an accurate description based on firsthand experience. I would advise most people to remain blissful in their ignorance. Knowledge, like wisdom, is accompanied by sadness and disillusionment. On this path, what you don't do, matters as much as how you spend your time. Everything in life, no matter how seemingly insignificant, matters. This is especially true for a Warrior seeking power. Those who surrender to sloth have failed to conquer their self-importance, and have overlooked the fact that death never rests. As lazy individuals die, they are riddled with regrets and remorse, knowing they have wasted their lives doing nothing. The happy drunk and local drug addict are perfect examples of average people. They've indulged in their weakness until it was all they knew, and now it is all they are. Warriors know there will never be enough time to do all the things they've wanted to do, and their time on this earth will be altogether too short. Although there are better ways to spend their lives, both the slothful and the Warrior will eventually die, making them equal. In the end, how you spend your life matters little, but everyone must decide for themselves.

Note to Reader

In addition to conventional grammatical use, italics are commonly used throughout this work to emphasize the distinction between a word's traditional description and its reference in terms of the Toltec discipline. Understanding this is of paramount significance to attaining comprehension of the concepts discussed and explained throughout this work. Please note that this is an independent publishing endeavor. I did not wish to subject myself to big publishing companies, who for profit would censor and restrict my work. This book is specifically written to assist Pathfinders, Seekers, and Warriors. As such, rather than conforming to industry standards, it has been designed in a workbook fashion. Line spacing has intentionally been made slightly larger, therefore providing readers with the option of keeping notes on any page. Additional space for note taking can be found at the back of the book. You may find errors in spelling, punctuation, grammar, formatting, and etc. I make no apology. Anyone concerned with such things in light of the awesomeness of the Toltec discipline, has many other problems which need addressing before they're ready to tackle sorcery.

The following are definitions of words and acronyms commonly used throughout this work. Please note that this is a basic list of basic descriptions, added for the benefit of the reader's comprehension. Complex concepts will not be expanded upon in this section, nor confined to such simplistic descriptions.

Pathfinder: A Pathfinder is an individual who is searching for the Warrior's path. They have become aware of the emptiness which their average existence has created in their lives. Although this inner void has led them on a search for a better way to live, they do not know what the freedom they desire will cost, or how to go about attaining it. Many Pathfinders are newly introduced to the Toltec discipline and have begun reading related books, searching for answers and a path to follow.

Seeker: A Seeker is an individual who is on the Warrior's path. However, they have not yet learned to silence their *internal dialogue*, *see*, or move energy. A Seeker's challenge is to become a Warrior via following the path they have found. This is done by living like a Warrior; deliberate application of the Toltec discipline on a daily basis. A Seeker must train himself to replace his average person's reactions to life's situations with a Warrior's response. Through deliberate, disciplined *focus* he will eventually learn to manipulate power, silence his *internal dialogue*, *see*, and move energy.

Warrior: A Seeker becomes a Warrior when his deliberate actions and responses are no longer a habit, but a part of who he is.

It is important to note that these words are used in an effort to explain complex and abstract information. There are no clear boundaries, as an individual's development is always in a continuous state of flux. Anyone can have a setback at any moment, just as anyone can touch the stars, if only for an instant.

96er: Another word for average person.

Four Percentor: One of the four percent of people who work to defeat their weaknesses.

Sorcery: The deliberate manipulation of awareness and deliberate implementation of discipline.

Tweak: S*hifting* the *assemblage point*, raising the ability to perceive. Influencing a person and/or situation via energy.

Average people, as well as Four Percentors, come in all shapes and sizes. Race, ethnicity, education, occupation, status, money, gender, age, and etc., does not matter. Behavior is all that matters. Warriors *see* everyone in terms of energy, and know that death makes all things equal. This makes the idea of any person believing their race grants them a level of superiority completely ridiculous. How can one biological creature be superior to another, if they are both going to die? In spite of this truth pseudoscience, racist government legislation, religious propaganda, and the ignorant masses have continuously perpetuated delusional ideals of ethnic superiority. I do not believe a description of someone's ethnicity should degrade them, nor should it compliment them. However, in the United States being called "White" is considered favorable in contrast to "Mexican," or "Black," and etc. My refusal to accept the inferior title assigned to me by those who demand I address them in a manner they see as superior, led to the impartial creation of a new method of categorization. Please note that this method is very general, and does not account for all the complexities associated with race and ethnicity. I simply refuse to endorse a system which unashamedly perpetuates delusional ideals of ethnic superiority.

DOEI [do-ee]: Descendant of European immigrant

NTOMA [nuh-toh-muh]: Native Tejano of Mexican ancestry

NCOMA [nuh-coh-muh]: Native Californian of Mexican ancestry

AMOAFA [uh-moh-fuh]: American of African ancestry

AMOASA [uh-moh-suh]: American of Asian ancestry

Texas escapee,
-don Jesus M. Ramirez

TOLTEC INSTITUTE
INTERNATIONAL INSTITUTE OF TOLTEC STUDIES

Toltec Institute was born via the determination of a band of Seekers of knowledge, united in their steadfast commitment to the discipline of the ancient Toltec Warrior. Comprised of members from various regions across the globe, they initially met in secret, both in person and via the advantages of contemporary technology. Their objectives were to discuss, understand, and develop strategies for implementing the discipline of a modern Toltec Warrior. Undermined by self-promoting, self-proclaimed spiritual leaders, gurus, and masters, these determined individuals struggled to find direction. This search continued until Toltec Institute members discovered *Sorcerer's Secrets, Book 1: Translated Secrets of Carlos Castaneda* by don Jesus M. Ramirez. This amazingly powerful book has swept away the competition with superior explanations of complex concepts, authentically translating secrets of ancient Toltec wisdom for modern application. Seekers of all levels and backgrounds can now benefit from following a previously nonexistent roadmap to spiritual freedom.

Toltec Institute was founded by its current president, don Roberto San Miguel, a student of many spiritual disciplines. Originally of México City, México, don Roberto now resides in London, England, and has written on many topics of interest to New Age enthusiasts. Although he has visited and lived in many areas known for their spiritual energy, such as Venezuela, South Africa, India, Pakistan, the deserts of México, and the American Southwest, he lives the life of a simple man. Following the discipline of the modern Toltec Warrior, don Roberto works unceasingly at defeating his weaknesses, and refuses to be photographed or have his image reproduced. In true Toltec fashion, don Roberto, like don Jesus, believes that to be a Warrior is the highest title or rank any man can aspire. As such he refuses to be called a master, guru, or leader, and rejects those who would claim such titles. He humbly considers himself a student, like any other, and continues to struggle to stay on the path of knowledge.

Of the hundreds of books that were reviewed, don Roberto, along with a dozen other Seekers, selected *Sorcerer's Secrets, Book 1: Translated Secrets of Carlos Castaneda* to be Toltec Institute's official manual. In exchange for permission of use, Toltec Institute has become acting administrator to don Jesus and his works. All letters, requests, questions, opinions, analysis, rebuttals, challenges, and reviews of the material within this highly controversial book can be sent to Toltec Institute via the email or physical address listed below. Direct contact with don Jesus or don Roberto is unavailable. All mailed material will be rerouted to the addressee. With the exception of information of an illegal or illicit nature, all material received will be kept confidential. All mailed material will become the property of Toltec Institute or the addressed recipient, and may be used as per our discretion. Replies are not guaranteed. Each letter is reviewed individually and independently of all others. Please note that due to the high volume of emails Toltec Institute receives, hard mailed letters to the physical address are given priority.

We welcome you to participate.

Toltec Institute Director,

-Roberto San Miguel

The Toltec Institute
PO Box 6552
San Jose, CA 95150

www.toltecinstitute.com
info@toltecinstitute.com

Notes

Notes

Notes

Notes

Notes

Notes

Notes

Notes

Notes